Bahaa Taher

Bahaa Taher was born in 1935 in Cairo, Egypt. He was active in the country's left-wing literary circles of the 1960s and in the mid 1970s was prevented from publishing his work. After many years of exile in Switzerland, he has recently returned to Egypt. Now one of the most widely read novelists in the Arab world, Taher has received the State's Award of Merit in Literature, the highest honour the Egyptian establishment can confer on a writer. He is the author of four collections of short stories, several plays and works of non-fiction, and six novels: *East of the Palms*, *As Doha Said*, *Aunt Safiyya and the Monastery*, *Love in Exile*, *The Point of Light* and *Sunset Oasis*, which won the inaugural International Prize for Arabic Fiction in 2008.

19 MAY. 2010

Dear Mum,
thought you
might enjoy
this!
Happy Birthday,
Love from
Alice
xx

Sunset Oasis

Bahaa Taher

Translated by Humphrey Davies

SCEPTRE

Originally published in 2007 as *Wahat al-Ghurub* by Dar el Shorouk, Cairo

First published in Great Britain in 2009 by Sceptre
An imprint of Hodder & Stoughton
An Hachette UK company

1

Sceptre is grateful to Sigrid Rausing for funding the translation.

A CIP catalogue record for this title is available from the British Library

Hardback ISBN 978 0 340 92487 7
Trade Paperback ISBN 978 0 340 91949 1

Typeset in Sabon by Hewer Text UK Ltd, Edinburgh
Printed and bound by Clays Ltd, St Ives plc

Hodder & Stoughton policy is to use papers that are natural, renewable
and recyclable products and made from wood grown in sustainable
forests. The logging and manufacturing processes are expected to
conform to the environmental regulations of the country of origin.

Hodder & Stoughton Ltd
338 Euston Road
London NW1 3BH

www.hodder.co.uk

For Stefka Anastassova

Author's Note

The real name of the district commissioner of the oasis of Siwa during the last years of the nineteenth century was Mahmoud Azmi, and it is to him that is ascribed an act that has left a permanent mark on the oasis, as the reader will discover at the appropriate place in the novel.

That act aside, no published historical information exists concerning the commissioner or his life story.

Part One

I

Mahmoud

He told me, 'Your wife is a brave woman,' as though I don't know my own wife! Isn't she willingly going into danger with me? All the same, it may be that I don't truly know Catherine. Not now! The important thing is it was no coincidence. Every word he utters is spoken for a reason, though Catherine isn't the problem at this moment. And anyway, I'll never solve any problem wandering the gloomy corridors of the Ministry of Internal Affairs, especially following that oppressive meeting with Mr Harvey.

There was nothing new in what he said, apart from the veiled hints, some of which I understood and the rest of which puzzled me.

I knew before I saw him that matters were settled. Brigadier General Saeed Bey had informed me that the ministry's advisor had forwarded the recommendation to His Excellency the Minister of Internal Affairs and His Excellency had issued a transfer order, to be implemented immediately. I had only a few days left if I was to join the caravan that departed from Kerdasa, and the brigadier general advised me, as a friend, to abandon the idea of taking my wife: the journey to the oasis was not easy, and the posting itself very difficult, as I well knew, though, in the end, the decision was mine; despite which, it was his duty to warn me of the danger of the journey, which, under the best conditions and with a skilful guide, took at least two weeks.

I'm confident that Saeed wasn't trying to scare me and I believe he did everything in his power to have me excused the posting. Our friendship is of long standing, though it may have waned over the years and these days is hardly more than the relationship between any official and his subordinate. However that may be, the stories and secrets of a bygone age form a bond. We haven't spoken of them for years, but each of us knows that the other still remembers. My other colleagues, of course, warned me, with suspect compassion, against the journey. Some were glad to have escaped the posting themselves and that it had fallen to me, and others had to make an effort to hide their delight at my discomfiture. They told me of the numerous caravans that had gone astray in the desert and been swallowed up by the sands, of small caravans that had lost the path and of a mighty Persian army on its way to take the oasis long ago that the desert had engulfed and buried beneath its sands for ever. They told me it was a lucky caravan which completed its journey before its supplies of water ran out and before the winds altered the features of the road, building dunes that had not existed before and burying the wells on which the caravans depended for watering the camels. Lucky too the caravan whose campsites were not attacked by wolves or hyenas and one or two of whose company were not stung by a scorpion or a snake.

All this was said, and more, but I paid no attention. My fear of the caravan's safe arrival at its destination is no less than my fear of its getting lost. I know very well I am going to the place where it is my destiny to be killed, and perhaps Catherine's too.

Was that one of the things Mr Harvey was hinting at in our meeting?

I had entered his office determined to provoke him. What did I have to lose?

It was the first time I had been in the office of this advisor, who held all the strings of the ministry in his hands. I found his diplomatic manner of talking affected and I found him affected too, as he sat there, his short body behind a huge desk, a tarboosh, from beneath which fair hair peeped, unconvincingly perched on his head. He didn't address himself to me but for most of the time directed his remarks towards an invisible point to his right, in the corner of the office. He repeated the things I had already heard from Brigadier General Saeed, but kept needling me on what he took to be my weak point: 'You must be happy, Captain Mahmoud Abd el Zahir Effendi – I beg your pardon, I should say *Major* Mahmoud now, of course!' he said, referring to my appointment as district commissioner for the oasis. He pretended to look through my service file, which was placed in front of him, and went on to say that under normal circumstances I would have had to wait long for this promotion.

I interrupted him with a smile, which I tried to make polite, to say, 'Especially if one takes into consideration, Mr Advisor, how few in the ministry would welcome such a promotion for themselves!'

He made no comment and didn't look at me. Instead, he turned the pages of the other file, on which 'Siwa Oasis' was written in large letters in English. He seemed to be enjoying what he was reading and muttered 'Interesting, very interesting' to himself every now and then. Finally, raising his face towards me with something like a smile on his lips, he said, 'So you know, my dear Major Mahmoud, that you will deal only with the heads of the families, whom in the oasis they call the *agwad*?'

'Naturally. Saeed Bey has given me all the necessary instructions.'

He went on, as though I hadn't spoken, to tell me that I was to have no dealings with the cultivators whom . . . and here he returned to the file in search of them and I reminded him that they were called *zaggala*.

Taking another quick look at the file, he echoed, 'Yes, yes. The *zaggala*. So long as they accept such a way of doing things, what business is it of ours? One is reminded somewhat of Sparta. Have you heard of Sparta, in ancient Greece, Mr Abd el Zahir?'

'I have heard of it, Mr Harvey.'

A certain disappointment appeared on his face at the thought of my having heard of Sparta, but he was determined to continue his lecture. 'Yes, indeed. Sparta. With a difference, of course! Sparta was a city dedicated to the production of warriors. They trained their children from infancy to become soldiers and they kept them apart from the residents of the city, which is how the whole of Sparta came to be an army living in a city, the strongest city in all Greece until Alexander appeared. And these, uh ... these *zaggala* in the oasis are also conscripted, to work the land until they are forty years old. Forbidden to marry or to enter the city and pass through its walls after sunset.' Speaking for himself, he thought this was a system for society and for labour that deserved consideration; he might even go so far as to say it deserved admiration. 'Observe, Mr Zahir, our colonies in Africa and Asia where chaos reigns because labour there—'

I interrupted him once again with a laugh and said, 'My dear Mr Harvey, *we* don't have colonies in Africa, or Asia.'

I managed, however, to prevent myself from saying, 'We're the colonized!'

He frowned for a moment, abandoned his musings on the matter of the colonies, and returned to his perusal of the file. Then he raised his head and gave me a sudden, crafty smile as he said, 'Naturally, the other aspects of this system of theirs that separates the men from the women in boyhood do not concern us. It is a matter of no interest to us. We have nothing to do with their primitive customs.'

I understood what he was trying to say but did not respond, so he started addressing the invisible thing to his right again. I would have heard, of course, from Saeed Bey, that they were divided there into two hostile clans.

6

My patience was close to exhausted. Yes, yes, and I knew that the battles between them were never ending.

He turned his face towards me once more and emphasized his words as he said, 'Even this is no concern of ours. These battles are a part of their lives and they are free to do what they like with themselves, unless, of course, it should be possible, through specific alliances with one clan or another, to turn this into a means to assure our domination. It is a tried and true method, so long as the alliance with one party does not go on too long. The alliance has to be with one group this time and with their opponents the next. Do you understand?'

'I am doing my best, Your Excellency. I am aware of the policy, but have no experience of its application.'

'You will learn, my dear sir,' he said, with, for the first time, a certain malice. 'Do not forget that your first task will be to collect the taxes. A difficult task, as you are aware. A very difficult task. Your survival instinct will teach you this, and other policies, Major.'

He stopped suddenly and smiled again as he said, 'There is, all the same, something comical about the whole business. These people built themselves a fortress in the desert and built a town inside the fortress to protect themselves from the raids of the Bedouin, and despite this, the blood that the Bedouin would have shed in the open they have taken upon themselves to spill behind their own walls.' He found this quite remarkable. He found it extremely oriental!

The blood rose to my face and I burst out, 'Battles like these, within one group of people, are to be found in both East and West, Mr Harvey. It's different from invasion from the outside . . .'

He looked at my face for a while and then said, in an amused tone, 'Major Mahmoud Effendi is still under the influence of ideas from the past. Though, of course, he no longer sympathizes with the mutineers?'

I was incapable of controlling myself and burst out once more, 'I never sympathized with any mutineer. I was performing my duty and nothing more, and I have paid the price twice over in unjust treatment.'

He shook his head. Anyway, I would be aware, naturally, he pointed out, that my work would be the object of close scrutiny.

I thought this would be my last chance, so I said, in a tone of voice I tried to keep perfectly neutral, 'I hope that my work, when scrutinized, will be found satisfactory. But what if I do not succeed?'

He replied curtly, 'You know that you will pay the price.'

Then he caught himself, as though he had read my thoughts, and said, 'In any case, the penalty will not be your return to Cairo.'

Suddenly he changed the subject. I had to know that Saeed Bey objected to my taking my lady wife with me. Out of concern for her safety, of course. He had, however, informed His Excellency that the ministry did not interfere in the private lives of officers. Moreover, the lady was, he believed ...

He paused for a moment and appeared to hesitate over his choice of words before continuing, 'The lady is a brave woman.' Then he repeated this, shaking his head. 'Indeed. A brave woman.'

I said nothing and he stood up suddenly. I stood too and he started talking to me in an official tone: 'You will travel with the Kerdasa caravan since it is ready to depart but I will send a number of horses' (and here the ghost of a smile appeared on his lips) 'which I hope will reach their destination alive, with the Matrouh caravan, which leaves in about two weeks.'

'Beaten by the British again!' I said to myself as I left his office. 'How I hate you, Mr Harvey. How I hate you all, along with this ministry. But there's no escape.'

I have to go home now and prepare for the journey. But what is there left to get ready? As soon as I told her that all efforts to excuse me from the posting had failed, Catherine gathered together everything we would need, and collected from the bookshops every book that discusses the oasis or in which mention of it occurs. She has left nothing to chance. Yesterday she told me of her remarkable plan to combat the bites of scorpions and snakes, so I referred her to a Rifa'i sheikh and convinced her that he had greater experience in dealing with poisons. She too, then, is afraid of such things – so what is the secret of her enthusiasm for this journey? I have made every attempt to convince her to stay, but to no effect. She knows the dangers awaiting me there but doesn't care. If I were naive, I'd say the reason was love, and that she didn't want her husband to perish alone. I do believe she loves me, but not that much!

I left the ministry, crossed el Dawaween Street, and proceeded until I reached Abdeen police station. In this station my whole life has been fashioned, and wasted, at a short distance from the only house I have ever known. It never occurred to me as a child, though, that I should end up doing such work.

Anyway, the time for regret is past. What do I have to regret? And what did I hope for when I was a boy? I gave no thought to the future. All I wanted was for things to go on the way they were. A happy childhood and a happier boyhood. My father denied me and my younger brother nothing. He forbade us no pleasure and never forced us to pay attention to our education or have done with it within a suitable period. My brother Suleiman liked to spend most of his time with my father at his shop in el Muski, learning the basics of the trade. For me, there was nothing to sully the bright days of my life. It was the last days of Khedive Ismail, the whole city was in commotion, and I dawdled away my time at the grammar school until I was almost twenty. I knew women and I kept company with slave girls and I spent my nights with friends moving from one café and bar to another. At our large house in Abdeen, there was always a feast being held and scarcely a night went by without guests, a party, and the most renowned singers, male and female. Thursday nights were the exception. On Thursday, the servants would remove all the furniture from the large room on the first storey, cover the floor with carpets, perfume the place with incense, and place brass pots filled with rose-scented water in the corners. That was the night of the 'People of the Way', of songs of praise for the Prophet, and of the circles of remembrance of God in favour of which my father, and I along with him, would abandon all other pleasures. I would chant with the chanters and sway with the participants in the *dhikr* till I was bathed in sweat and my limbs exhausted, and then a calm, deep sleep would come that lasted all night. And in the morning, I would go early with my father and Suleiman to Friday prayer at the mosque of el Hussein. The same night, however, the cycle would begin again, until, one evening, I found myself by chance with my friends at the Matatia Café on Ataba Square. There I beheld that turbaned man who spoke Arabic like a Turk, or a Syrian. I had never before heard the like of what he had to say, or perhaps I had but had paid no attention. Nevertheless, the words of Sheikh el Afghani and the enthusiasm of the disciples around him forced me to listen and pay attention, and thus I became addicted, in addition to wine and women, to the gatherings of the sheikh and the reading of the newspapers edited by his disciples – *Misr*, and *el Tigara*, and *el Lata'if*. Whenever the Khedive had one of them closed down, I would transfer to another, new one that would repeat what its sequestrated sister journal had said, all of them attacking the rulers who had plunged Egypt into debt and brought it to bankruptcy, and all of them burning with anger at the domination of the Europeans, who had even become ministers of the country's government and were employed in every ministry. During the same period, I heard that the sheikh and some of his pupils had embraced Freemasonry, whose adherents belonged to every religion and were bound together by their faith in freedom and brotherhood among people of every race. I too therefore hastened to join a Masonic lodge and waited for the day when the whole earth would become one great lodge for a world of free brethren. I also heard of the formation of a secret nationalist party. After reading its manifestos, with their slogan of 'Egypt for the Egyptians', I was caught up by enthusiasm and wanted to join, though I didn't know how to get in touch with the party. I was held back, too, by the first betrayal to change my life, which was when my father's business went bankrupt. To this day, though, I still fail to understand how I could have done all these things with so little reflection.

Each one succeeded the next without causing me any anxiety or self-reproach, as though it were very natural that I should get drunk, attend the Masonic lodge, sleep with women, go to Afghani's gatherings, and turn with my father and the Sufis in the circle of remembrance. I even thought in those days that I ought to pay some attention to my studies, so as to obtain a diploma and enter the College of Law, as most students dreamt of doing. I believed I would have been well suited to that because what most caught my fancy at school were the classes in rhetoric and literature. My father, however, went bankrupt. A Greek merchant seduced him with promises of large profits from the import of olive oil from his country, then inveigled him into debt, and interest on the debt, until in the end the Muski shop was wrested from him. No source of income remained to support the large house full of slave girls and servants. My father made a great effort to have me enrolled in the police, and it was possible at that time for me to become an officer with the education I had acquired and some months of training. Thus my father was able, before his sorrows and illnesses incapacitated him, to set his mind at rest, knowing that my salary would be enough to support my mother and brother and keep the house open, albeit without the feasts and the singing and the circles of remembrance. The visitors disappeared and, along with them, even the Sufis and the singers of religious songs. I returned to the circles only once, after many years, when Brigadier General Saeed invited me to a night of chanting with the Sufi order to which he belonged, but I never repeated the experience. It failed to inspire any of the ecstasy that had swept over me in the long-gone past.

And now I ask myself – has all that distant past disappeared? I ask whether the parts of that young man, with his divided spirit, have come together, or whether the days have flung them farther apart. When I married Catherine, after much hesitation, I dreamt that my unruly self might finally calm down. A family, a house, an intelligent and courageous wife – why did that settledness never come? Why does it remain elusive and out of reach? The only certain thing is this uniform that I wear, and this profession that came to me without my wanting it and than which I have known no other, despite all the vicissitudes of the years.

And now this oasis.

2

Catherine

I know Mahmoud will miss this roomy house. In the silence of the desert he'll yearn for this quarter where people are in constant motion and the cries of the street vendors never cease. Of course, he won't miss the Khedive's palace next door to us, where our feet have never trod, though I have become fond of what can be seen over the walls of its beautiful green gardens. Mahmoud can't imagine life far from his house, which is the only one he's ever known. I, on the other hand, have moved three times and no one house fills me with a sense of nostalgia. Places come back to me only when I think of the people who live in them, and then I recall even their familiar smells and forgotten corners, and am astonished by the games memory plays.

Mahmoud is a little late. He went to the ministry to complete the formalities and said he'd come back afterwards to help me pack. Not much is left to do; everything is ready for the journey except Mahmoud himself. I long ago got used to his endless changes of mood. He used to astonish me at first when he'd say one thing and then its opposite, or do contradictory things with no forewarning. This time, though, things are different. His sorrow is deepening.

He wasn't happy when I met him, and nor was I then. Nevertheless, we managed to seize happiness, and we lived it for a while. I always see him as I saw him for the first time, on the bridge of the *dahabiya* where chance threw us together on the trip to Aswan. I noticed him standing there, with his towering stature, wearing his police uniform and tarboosh, from beneath which the grey hair, framing his youthful face, protruded. His handsome features caught my attention immediately, but it wasn't them which attracted me to him. From the beginning I found him different from the other officers I had met in Cairo, different in fact from all the men I had met here. These usually spoke to me, as a foreigner and a British woman in a country occupied by the British, with total subservience, while looks of supplicant lust flowed from their eyes like beggars' tears. When I approached him, his tarboosh looked to me like a pharaonic crown on his head, his stern face with its wide black eyes and regular features the face of a real king transferred from the walls of a temple to the deck of that *dahabiya*. I asked him how much time remained before we reached Aswan. He didn't turn towards me, eyes lowered, like the others. On the contrary, I noticed a fleeting look of hostility in them. He looked around him, however; there was nothing on the horizon except fields on either side of the river and identical villages at the ends of the fields. Then he looked into my eyes and said, in what was in those days his poor English, 'I don't know. I am here with the guard of the *dahabiya*.' He was a member of the guard of, as far as I remember, some travelling prince or minister, and when I remained standing in front of him, he said, unenthusiastically, that he could ask one of the sailors if I liked. So I said, 'I'll come with you.'

From then on I stayed with him – on the *dahabiya* on the Nile, in the streets of Aswan, in the temples of Luxor, and then in Cairo, where we got married. For a long time he was hesitant in his approaches to me and I was the one who did most of the talking. I think the turning point came when he found out I was Irish and I hated the British for occupying my country, as they had occupied his, and felt shame at bearing their nationality, which I would be rid of the day Ireland gained its independence. After this, the barriers between us collapsed. His resistance, which I could see in his eyes just as I could the love, came to an end. Or was I deluding myself?

Was it love or desire? It didn't make much difference to me at the time and he warned me at the start of our relationship that he had promised himself never to get married, though that promise did not hold for long.

The sheikh who notarized our nuptials in Cairo seemed miserable to see a Muslim man, and a respectable officer, marrying a foreign woman not of his religion. He'd ask a question and the alarm in his eyes would grow yet greater and he'd repeat the answer as though he couldn't believe his ears. She's not a virgin? A widow? Two years older than he? There was no father or brother to act as her proxy for the marriage contract? She was giving herself away?

Mahmoud told me that there was nothing in all that which contradicted their religious law, but I saw the notary bury his face in his papers and record in them what he heard without raising his head, so that we shouldn't see the look of indignation in his eyes. He was, however, the epitome of politeness compared to the British when I went to the consulate to register my marriage. You're marrying an Egyptian? And according to their laws too? And before coming to us? Are you aware of the rights you have lost? I responded in like fashion. I told them their law appealed to me more than that of the British in Ireland. My marriage had at least taken place of my own free will and no one had imposed it on me by force. When they heard this they rushed through the formalities, so that I wouldn't stay long at the consulate.

Mahmoud didn't expect the British advisor at the ministry to agree to my travelling with him to the oasis. I think he agreed with the greatest of pleasure, in the hope that I'd perish there as quickly as possible!

During our first days, our first months, I knew with Mahmoud a happiness that I didn't think possible in this world, after my wretched experience with Michael. And from the beginning I discovered that Mahmoud could not tolerate any talk of love – he didn't speak of it himself and he didn't want to hear it. Love, for him, was lovemaking, no more, no less. He was a king in that too. Ever ready to give, always able to awaken my passions, and bringing a knowledge gained through numerous experiences dating from his youth and which he didn't seek to deny. I learnt through my instincts alone – the instincts that I'd forgotten with Michael – to keep pace with his greater knowledge. And I may have taught him something myself too. I made him understand that I didn't like the violence and ravishment that he imagined were the marks of manliness, that I liked soft touches and for the two bodies to respond together slowly and fluidly, moving from the pleasure of closeness and caresses to the peak of ecstasy and fulfilment.

Gradually he started to adjust to me and we lived in uninterrupted nuptial bliss for months. He didn't hold back and I didn't hesitate. I hadn't believed that I'd ever be capable of accepting this understanding of love and life, but I became his utterly willing, utterly happy, partner. Was that because he caused so many delusions to fall away from me, or was I ready from the beginning, and all Mahmoud had to do was rip away the veil of prudery?

With him too I accepted things I never could have imagined I'd accept. After our first months, I became aware that I was not alone in his life. Once, when he was with me in bed, I smelt another woman and her sweat; I felt the ghost of another woman between us. Then, when I found his ardour the same as ever, or even greater, I told myself I was mistaken – but I knew my body was not betraying me; there was someone else who shared him with me. An unbearable jealousy swept over me and I spent a whole day pulling myself together and ordering my thoughts so that I might confront him. But when he returned from his work, all the thoughts I'd carefully assembled left me and I asked him the moment he entered and as we stood in the main room, 'Mahmoud, are you being unfaithful to me?' He responded with a question: 'Do you mean, "Do I have women other than you?"' I nodded and he said calmly, 'Yes.' I burst out, my whole body shaking, 'So be it! And what if I were to have men other than you?' He answered simply, 'I would kill you immediately.' 'So why shouldn't I kill you now?' I screamed. He said nothing for a moment, as though thinking. Then he took his revolver out of its holster and held it out to me, smiling. 'Indeed, that would be just,' he said. 'It's your right too. Take it. I won't stop you.' I pushed his outstretched arm aside and rushed to my room, shouting, 'I can't live with a madman!' and locked myself in and started gathering my clothes and other things in readiness to depart.

I didn't speak to him for four days, and on the fifth we were together again in bed. Holding me to him, he said, 'Lying is the easiest thing to do, but I don't lie. My body is the problem. One woman isn't enough for it and divorce is so easy. You too could leave me at any moment, but you won't. Each of us needs the other and that's why we got married.' I mumbled a question, 'Where is love in all that?' and he rolled on top of me and kissed me.

I have accepted this sort of love and this sort of marriage. Is it a life of utter truth or of utter falsehood? He wasn't mistaken. Each of us needs the other. Why? And for how long? I feel now that even this relationship that we took on jointly has changed. It isn't a matter of women this time, but Mahmoud is withdrawing into himself in a way that has never happened since I have known him. Is it all because of the posting, which he has hated from the moment he heard about it? He made every possible effort to be excused but didn't succeed. I know of the danger that awaits him, but Mahmoud is no coward. He will do his duty there as he has done all his life, whether he liked that duty or hated it. I am sure of that. He ignores even the pain that afflicts him from time to time in the place where the bullet smashed the bones of his arm. The pains are worst in the winter, in the cold,

17

but I discovered that only from the changes on his face when he presses his arm hard with his hand. He never complains, though, and never says a word. I said to him jokingly once that at least he'd never suffer from the cold at the oasis, as it was hot all year round. He shook his head and said, 'I wish the problem was just the heat!'

I am not ignorant of the true problem. I have read everything about the oasis written by the historians and travellers. I know its history, ancient and modern. I may know more about the ancient history but I've also studied everything that happened there since the beginning of this century, when the army of Egypt's governor, Mohamed Ali, took it. The Basha incorporated the oasis into Egypt and put an end to its independence, which had lasted hundreds of years during which Siwa had been subject to no outside state or force. I have read how they resisted Egyptian rule, ceaselessly rebelling and rising up against the soldiers and fighting them, while the Egyptians ceaselessly repressed their uprisings with a savagery that gave birth to new rebellions and new uprisings. And I know, as does Mahmoud, that the district commissioner, who is the ruler of the oasis, will always be a prize trophy for them. At the beginning, they murdered the local mayors that Cairo chose from among the Siwans, their murder being a message to the district commissioners that they were not beyond their reach. In the last two rebellions, however, they murdered the commissioners themselves and the government sent a large army, later withdrawn, to restore calm. Does that calm remain?

I hope so. Long ago, I dreamt of a journey into the desert without imagining that the dream would be realized in this fashion. I dreamt that I saw the oasis whose sands were trodden by the feet of Alexander the Great and where he lived the disturbing events that haunted him till he died. I have other dreams to realize there that I don't even dare to think about right now. Everything in its own good time. The important thing is that we should be there, Mahmoud and I, together and on our own. There will be no danger of another woman competing with me there. The other dangers are not an excessive price to pay to restore our life to the way it was in its first untroubled days.

Mahmoud is very late.

Perhaps he's still at the ministry, or maybe he's saying goodbye to the streets of his city and thinking now the same thoughts as me – making an inventory of his life and working out how it brought him to this moment, that of moving towards an unknown destiny with this Irish woman whom accident threw in his path.

And me too, how many accidents has it taken to lead me to this moment? No, not accidents. I am responsible for everything and I regret nothing. It may have been my father who set me on the path, but it was my own will that brought me this far.

If he were alive now, he'd see a well-deserved punishment in everything that has happened to me with Mahmoud. Being a zealous Catholic, he would never have agreed to this marriage from the outset. All the same, the first thing he taught me was to love the East and be passionate about its antiquities. Indeed, he excited my curiosity specifically over the unknown antiquities left behind by the Greeks and Romans – on condition, of course, that I kept a distance from the living people of the East, who were a mere repository of history. I was always to remember that I was Irish, and a Catholic.

I shall never forget how angry he was when we talked once about religions and were speaking of the Ancient Greeks, his favourite subject. The conversation turned to their gods, and I said to him that the Greeks of those days, like the Ancient Egyptians and for that matter everyone before and after them, worshipped the Creator as they imagined Him, and that given that the Deity was the same at all times and in all places, He must accept the prayers of all who worshipped Him. I was young then, maybe fourteen or fifteen, but my father didn't try to discuss the matter with me or teach me. His face flushed. 'So you'd put those who worship the True God on a par with those who worship a statue or a tree or any other false god? You'd put the believers in the Lord our Saviour on a par with heathens and savages who pray so that their gods may help them in hunting and war?' Despite my fear of his anger at that moment, I answered him back. 'I don't mean that at all, Papa. I mean that everyone looks for the Creator and worships Him out of faith and with good intent, and even if they choose wrongly, He must surely know that their intentions are pure because He knows everything.' My father, however, would not listen to me and insisted that I go to church to confess my sin to the priest and seek absolution. I went, of course, because I too was a loyal Catholic.

How much I miss him now, in spite of everything! If he were alive, I'd ask him to help me in my search. He was the one who taught me Greek and Latin and said I was gifted at languages and should put my talent to use. I think he wasn't wrong. I have taught myself to read hieroglyphs and their derivatives and after I married Mahmoud I learnt Arabic. My father would be proud of me, in that respect anyway. He used to read his papers and translations from the Greek to me and he encouraged me too to translate and enthused over everything I wrote. All the same, I am sure I couldn't have convinced him to accept my marriage to Mahmoud. Impossible.

I haven't seen my mother either since I came to Egypt and I don't know what her feelings are now. She writes to me sometimes, briefly, just for form's sake. She wasn't pleased by my first marriage and I suppose her to be even more set against the second. My sister Fiona was the only one to understand my marriage to Mahmoud straight away. Just as she forgave my marriage to Michael, she blessed my marriage to Mahmoud. She forgave me for the business with Michael, even if I haven't forgiven myself. No wonder my father used to call her 'the Saint'. She writes me her long, loving letters all the time. Will she come to Egypt one day as she has promised? And how would she be able to get in touch .with us if she did, with our leaving now for a place so far from civilization? I have written to her telling her to postpone her travel plans.

But let me think this through to the end. Do I truly want her to come or do I want her, despite my missing her, to remain distant? I don't want things that remind me of that painful experience. I recovered from it only with difficulty. I'm certain, of course, that she'd never do anything to bring back the memory; perhaps she'd not even mention Michael's name if we met. It's not she that's the problem, it's me: it's my feeling that I stole him from my sister. If only Fiona knew how lucky she was to have been saved from him!

Our close neighbour, a friend and youthful companion of my father's, like him a teacher, with the face of an angel and soft spoken, he was joined to my father by their interest in the study of the language and the civilization of the Greeks, though while my father was content all his life to be an amateur, Michael published articles in a small local journal, and sometimes they'd accept essays from him in a well-known history journal. I believed, like everyone else, that when he visited the house it was because of his interest in Fiona. He would spend hours in conversation with her in the garden, and there was nothing strange in that. Fiona was the more beautiful, the younger, and the more congenial. Just to look at her shining face was a pleasure. I know my body is acceptable but my face is ordinariness itself. Despite all that, one year after my father's death, from the shock of which I had yet to recover, he surprised me with a proposal of marriage.

I entered my father's study one sunny morning and found him toppled over a book he was reading. He had never been sick before and complained of no ailments; indeed, on that particular morning he had been more than usually cheerful. Mahmoud told me he'd experienced a similar shock. I didn't understand the meaning of that death. I don't understand what meaning death has, but since it is inevitable, we should do something to justify our lives. We should leave a mark on this earth before we leave it.

When Michael came to me in the garden, I asked him, 'Why me?' and he replied, 'Because I love you.' 'And Fiona?' And he repeated, 'You are the one I love.' My mother, in great anger, said, 'He led us all to believe that he wanted Fiona and now he wants to get engaged to her sister? Anyone would think there had been a scandal! Has anything been going on between you that we don't know about?' I swore with perfect honesty that I hadn't thought about him at all, and that his offer had taken me by surprise, not to mention that I myself didn't want him. But it was Fiona herself who settled things. She said she had never thought of Michael as anything but a friend of her father's and the family's, and even if he had proposed to her she would have refused.

If that was true, then she was not only the more beautiful but also the more intelligent.

No doubt she understood him better than I. She said she wouldn't accept Michael under any circumstances and left it up to me to accept or refuse him. I thought a little and then agreed. I told myself that beautiful Fiona would surely find better opportunities.

Why did I ignore my mother's insistence that, whatever my sister might say, this marriage would be a betrayal of her? I should have understood, as she did, that he was not a person to be trusted, but at the time I had no way of knowing his other characteristics. It was only after the marriage that I experienced his insane jealousy of other men. He imposed on us a complete isolation during which we neither visited nor were visited and hardly even left the house. His jealousy extended even to books.

He'd been used to seeing me studying with my father and had demonstrated in his presence a concern for the encouragement of my studies. Then, after we married, he came to hate the sight of me holding a book. He would mock my readings and my translations. What was I going to do with them when I had no employment? Wouldn't it be better if I concerned myself with the housework? And all the time he would accuse me of ignorance and expose mistakes in my readings of the Latin or Greek.

At the beginning, I tried praising his work. I would display an exaggerated admiration for his articles and studies, which I knew he copied from others with minor alterations. It was no use. At least he knew that I was playing the hypocrite with him and that my admiration was false. He refused, however, to acknowledge that there might be any truth to the criticism he perceived in my comments; rather, he would insist that I, like other readers, had failed to grasp the central idea of his article. That also was my fault. I was responsible because his ideas were beyond us.

And from the start of the marriage, too, I discovered his miserliness. He wasn't just a miser with money. That's no great sin in a poor country that doesn't permit its people to live in luxury. But he was grudging in everything, even his feelings.

On the few occasions when he made love to me, he behaved as though he were bestowing on me a great favour, and one that he was in a hurry to be done with. I only really discovered my body with Mahmoud, after the failed attempts with Michael. With Mahmoud, I came to know that the practice of love is a sublime moment in which two bodies fly together, leaving the world's orbit for a pleasure that is new every time. A unique grace would descend, as though each occasion were the first, and as though that final gasp were a new birth, or a new resurrection – something I never knew with Michael, something utterly different from the stickiness of the sweat, the revulsion and the tension of a body desperate to be watered and, with that, relieved of the torture of an entangling that led only to disgust at oneself and one's bedmate.

Once I asked him, 'Why did you marry me?' to which he replied sarcastically, 'To torture myself.' Maybe he was telling the truth. A man can't marry a woman he doesn't love unless he wants to torture himself. But why? To the end of his life I could see in his eyes a sad and abject look when he gazed at Fiona. So why didn't he marry her and why did he choose me? I have known men in my life who avoid beautiful women for fear of the looks of others who ask, 'Does that man deserve that woman?' Perhaps he too was that cowardly, or maybe he was indeed sure he didn't deserve her, so he chose the ordinary sister for whom nobody would envy him to torture himself, as he said, and to torture me along with him for four long years.

All the same, he found out, after my first few attempts to placate him, that I was not the sort of person he had imagined. I am not one to endure a slight. I gave him cruelty for cruelty and hatred for hatred. I suggested to him when we were first married that we take a journey to Egypt, because Ancient Egypt had for so long bewitched me and because I hoped that if we went somewhere far away we might succeed in growing closer and understanding one another better. I said we could divide the costs of the trip because the money left me by my father was enough for my share. But Michael considered the very idea a sign of madness. Meaningless folly and dissipation. I could learn everything I needed to know about Egypt from books, if indeed my mind was capable of taking anything in. I challenged him. I began to study the language of the Ancient Egyptians. I studied hieratic and demotic on my own. None of this pleased him. He would snatch the books from my hand and tear them to pieces because I was wasting my time on things of no value instead of working in the house; I should make an effort, at least, to perfect the languages that I had started on. I would get up very calmly, take a book from his library, and start ripping it up. He would fall on me and beat me and try to stop me, and I would take more books and hit him with some of them and tear up what I could. We almost killed one another with the books in those battles, and with our fists in others. Indeed, things would have ended with a crime or a scandal, for I often thought of fleeing the house and the whole country and would have done so but for my apprehension about what would happen to my mother and Fiona, and had not his miserliness and stubbornness killed him first.

He insisted on considering the cough that racked his chest an ordinary bout of cold. He treated himself with herbs, hot drinks, warm rum, hot and cold baths, and all the remedies that he had ever tried or heard about before. We watched as his body withered and his cough turned into a bark whose mere sound inspired terror. Neither my urgings, nor those of Fiona or my mother, were of use in making him show himself to a doctor. It wasn't worth it. The last remedy he had tried, or the last drink he had taken, was the tried and true cure that would put an end to the illusory cold. In the end, when he started spitting gouts of blood with the cough and went to the doctor, it was too late.

The sight of him in bed in the hospital, his face the colour of chalk as he gasped for breath, incapable even of coughing, horrified me. The horror was there, but when I searched in my soul for some true sorrow, I could find none, even when he looked at me with panic-stricken eyes as though asking for a rescue I couldn't provide. And I was alarmed at myself when he died, because I found within myself, and in spite of myself, an exhalation of relief that shouted, 'At last!'

It wasn't intentional. I didn't kill him and I didn't wish death on him, but he came to an end as a result of his own acts, and what fault of mine was that? Despite this, I did my duty for the period of mourning and gave a good performance of all the required outward shows. Fiona's grief, though, was real. How should I know? Maybe she truly did love him even though she denied it. Or perhaps it was her heart, which felt for everyone. How should I know? As though my life weren't complicated enough already!

Four years with Michael killed many things in me, and two years with Mahmoud brought them back to life again. It's true. Nothing less than the genuine resurrection of a new woman. The cure may have started with the journey to Upper Egypt that I was able to make with the money Michael, who had saved it penny by penny, had left me. As I moved among the antiquities looking at the pictures and statues and reading by myself the writings carved on the columns and walls and entering them in my notebooks, I felt that this was a pleasure above any I had dreamt of. Then I met Mahmoud. What a blessing to find someone who was Michael's opposite in everything! He gives without stinting and knows no limits, not even to the contradictions and shifts of his moods!

Here he is at last.

I hear his familiar footfall on the stairs.

Come, Mahmoud! We shall travel to the desert together. We shall be reborn there together too, and in that rebirth I shall not let you escape. You will be mine.

3

Mahmoud

So this is the 'garden of the spirit', as Saeed called it! His spirit maybe, not mine. It moves nothing in me, this yellow 'garden'. Except anger, perhaps.

The desert stretches away before my eyes and there is nothing in it but sand, dunes, rocks, and the mirage that shimmers in the distance. Searing heat by day and biting cold by night. From time to time, chains of grey mountains like the remnants of a single mountain transformed by a bolt of lightning into splintered rubble.

Catherine and I ride on camels at the front. She wears riding dress, the trousers puffed out at the thighs, and is the only one with a saddle with an awning of thick cloth, like an open howdah. The guide, and the Bedouin of the caravan, show concern for her. They put up a tent for her at night while they themselves sleep in the open, sheltered from the winds by their kneeling camels. The ten soldiers who joined the caravan with me ride at the rear, with the exception of Sergeant Ibraheem, my orderly, whom Brigadier General Saeed attached to my service before the journey with his personal commendation.

As each day passes on the road, a deeper silence reigns over the caravan, and all eyes are directed to the front, gazing into the emptiness. What does each of them think about? I don't know, but the silence floods my mind with cries and images that awaken all the past – all who are alive and all who have passed away. It may be that this started before the journey. I think about many things, especially the end.

Am I afraid of death? Of course. Who isn't? I ask myself how it will take me – at the oasis with a bullet? Or as an ordinary death after an illness, long or short? In some passing accident? By strangulation in the bathhouse or poison put in my food? Will it come without any preamble whatsoever? Hundreds of shapes hide in the dark corners of the road, waiting to pounce on me in a single leap that is itself the end. I make every effort to forget my mother, but on this trip I cannot. I see her waiting for me that night when I came home, sitting in her large chair next to the bed, the maid lying on the floor, fast asleep. I knew that my mother never went to sleep until she had assured herself of my return and asked her customary question – had my brother Suleiman sent a letter from Damascus? Usually there was no letter, but I would reassure her that I had heard that he and his children were well. I kissed, as usual, her head and hand and asked her whether she needed anything. She asked for a cup of water because she couldn't bring herself to wake the maid. Before I reached the door, she cautioned me, 'From the brown jug.' Then 'and in the brass cup' caught up with me. I went to the main room, where the jugs were kept on a tray on the sill of the north-facing window, and I lifted up the brown jug, which she would always perfume with mastic and cover with a fine pierced cloth, and which really did cool the water more than the others. I poured the water into the brass cup decorated with coloured foliage and returned to the room, having in mind to tease her about the cup, which was the only one she would drink from because my father had given it to her one day. A minute or two had gone on these things, and when I opened the door, cup in hand, I saw her head drooping on her chest. I went up to her, calling out, but she didn't answer me and I discovered she was gone.

I went two months incapable of taking anything in. I would repeat to all who offered me condolences everything that had occurred between my leaving the room and my returning to it, as though these details concealed some secret or riddle that would explain what had happened. And my

28

legs shook when I walked. I didn't understand and I still can't understand.

Yes, I fear death, but despite that I was prepared, at one time, to meet it without hesitation. In those days there was meaning, but that's over and done with. The only thing that still reminds me of it is the intermittent pain left by the bullet that smashed the bones of my arm. Now, though, what am I supposed to die for in this forgotten oasis among these Bedouin whom I hate? Catherine says the inhabitants of the oasis aren't Bedouin, but all the inhabitants of the desert are Bedouin and I know them more than well enough. She too will regret her insistence on making the journey. I warned her often and she kept repeating that nothing could make her regret so long as she had chosen. Despite this, I can't understand the secret of her eagerness to make the journey. I think that, once again, it's about the antiquities. She exhausted me at the Luxor temple and in Upper Egypt and at Saqqara and Dahshur, and in the end I grew accustomed to leaving her to go where she wanted with an orderly as guard. Now she speaks with passion of Alexander the Great and his visit to the oasis and can't believe that she's travelling where he travelled! She wants to cross the desert so she can follow in his footsteps and search for his remains, and it doesn't matter if it costs her her life. A brave woman? A madwoman! I was only just able to convince her to abandon her idea of letting ourselves be bitten by snakes before the journey so that we could gain immunity to the reptiles of the desert! The sheikhs of the Rifa'i order I had advised her to consult contented themselves with giving her phials containing liquids of whose benefits I know nothing. But it may be that it is this madness which binds me to her. No sane woman ever convinced me to take on the bonds of marriage. Of course, before her there was Dusky Ni'ma, but I was the one who drove her away and it never occurred to me to marry her. Enough!

29

In any case, I am not travelling now for the sake of Catherine or the promotion which Harvey insisted on reminding me of. Perhaps, had it not been for the stigma of the court martial to which Saeed alluded, and had I not been ignorant of any other profession, I would have refused the promotion and the journey with it. Enough! Let happen what may. I remember from my school days a line of verse that goes:

> Of today I know what may be known, and of the day
> before,
> But to tomorrow I am blind.

Would that it were the other way around – that I were ignorant of what happened yesterday and knew what will happen tomorrow. In fact, I'd even accept blindness to what tomorrow might bring on condition that yesterday would go away too. I'd agree to even less – that morning would come and I'd live one day at a time, with all memories gone from my mind. What a comfortable arrangement of life it would be if we could live today without the disquiet of either yesterday or tomorrow! In this desert, though, there's nothing in my mind except yesterday, and I do not like it.

By day, the same scenes are repeated, their monotony broken only by tracts, each far from the others, where the colour of the sands changes from red to white, or the appearance of dunes, which the camels make hard work of climbing, their pace slowing. Every two or three days, the guide cries out, giving us the glad tidings of our imminent arrival at a well or small, uninhabited oasis where we rest in the hope that the camels will find water. My eyes pass fleetingly over the landmarks, but I steal a glance at Catherine and behold her on the back of her camel, turning her head right and left with an unquenchable amazement in her eyes. Does she too see the 'garden' of Brigadier General Saeed? What is there new to keep catching her attention like that?

I asked her one night as we sat in front of our tent and she was gazing in absorption at the sky with its host of stars, and she answered, 'Can't you see for yourself? These stars, for example. Never in the city have I seen them so many or so bright.'

I raised my eyes to the sky, saying, 'Because the moon is still small.'

She responded, 'I know. But here the stars seem to me bigger and closer. They twinkle as though they were in constant motion towards me, so that I can almost touch them with my hand, as though they were swimming fast through the sky and will soon fall to earth.'

I laughed quietly as I said, 'I know a lot of Irish are poets but the desert affects us all differently.'

'And how does it affect you?'

'I have another desert stretching inside me, with nothing in it of the silence of this desert we are crossing – a desert full of voices and people and images.'

'That's very beautiful.'

'It would be beautiful if the images weren't also sterile, like the desert. All of them hark back to a past that is dead, but they pursue me all the time.'

She sighed as she said, 'It may not be the desert's fault. Perhaps you brought these things to it.'

'Perhaps,' I mumbled, as I stood up.

Our conversations on the road grew shorter too, day after day.

Despite which, the desert had something else in store for us.

On the ninth night of our journey, the caravan came to a halt far from any of the small wayside oases. In the morning, the light was pallid and the sun's rays did not bathe us. It remained a mere orange ball in the sky, veiled in mist and thick flying dust. The guide looked grim and irritable. He was urging his men to hurry with the loading of the camels and to tie the loads well when a light southerly wind, accompanied by a low whistling sound, began and stirred up scattered devils of white dust that flew here and there in little vortices, then fell back on to the sand.

When the guide passed close to us as he trotted by, he advised us to wrap our faces well to protect our noses and eyes. The caravan started on its way as usual, however; indeed, it advanced faster than normal. It seemed to me that the winds were driving the camels over the sands like boats over water. The men's robes ballooned out behind them and we all bent our heads to avoid the rushing air and the sand. Then the camels started to cry out, sometimes running and sometimes stopping, and on the far horizon a large oval cloud appeared, like a spiral-shaped hill, which crept slowly towards us over the sands. Screaming at the top of his voice, the guide ordered the whole company to dismount, make our camels kneel, and take a firm grip of their reins, but by the time the command was issued two camels had shaken off their loads and set off, running aimlessly in different directions. One load of fabrics flew into the sky, scattering like coloured sails escaping into space, and metal pots and pans tumbled against one another with a repeated ringing sound that could be heard through the roaring of the camels and the shouting of the men, while the spiralling hill crept quickly towards us, driving before it wisps of sand that penetrated to our muffled faces like arrows. As the cloud got closer, the whistling of the dust devils was transformed into a thundering roar and no one could hear any longer what the guide was screaming. Catherine threw her arms around me and we staggered like the rest, were forced to our knees, then got up and staggered about again in the middle of the circle of kneeling camels while I tried to protect her and myself from the hail of gravel and small stones that pelted us. Then total darkness fell upon us and the roaring enveloped us. I could no longer hear the voice even of Catherine, who was screaming at me as she clung to me. All that existed was a deluge of sand and stones that came from all directions and piled up on top of us, so that every time I tried to shake them off they weighed the more heavily on my head and shoulders and I thought to myself that they would bury us for ever.

And in those moments when I was incapable of breathing and a terrible constriction pressed down on my chest, I wished for death with all my heart. The thought 'Let it come!' flashed into my mind as I held Catherine's shaking body to me. It was painful but not frightening. Let it come quickly! I want the end, as a beautiful relief from a burden I can no longer carry. Let it come!

But it didn't come.

Rather, everything suddenly stopped.

Just as the storm cloud had caught us and flung us in all directions in the desert, so it quickly receded and moved on to a place unknown. Quiet reigned and the sun shone. We, though, continued to cough and spit out the yellow sand which had filled our throats and mouths and I heard the panting, disjointed voice of the guide ordering his men to gather up whatever could be retrieved of the goods scattered over the desert. One of the Bedouin cried out, 'But we've lost two of the camels,' to which the guide replied, 'If they're alive they'll come back. Redistribute what's left of their loads among the other camels.' Catherine, who had kept her head buried in my chest the whole time, raised a pale and dust-stained face as she ripped its covering off, let out a long breath and tried to smile.

Still in a state of astonishment at myself, I said, 'It wasn't very frightening.'

'What wasn't?' mumbled Catherine.

'Death.'

She drew back a step, raised her gaze to mine, and asked me, 'You mean, it wasn't very close?' I thought for a second before answering, 'On the contrary, it was very close.'

She was no longer listening to me, however. Breathing hard and coughing, she was carefully removing the sand from her face and clothes, and I was incapable of explaining to her how it was the nearness of death which had made it familiar and desirable. At the same moment, I found Ibraheem, the orderly, before me, his face hidden behind a mask of clinging yellow grains that left only the eyes and lips showing.

'Are Your Excellency and madame all right?' he asked me.

'We are. And what about you, Ibraheem?'

'As you can see, sir, I'm an old man. When the darkness fell on us, I recited the double profession of faith, but more time has been written for us, praise God.'

Ibraheem is the only one among the soldiers who has undertaken the journey to the oasis before. In his youth he took part in one of the military expeditions against Siwa, and Brigadier General Saeed commended him to me for that reason.

Catherine was following our conversation and she gestured towards Ibraheem and said, 'Now do you see?' but I didn't ask her what she was talking about, nor was there time to ask. The whole caravan was bustling with activity and the kneeling camels had started to rise in preparation for departure.

The caravan continued on its way in the midst of complete quiet. The noise of the winds and the roaring of the camels had disappeared and the caravan pursued its path over smooth, still sands, as though the desert had never known a storm. The tired camels moved forwards slowly and the drivers, exhaustion drawn on their faces too, didn't try to hurry them. At midday we reached a small well edged with a few trees, most of them withered, and there we found one of the two camels the caravan had lost. It was kneeling and moaning, its body bearing long open wounds like the parallel strokes of a whip.

The guide patted its neck and told it, 'You should have stayed quiet during the storm, my friend, not run from it to your destruction. Haven't the desert and the caravans taught you anything?'

Then he bent over and started anointing its wounds with oil that he poured from a metal flask. He turned towards me while I was observing what he was doing and said, as though in self-defence, 'This isn't the storm season. It came at least a month early. I've lived with this desert all my life and know it like the back of my hand. I've memorized its tracks and its seasons, but it's treacherous. No matter how long you live with it and how safe you feel in it, it can still betray you.'

'Not so much as men.'

Busy doctoring the camel with both hands, he asked me, 'What did you say, Excellency?'

'I asked you how much longer we'll stay here.'

'The camels have to rest. We'll spend the rest of the day and the night here.'

The guide gave orders that we, that is Catherine and I, should be the first to use the well and kept the rest of the caravan away from us. After we had washed and changed our clothes, which were full of sand, we moved off a way and the men approached, cheering and jumping into the muddy pool surrounding the well. We stood in the shade of a palm tree, where their laughter and shouts reached us as they frolicked in the water, and Catherine said, smiling, 'It might be said that those men are happy to have been saved from death. And it might be said that they did indeed find it frightening.'

'And it might be said too that I was as afraid of it as they were, but when it came close to me and I touched it, I found it smooth and soft, and it whispered to me, "Come. The faster you come, the better." It's not the first time I've faced death. But here, in this desert, there's something I can't explain, something beckoning, or calling.'

Catherine burst out angrily, 'That's enough! You know I'm not afraid of death. It will come at its appointed time. But I don't yearn for it and I don't woo it. This life is for us to live,

35

so let's try to give it some meaning. The truth is it's you that is scaring me now.'

'Pay no attention, then. It may just be a passing moment. Ever since beginning this journey I've never stopped thinking about what has happened to me in my life. Few pleasures, heavy sorrows. As though the desert were asking me, "If this is how things stand, isn't it true that the faster it comes the better?"'

'I told you, it's not the desert's fault. It's not your gloomy thoughts about death that are upsetting me now because you're not the only person to have discovered them, and most people perhaps think that way in moments of crisis and sorrow, but ... there's something beyond that that's been inside you for a while and which is no fault of the storms or the desert. So what is your crisis, Mahmoud? You're the only one who knows. All I know is that this desert will fight us and so will the oasis and so will enemies known and unknown and, of course, we will die in the end. We shall die like everyone else, but we have to die undefeated.'

'And who said I want to kill myself?' I replied. Then I laughed. 'The people of the oasis are going to take that task upon themselves! Why would you even imagine I'd kill myself? What do we have, in fact, other than this life? We have to live it to the last instant.'

Catherine raised her hands and her eyes widened a little as she said, 'How is it I still haven't gone mad?'

At that moment, Ibraheem approached us, the water still dripping from his hair and running over the wrinkles of his brown face. 'Does Your Excellency require anything?' he said.

I smiled as I asked, 'And what can you do for me in this place, Ibraheem?' Ibraheem turned in the empty waste and pointed to a tall, emaciated palm tree, saying, 'It's date season. If this palm tree were to produce any, I'd climb it for Your Excellency.'

'What a hypocrite you are, Ibraheem! If you climbed it, you'd break your neck, and what good would that do me? And you want to go on living, don't you?'

He spread out his hands and said, 'For the sake of the little ones, Your Excellency.'

Catherine said, 'Instead of climbing the palm tree, then, tell us something useful about the oasis before we arrive.'

'But I've told you everything I know, madame. It's like no other place and its people are like no other people. Say what you like about them, they're the bravest people I've ever seen. When I came with the army twenty years ago, we bombarded the town with artillery and the only weapons they had were small rifles, which they fired at us from behind the walls. But despite all their dead they didn't surrender until their ammunition ran out. They have their feuds, but they always form one front against outsiders. And they also don't allow . . . outsiders in their houses.'

'Especially infidels, isn't that so?' said Catherine, laughing.

Embarrassment appeared on Ibraheem's face as he mumbled, 'I'm sorry, madame.'

Catherine turned to me and said, 'Indeed, I read that they hate Europeans especially and that they have killed a number of European travellers who went to explore the oasis.'

'When I think of all the disasters the Europeans have brought to our country, I can't blame them,' I said. 'And don't forget,' I added, 'I warned you more than once. You're the one that insisted.'

'And still insist,' she said, lightly. 'You shall see. I will tame them.'

Turning to Ibraheem, I said, 'But I imagine they hate the government more!'

Ibraheem answered in a low voice, 'They hate paying the taxes and I think they're . . .'

Then he said no more, asked permission to leave and went back towards the well.

'So they'll be welcoming me with open arms from the outset!' I said to myself. I have been told above all to collect the outstanding taxes. I am to send to Cairo immediately on my arrival two thousand camel-loads of dates, five hundred camel-loads of olive oil, and a late fee in cash of five thousand rials. Mr Harvey chose well!

The rest of the caravan was making its way towards us, some of the men wringing out the clothes they had washed. One of them came over to me at a trot and said, 'The guide has changed his mind. He's decided that we should rest here now and resume the journey at night. He says the desert is safer than this pool, which attracts wolves and hyenas in the dark.'

Slapping a gnat on my cheek, I said, 'And what are these hosts of gnats going to be like at night?'

They put up the only tent and Catherine went in to sleep. She's fortunate. Sleep comes to her quickly, whenever she wants. Unlike me, she doesn't have to do battle with it each time. The men – Bedouin, traders and soldiers – slept too, and the camels settled down to rest in preparation for the night journey. The desert, comatose, stretched to the horizon – a calm sea of spreading sands, without movement or sound, it, the camels and the humans recovering their strength after the storm. How deep the calm! Brigadier General Saeed told me, 'Believe me, in some ways, I envy you for going into the desert, paradise of prophets and poets. To it flee all those who would leave the world behind them to find themselves and in it the withered soul puts out new leaves and the spirit blooms!' What a good and simple man you are, Saeed! As though all that a man has lived through and has accumulated in his bosom could evaporate simply by virtue of his moving from soil to sand! You're like Catherine, who sings songs of love to the desert and says that it's changing her. This really amazes me, for she's no Sufi, like Saeed, and I don't believe that the things of the spirit concern her. And how can she claim with such confidence that we shall defeat the world? What weapon could I, for example, have brandished in the world's face when all the rest had put their weapons away? The good ones, like Brigadier General Saeed, were content merely to stick their weapons in their scabbards. The others, though, stuck them in the country's chest. I beheld with my own eyes the stab in the back that broke Urabi, and then I beheld the greater betrayal that followed, right next to my own house, to be precise, in the square that had witnessed the glory and the joy, with Urabi on his horse waving his sword and berating the Khedive, who had humiliated them for so long – 'God created us to be free men, not chattels or property to be inherited. I swear by God, than whom there is no other, that we will never again, from this day on, be handed down from one master to the next, or treated as slaves' – and the people came together in droves from the streets and the alleyways, strangers embracing strangers, tears of joy in their eyes. A day of rejoicing in the Protected City! And in the very same place, just one year later, I saw the gilded carriages, drawn by horses in splendid harness, descending one after the other into the broad square, carrying the great men of the country, the bashas, the beys and the members of parliament who had delivered fiery speeches against the British in the days of the revolution – I saw the very same men in all their grandeur, with their embroidered coats and gilded medals, alighting from their carriages to join the Khedive on his dais, from which he reviewed the army of occupation with, on his right, Admiral Seymour, the cannon of whose fleet had demolished Alexandria, and, on his left, General Wolseley, who, with the help of traitors, had annihilated our army at Tell el Kebir. A few days later, I read that the same bashas and beys had collected a huge sum of money and used it to buy expensive gifts to present to Seymour and Wolseley, and I wept for my country and myself. And Catherine asks me what my crisis is?

But what in fact is my crisis? All that is an old dispensation and has passed into oblivion, so what is the problem now?

I got up and walked, turning my back on the tent and the uninhabited oasis. Nothing but sand and distant brown hills like carvings of crouching beasts. I saw the men sleeping scattered over the sand, each taking refuge in whatever shade he could find – under a palm or other tree or in the shade of a kneeling camel, some covering their faces with large kerchiefs. They too had been able to find peace and sleep in this heat. I alone then was incapable of sleeping. I have spent days and years concocting short-lived peace treaties with myself. No sooner do I tell myself that I did what I had to do than something inside me mocks me, and I run to drink and women just as I did as an adolescent and a young man. Where now, though, is the innocence of my early years, when things were easy and straightforward and peace of mind came without effort or complication? And what is the point of thinking about such things anyway? All the same, there's no escape from the faces that crowd the emptiness and impose themselves suddenly and importunately. My father peers down. I see him in his shop in el Muski, with the confident, beaming face of his glory days; then he comes at me with the face of an old, broken man, after his defeat. My brother Suleiman, whom we haven't seen for so long, appears and I try to make out his features. And I see the face of Dusky Ni'ma, the one and only, for whom I search in all other women. The face of Tal'at, friend and companion of my youth, rises to the surface, but with his appearance all the other faces disappear and the roar of the cannon reverberates in my ears. I deliberately push him away and return to Ni'ma. Why didn't I appreciate her worth when she was mine to do with as I liked? My ruse doesn't work. It is Tal'at who pushes her aside and lays siege to me.

I decided to go back. My legs would not bear me for long in the burning sun, so I returned to the tent in the hope that sleep would come. To no avail. No sleep came to my eyelids and I could not even close my eyes. No escape from the face of Tal'at. I left the tent and sat on the ground in its shade.

Those hours and days with Tal'at remain engraved on my memory no matter how hard I try to erase them. I see us running together on the shore. We're running from one fort to the next with our little patrol of troopers, waiting for the artillery bombardment to stop, then we join the throng of people rushing blindly towards the sea and the site of the latest battle. All our clothes are bloodied. There's no time to think about anything, not even what's going on before our eyes. We have to hurry. Splinters from the British shells, coming from many points at sea, fly over our heads. We scream at the top of our lungs as we force our way through the throngs milling in the streets of Alexandria so that we can open a way for the horses pulling the carts. Sometimes we dismount and force a way through with our bodies, then get back on the carts, which are piled with soldiers from the forts, who are tied on top of them in mounds so that they don't fall off on to the road. Among them too are the ordinary people who volunteered at the forts and have been injured. We have nothing with which to respond to the pleas and moans of the wounded and nothing with which to stem the blood dripping from the carts and forming a trail along the route from the fort to the door of the hospital at el Raml. At the hospital we leave them to the people there to sort into dead and living and hurry back again along the beach, searching for a senior official or high-ranking officer to direct us towards something useful we could do. We were just two young lieutenants whom they'd transferred to Alexandria after the massacre in which a number of foreigners had been killed and which the British took as their excuse for war. But we can't find a single superior officer to ask.

I can see myself with Tal'at on the top of a rise, watching from afar what is happening to one of the forts. Tal'at says in

41

a choking voice, 'It's slaughter, not war,' and I reply, 'You're right.' We see the British ships shelling the fort as though carrying out a leisurely review, with three large ships in a geometric formation pointing their guns at the fort and then shelling it very precisely, and then the fort responding – those who remain alive inside it, that is, responding – by firing their ancient cannon, the shells falling far, far from the ships, and even those that reach the fleet being rebuffed by sheets of steel that clad the ships so that a giant white fountain explodes out of the sea at the place where the shell hits it without inflicting any damage. The revenge comes immediately, however. The serene battleships move closer to the openings from which the cannon peek and strike them with machine-gun fire. The artillerymen, who have no sheets of steel, or even of stone, to protect them are cut down and the firing doesn't stop until the fort is blown up, along with its soldiers. And we run towards it. We strain to hear the sound of the ambulance horses and their bells, but the bombardment continues, even after the forts have raised white flags and not one cannon in them remains in a condition to fire.

On our way back from the military hospital we see fires in the city, in el Manshiya and Kom el Dikka, and in one street we see gangs of Bedouin riff-raff breaking into the locked shops and plundering them. They throw torches to burn what the guns of the British have not already burnt. We corner them and fire at them with our revolvers and rifles and they fortify themselves behind the walls and return fire. Their weapons are much better than ours. Then one of their chiefs orders his men in a loud voice to stop shooting and comes towards us, his hands in the air. He stands in the middle of the road and asks us in astonishment, 'Why are you firing? Didn't you get the orders?' They were carrying out orders, he says, so why were we standing in their way? Tal'at asks him, 'What orders, you madman?'

I see Tal'at's reddened eyes and the blood clotted on his military jacket and on his hands, as it is on mine and on those of all the soldiers of the patrol. He's the one whose looks speak of madness, while the tribesman stands in front of us in his flowing white robes addressing Tal'at calmly and arrogantly, saying, 'Those of His Excellency the governor, my dear lieutenant. Have you forgotten how we helped you out a month ago, the day the Greeks were killed? Didn't Umar Basha give you orders that day not to interfere with us when we struck at the foreigners? Will you not carry out the orders to bring down Urabi, who is in a state of mutiny against Our Master the Khedive and bringing ruin on the country? What is different now? Why are you shooting at us?'

Tal'at started letting out short laughs, like exclamations, as he looked towards me and said, 'Did you hear? Let's be off, Mahmoud. Back to the station! Or to our houses! Are we to disobey the orders of His Excellency the governor? Or those of Our Master the Khedive? Or of Our Lord Admiral Seymour? Back to our houses!' He went on laughing his strange laugh and gesticulating with the hand in which he was holding the revolver and the tribesman sensed danger and started to retreat in the direction of his men, who had fortified themselves behind the walls, but Tal'at yelled, pointing his revolver at him, 'Wait! Wait! Take this for yourself! And this for Our Master the Khedive! And this . . .' and he couldn't name the one he wanted the third bullet for because of the volley of fire directed at him by the followers of the chief, who ran to join his men. I threw Tal'at to the ground and flattened myself next to him. I managed to hit the tribesman and he fell to the ground and went on crawling to get to the others, and a bullet hit me in the top of my left arm, at the shoulder. But for the Alexandrians, who came at the sound of the shooting carrying rifles, staves, and knives, we would not have got out alive. Most of the Bedouin took refuge in flight, but I was able to catch a number of them. We made our way to the monks' hospital on Saba' Banat Street where they bound the men's wounds, and there I left Tal'at and the wounded soldiers and Bedouin, and drove the captives before me to the Labban police station.

The Italian station chief looked at my arm, which was bandaged and tied in a sling, and said nothing. He pointed to the Bedouin I had caught, however, and asked me, 'Who are they?' I told him what had happened and he gazed into my face for a while before indicating to his men that they should take the Bedouin to the gaol. Then, for the first time, he gestured at my sling and said, 'There are still fires in el Manshiya. If your wound isn't serious, take a patrol there quickly and help evacuate the civilians.' And that was the sole mission I was entrusted with on that day. I asked the police chief what he was going to do with the Bedouin and he responded in Arabic, which he neither spoke nor understood, 'Look to your business!'

But there was no work that I or the soldiers could do in el Manshiya or anywhere else in the city. Alexandria had been turned into a bonfire under renewed bombardment from the fleet, the shells failing to discriminate between fortifications and houses or soldiers and civilians. For two days, thousands of men, women and children rushed towards Rasheed Gate to get away from the burning city – an uninterrupted flood of humanity that swept up with it the soldiers of my patrol, so that I found myself alone, moving from one place where the tongues of flame were encroaching to another to which the marching crowds, the crackling of the flames, the weeping of the children, the wailing of the women and the insults of the men, who cursed the British, the Khedive, the army and the police at the tops of their lungs, pushed me. Some of the men pointed at me and said, 'Traitor!' They were right: on that day, when their city had been burnt and they had lost sons and fathers, who could sort out the traitors from those who had remained true? The Khedive moved from palace to palace to take advantage of the protection of the fleet that was invading his country, the army withdrew following the destruction of the forts without explaining to the people why they were leaving the city, and the police left them without protection from the arsonists and plunderers. Among the flames of the burning buildings and the chaos, the page on which the courage of the soldiers of the forts and of the people of the city who had fought with them had been inscribed was erased. How, then, could I tell those refugees who insulted me that I, I alone, had not betrayed them?

All that remains in my mind of those days is disconnected images. I see myself in the midst of thousands blocking the streets, donkey carts loaded with people and possessions all brought to a halt by this human dam, while everyone quarrels with everyone else, and I see a cloud of dust and smoke hanging over their heads and spreading darkness at the height of the day, and I join a troop of soldiers seizing the thieves who were looting the abandoned shops, and executing them on the spot, and I see columns of soldiers making for Rasheed Gate to get out of the city; but I don't remember whether I slept or where I slept or what I did exactly during those two days. I went of course to the hospital to change the dressing on my wound, which was extremely painful, and to see that Tal'at was all right. He had been struck by bullets in his belly and legs but his life was not in danger. (Would that it had been! Would that he had died at that moment when he was true to himself! And would that I had departed with him!) And I saw my Italian superior officer when I went to the police station. He pointed with revulsion at the filthiness of my uniform. He himself hadn't left his office throughout the bombardment of the city and his badges of rank shone on the shoulders of his clean uniform, which fitted his plump body perfectly. And I remember him handing me that small paper crowded with official stamps that cancelled my transfer and ordered me without explanation to return forthwith to Cairo. In Cairo, however, I discovered that he had sent a telegram accusing me of dereliction of duty and saying that

45

I had been absent from my work for two consecutive days – during which period he suspected that I might have aided the mutineers who had spread civil strife in Alexandria – and requesting that I be investigated.

My investigation by Captain Saeed Effendi didn't take long. Conditions in Cairo were quite different from those I had left behind me in Alexandria. The 'mutineers' of the latter were heroes in Cairo the Protected. A council, formed of all Egypt's communal groups, had commissioned them to defend the country against the invaders.

During the interrogation, I related everything that I had done, starting with the bombardment of the forts, and made a point of mentioning what I'd heard from the Bedouin about the instructions of the governor, Umar Basha Lutfi, on the day of the massacre and during the fleet's shelling of the city. I also put on record what had happened from the time we were fired upon until we handed the captured tribesmen over at the Labban police station. The Italian police chief's telegram had made no mention of these or of their firing at and wounding us. And I presented my testimony regarding all that had befallen Lieutenant Tal'at, who was still being treated in Alexandria.

Captain Saeed recorded my statements and ordered that the investigation be shelved and I return to work. We were, both of us, preoccupied with helping the police maintain order in Cairo during the period of the war. I even neglected to have my deep shoulder wound treated, resulting in a delay in its knitting and mending. With everybody else, I followed with pride and enthusiasm what happened in the fighting at Kafr el Dawwar – the steadfastness of our army, the inability of the British to break through their fortifications there, and their withdrawal in the face of the attacks by our troops.

But the interrogation was reopened two months later, by which time everything had changed.

All the time I ask myself about the betrayal. I asked myself often then, 'Why were the bashas and the great men who had everything traitors? And why did the little people always pay the price, dying in the war and being imprisoned after the defeat, while the great ones remained free, and great?' I asked myself, 'Why were the little people also traitors? Why did the officer Yousif Khunfis betray his country's army at Tell el Kebir and guide the British so that they could make a sneak attack on it and destroy it by night? What was he thinking as he watched the British guns mow down his brothers and the companions-in-arms with whom he had eaten and slept and laughed? Did his eyes happen to fall on his brother officer Mohamed Ebeid as he crouched in the midst of the chaos and defeat, firing at the British till incinerated by the heat of his gun, as we heard? How I and the people all loved him! They refused to believe he was dead, saying that he was only 'absent'. They call him 'Sheikh Ebeid' and say that he has been seen, once in Damascus and once in Upper Egypt, and await his return to resume the war against the British! Despite which he remains a dream, while Yousif Khunfis is the reality we're left with. Why did Sheikh Ebeid depart in the flower of his youth, like a bird that swiftly crosses the sky, while Khunfis lives on, as though he will never die? Why do we betray others? The guide says the desert is treacherous, just because a storm came out of season! Come here, and let me tell you what real treachery is!

4

Catherine

Mahmoud sinks deep within himself. I see him sinking deeper
and deeper. Now he's riding his camel, his head bowed as
though sleeping and looking at nothing around him. I had
thought this desert would bring him out of his shell a little,
that he would see how different it is from any place in Egypt
we've seen together, but he asks me in amazement, 'What it is
that you like about it?' How can he not see? I read everything
about this desert and about Siwa before we began the journey
– all the books of the travellers and historians that I brought
with me from Ireland and everything I could find in the
bookshops of Cairo. I thought I'd never find out anything
new and that nothing would surprise me. I studied everything
written about the route and the wells, the dunes and the
storms, but the books didn't tell me about the real desert.
I didn't learn from them how the colours change above the
sea of sand through the hours of the day, and I didn't find a
word in them about the movement of the shadows as they
trace a thin grey cowl over the peak of a yellow hill or open
up a dark door in its centre, and they didn't teach me how
the small high clouds are reflected on the dunes as hurrying
flocks of grey birds, and they didn't speak to me of the dawn
– above all the dawn – when it shifts from a thin white line
on the horizon to a red blush that slowly pushes the darkness
aside until, with the first rays of the sun, the sand blazes like
a golden sea, at which moment a smell penetrates my nose
that I have never known before, of the mixture of the dawn's
dew, the sun, and the sand. An erotic smell that not only steals
into my nose but to which all the pores of my body open

themselves so that I could almost, were it not for shyness, and were it not for the cries of the men of the caravan, who have woken up outside my tent, seize Mahmoud's hand and say, 'Come here, right now! On this damp sand!'

And I ask myself in amazement, 'How can he not also feel what I feel? Why doesn't he embrace me, or kiss me at least?'

At every moment, this desert brings me something new, but it is Mahmoud that takes me by surprise. He says the desert reaches are inside him. Would that were true! How rich this desert is! But I hadn't previously noticed in him any attraction to nature outside the desert. He never stops in front of trees or flowers. He has never said that the sea enchants him, or rivers. And when we visit antiquities, boredom overcomes him in five minutes. He never contemplates the construction of a building, or a painting on a wall.

I don't mean to say that I am more intelligent than he or that I see things he is incapable of seeing. It may be that it is I who am incapable of understanding what interests him, though I have tried and am still trying. This is the man I'm in love with. I encouraged him to take the posting in the hope that the long journey would change him and the danger revive his flagging spirit. Though I'm not being wholly honest when I say that. I too am crossing this desert to carry out a mission! But let us wait now; it's still too early to think about that and you, Mahmoud, right now, are my mission, you are my real work. What was it that made you so delighted with the idea of dying in the sandstorm instead of its driving you to cling on to life, like Ibraheem and like all of them? And did you change your mind suddenly to please me, or was that an example of your switches of mood, which are incomprehensible to me? And among all these moods, where shall I find the true Mahmoud? I shall find you out, no matter how long it takes. And perhaps, along with you, I shall find a real Catherine of whom I'm ignorant. Who knows?

49

The caravan makes its way over the desert towards the west and day by day draws closer to the oasis. I truly long to reach it. Everything about it is like a myth – the place, the people, the history, the geography. It is, as I have read, part of an ancient sea and even now, in its sands and hills, seashells are to be found. Its inhabitants belong to the west, not the east, to the Zenata tribe of Berbers in Morocco, and they speak a Berber dialect. Despite this, in ancient times they were part of the Egypt of the pharaohs and a centre for the worship of their great god, Amun. And there's the story of the forty men who left the village of Aghurmi with its ancient ruins to build to the west of it, in the midst of the vast desert, and to surround with walls the city where now they live.

I truly long to see all that and understand it and I am convinced that the oasis will meet my longing with its own. I don't suppose anyone like me has visited it. All those who visited it before me were content to describe its ancient ruins from the outside, and some of them drew them, but which of those could read the language of the Ancient Egyptians or of the Greeks? Even those who copied the carvings from the temples made horrible mistakes, because they copied the hieroglyphs as though they were just pictures. I could tell the mistakes just by looking at them. Only I am capable of revealing your secrets, Oasis!

A modicum of modesty, Catherine!

Why? Isn't that the truth? Nevertheless, I shall hold my tongue, lest I be afflicted by that hubris which the Greeks believed to be the origin of all life's tragedies. Let me be humble, then. I have no need of new tragedies. All I need to do is open my eyes to the grandeur of this desert.

The mounds and hills have disappeared now and we are moving through soft sand stretching to a horizon in whose expanse only the blue shimmerings of the mirage can be seen. Despite this, as we cross these flat reaches of yellow sand, we are surprised by vast lakes of white sand, or by round dunes like little shrines or jutting breasts on the desert's bosom. I sense that the camels' pace increases when passing over these smooth sands and that the ground gives way beneath their hoofs, the camels moving forwards nimbly and energetically, as though skating over the sand. Do their hearts beat hard to the joltings of the descent, as mine does? I realize that we have entered at last the large depression that leads to the oasis and which centuries and centuries ago was a part of the great blue sea. For the last three days we haven't come across anything green on our path, not even those little cacti that defy the dryness and get their water from the drops of dew. At the last well that we passed, the guide said we should take all the water we needed because we wouldn't see another until we reached the oasis.

On the appointed morning, I heard a view halloo and sudden shouting among the Bedouin and traders of the caravan. At last, in the distance, the far distance, the sands gave way to reveal the tops of palms, and everyone waved, myself along with them, at the life that had suddenly been born out of what was dead, and the exhausted camels ran, sharing in the clamour and understanding that they had at last reached the end of their toils.

As we arrived, men of the small village on the outskirts of the oasis came to meet us in an open courtyard surrounded by walls. I noticed that they were wearing neither the flowing robes of the Bedouin nor the trailing *gallabiyas* of the peasants. Their *gallabiyas* were white and short, like wide shirts, and under them they wore long drawers, and most of them were barefoot. They surrounded us and offered us sugary dates and almonds from baskets of palm fronds, then gave us milk to drink in vessels of earthenware.

Mahmoud was standing by my side with the soldiers around him. I noticed that whenever they came close to us looks of hostility, which they attempted to hide by lowering their eyelids, darted from the eyes of the natives, who were exchanging conversation and laughter with the Bedouin and traders, and that they would hasten their steps so as to get past us as fast as they could, then move away muttering angrily. Sergeant Ibraheem told us in embarrassment that they were astonished and perplexed because this was the first time they had seen an unveiled woman, dressed like a man, in the oasis. I smiled into their faces and raised my hand in greeting but they gathered far from me in small knots from which they directed surreptitious looks towards me and whispered to the Bedouin of the caravan, who had likewise avoided me throughout the journey. I supposed that they were most probably asking them about me, and I noted that a few of the people of the oasis spoke Arabic with the Bedouin, though among themselves they loudly spoke their own language, which we could not understand. They went on muttering, shaking their heads, and shifting their glances from me to Mahmoud. He noticed this and remained by my side, holding on to my arm the whole time, the soldiers in attendance. I myself paid no attention.

I started moving around from place to place in the crowded courtyard, my inescapable guard sticking close, and I enquired of Ibraheem what was going on between the traders and the village men who had gathered around them. I asked him, 'Why are the traders offering only perfume bottles and bead necklaces and not selling anything else from their stock of goods?' and he whispered to me that they postponed their real work until they reached the main market of the town and met with its traders. Here, however, they might sell some clothes, for this was the custom of the oasis from ancient times: they wore only clothes that were made especially for them in Kerdasa and brought to them in the caravans.

Evening came and it was decided that we should spend the night in the village to rest the exhausted camels, which they drove off to be watered from a nearby spring. Mahmoud ordered the men to set up the usual tent in this space with its surrounding walls.

I asked Mahmoud, 'Have you noticed that we haven't seen any of the women of the village? Even the children were all boys.'

Mahmoud smiled and said, 'I'm not thinking about women at the moment.'

Then his face turned serious and he said, 'We have to think about work now.'

He called Ibraheem and told him, 'Ask if any of the *agwad* are present in this village for me to speak with.'

Ibraheem laughed and said, 'What village, Your Excellency? There's no village here.'

I asked him in confusion, 'And these men who came to meet us, then, where do they live?'

'These, madame, are cultivators, *zaggala*. They work and sleep in the gardens around here, which are enclosed behind walls. The *agwad* and great men who own the gardens live in the large town which we shall be making for tomorrow morning, and that's where we'll see them. They will certainly have sent one of the *zaggala* by now to inform them of the caravan's arrival, and of that of His Excellency the district commissioner.'

Mahmoud said, 'Brigadier General Saeed Bey wasn't wrong when he told me that you knew a lot about the people of the oasis.'

'No one knows much about them, Your Excellency. I came here, as you know, with an army expedition twenty years ago and stayed a while, during which all I saw was war and fighting . . .'

Smiling, Mahmoud asked him, 'Why, then, did you come back?'

'I told Your Excellency that too,' said Ibraheem. 'For the sake of the little ones.'

Ibraheem was truly an old man. His face indicated that he was past sixty, though his leanness and agility might make one think that he was younger. So what did he mean by 'the little ones'?

I interrupted and asked, 'But surely your children are grown now, Ibraheem.' He avoided answering me directly and said after a moment of silence, 'They're my grandchildren, madame.'

I sensed that there was something there, so I stopped talking, but Mahmoud asked quite simply, 'And where are their fathers?'

Ibraheem raised his face and said in his village accent, 'Fate and fortune!' Then he fell silent once more.

Mahmoud fell silent too, but Ibraheem resumed quite naturally, 'As Your Excellency can see, they choose as they will. My children went in the prime of youth. I wish I could have taken the place of even one of them when the plague struck our town, but it was Divine Providence. They left me a tribe of grandchildren that the cholera passed over just as it did me. It may be for their sake that God has given me long life. It's for them that Brigadier General Saeed Bey, God protect him, helped me to get work with you here, so that I could put a little money aside for them.' Then Ibraheem attempted a smile and said, 'As you can see, I survived the cholera, and the war of the oasis and the war of the British that they call "the Riots", and here I am before Your Excellency, as strong as a horse.'

'God grant you long life, Ibraheem,' said Mahmoud.

He replied with a small laugh, 'More life? All I ask of God is that He send me back safe to my village.' Then he suddenly changed the subject with another laugh and said, 'Did you hear? The Bedouin asked the *zaggala* to put on a drumming party for us tonight. You'll see something you've never seen the like of before! If you'll excuse me, Excellency, I'll put the tent up.'

When he had left, Mahmoud said with a certain astonishment, 'He takes life just as he finds it!'

'Is there any other way, Mahmoud?' I responded.

'I don't have time even to think about that now. The *agwad*

54

are getting ready for me and I must get ready for them.' Then he left me, saying, 'Hold on a moment, Ibraheem!'

No one learns anything from anybody!

The drumming party, as Ibraheem called it, did, however, teach me something.

The whole caravan attended the singing, which took place in the sandy enclosure, open to a black sky and a large moon by whose light people appeared as animated shadows. The chanting of the *zaggala*, who sat in a circle on the ground surrounded by a few high torches, started to the accompaniment of great excitement and shouts of encouragement from the Bedouin, who were, I believe, as ignorant as I of the meaning of the words of the songs and merely pleased, as I was, by the chanting. This started so softly that it was close to a woman's whisper, full of drawn-out sighs, and moved seamlessly into a drumbeat of screaming roughness as rapid as the crackling of bullets, while primitive oboes emitted their own moans and shrieks. The singers then stood up, to be joined by the other men, with dozens of hands clapping to the rapid rhythm, the melodious cries growing louder till they seemed to be coming from everywhere in space. And they were not finished yet, for the chanters then formed a circle, each of whose members took hold of his companion's waist, and they revolved in a headlong ring, the dancing bodies staggering to the beat of the lewd singing, which rose to a tumultuous roar. I felt my heart racing as though it were about to burst with the reverberating rhythms, and I looked surreptitiously around me and found that even Mahmoud was spellbound by that vortex, as were the Bedouin, who sat silent and open mouthed.

That night, in the tent, Mahmoud made love to me, or I made love to him, with ardour and passion, the two of us sating our bodies after a long hunger, though careful, all the same, to make no sound. The sounds that we suppressed, however, increased the tension of our bodies, and how we pounced, taut as bows, each separately burrowing into the other's skin, seeking release, and the two of us together burrowing into a soft cradle of sand.

Not a bad beginning for the oasis!

At sunrise, the caravan resumed its progress towards the main town. The camels, which had baulked at the brackish water of the desert wells, had drunk sweet water and appeared refreshed and happy, and I too was refreshed and wide eyed at every new thing that met us on the road. For most of the way, it was still sand, hills and small brown mountains far off to the right, but from time to time we passed wells and lakes from which branched channels that extended to the cultivated lands behind the walls, above which nothing could be seen except the fronds of tall palm trees embracing clusters of dates, some of which were still green, though I could smell the penetrating scent of figs and other fruit and became aware of the incessant singing from behind the walls.

I realized that these were the work chants of the *zaggala*, of which I had heard – songs for every type of sowing and harvesting. Whenever one singer stopped chanting, I would hear another take up the song, from the same garden or from behind the walls of another, and the song, unbroken for the length of the road, completed the enchantment of the previous evening's party. At the same time, I recalled that, in the context of the rivalry between the oasis's two clans, battles had arisen over the right to the sole use of these songs. Could they have reached a solution by which the songs had become common property?

On our way, we passed a broad lake shining with the blue of the sky in the midst of the sand, and on which little waves shivered. It must have been a salt lake.

The caravan had not spent more than two hours on the road before we reached the heart of the oasis.

We had come across no buildings beside the track, only the walls of the gardens, which no one can see inside. From the moment we had entered the oasis, my attention had been drawn to the large number of palm trees near the springs; indeed, I had even seen palms drowned in the lakes, only their tops showing. Now, however, suddenly, as we crested a hill, the whole horizon turned green before my eyes – a forest, too large for the eyes to take in at once, of palm fronds interlocking in space, a dark green sea, thick and undulating, above which the town, with its grey walls and yellowish-brown dwellings, rose like an island, atop a pyramid-shaped hill.

Mahmoud brought his camel up alongside mine and stood, looking out like me at the town, in silence. Taken aback by what my eyes beheld, I said to him, without turning my head, 'I've never seen anything like it in my life – a grey volcano emerging from green waves.'

'Or a step pyramid such as none of our ancestors ever thought to build. A pyramid with a round base,' said Mahmoud.

He was right. The greyish-yellow houses, each stuck to the other, climb up in narrowing ranks to the top of the hill, after which there is nothing to be seen but the blue of the sky.

I didn't take my eyes from the town when the caravan started to move once more towards it, and Mahmoud startled me when he repeated, 'Indeed. A large pyramid, Catherine. And what did our ancestors use the pyramids for?'

5

Sheikh Yahya

I love the first glimmerings of early morning. My spirit comes awake each day on this journey before the sun has risen that takes me from my house in Aghurmi to the council of the *agwad*. My worn-out eyes can no longer distinguish forms. Before, I used to be fond of following the withdrawal of the dark and the emergence of the forms of things into the faint blue light – as though I were witnessing the transition from chaos to creation. My heart would tremble when, with the rays of the rising sun, the green of the trees in the gardens would appear and innumerable mirrors would shine in the waters of the springs and the mountains and hills would float above the darkness. Now I see it in my heart more than I do with my eyes. Even these spectacles, which I've had so long, reveal only shadows and phantoms. I hate having to fix round my ear the piece of string that does duty for their broken arm but my nose still helps me out, sniffing the scent of the dew that we pass on the road, sorting out the smell of green cactus from dry, smelling the pure water in the spring and distinguishing between that and the muddy water in the irrigation channels.

This morning, however, what my nose smells before all else is the smell of war. May God prove me wrong! Hasn't this land had enough blood yet?

I proceed down the road, my donkey behind me not braying, scarcely making any sound at all. He's still trying to wake up and the silence that surrounds us has infected him.

The same silence takes me back to my days, years ago, in the desert, when I abandoned everything in anger at my people but without any aim for myself or care for where I dwelt. How many months was it I spent in the wilderness, or how many years? I've often cudgelled my brains to count those months or years and failed completely. It's as though all that wandering in the desert had been one day of endless toil in quest of food and water and in search of shelter, fleeing the sun, the wild animals and the cold. What did I learn from that endless day? I know not.

I still insist on undertaking the trip to Shali on foot, but am reassured by the fact that my donkey is following me, so I can ride him when my legs start shaking or my feet give out. You're an old man now, Yahya, but you still have your anger. They continue to have some respect for that anger in the council of the *agwad*, even though you possess no influence over them. They never used to do what I said in the past and they don't do it now, so what's the point of anger? I shall keep a hold on myself today.

The invitation sent by Sheikh Sabir yesterday puzzled me because it said that the meeting of the *agwad* would be at his house today instead of at our daily meeting place under the open lean-to at the entrance to Shali. My suspicions of Sabir do not stem from his being the leader of the Easterners. God knows, I don't distinguish between Easterner and Westerner, and they all know my story. It was my right to preside over the council of the *agwad* because I'm the eldest, but I conceded my claim of my own free will even though that angered my people, the Westerners. Let Sabir enjoy the presidency, then, but I still regard him with suspicion.

Why is he having us assemble at his house? Is it a council of war? I'm still not comfortable with him. He doesn't reveal frankly what he's after but keeps weaving and ducking. He doesn't say, 'Yahya, I'm better educated than you,' but is always boasting that he studied at the Zeitouna mosque in Tunis and repeating that there he understood them and they understood him because they speak our language. What he means is that they're not like the Egyptians who are ignorant of our language and with whom I studied when I spent a few years of my life as a boarder at the mosques of Ibraheem and Abu el Abbas in Alexandria. He looks at me while speaking as though I were responsible for the Egyptians' not knowing the language of Siwa, and I smile to myself. I feel like telling him, 'Let it go, Sabir! Your stories of Tunis and the Zeitouniya have given us headaches. You're educated and I'm ignorant. Are you happy now?' In fact, I may have actually told him that. I don't remember.

I do think I challenged him on the prophecies. He has in his possession a book which he obtained from I know not where that includes prophecies that he repeats every time the council meets. He chants them as though he were reciting from the Koran: 'It is written, O Earth, that a time shall come when you shall be as a widow who strews dust upon her bowed head. It is written that strangers shall walk your paths in pride and your people shall walk with their eyes cast down. It is written that the voice of the fool shall ring out and the wise man shall talk into his sleeve.' After these gloomy prognostications, his eyes roam over his listeners and he says, as though gloating, 'The hour of prophecy and accounting has come. How could it not, when you drink wine publicly, perpetrate abominations both open and concealed, and deliver yourselves to perdition with your own hands? Why should not torment be your just reward?'

When I hear him saying such things, I rebuke him and shout out the prayer 'May the mercy of God reach us before His anger, and may He spare us above all from the cawing of crows!' Only with difficulty do I restrain myself from asking him, 'Are those the only sins, my dear sheikh? Isn't the desire to bring about ruination also a sin? And you – are you not a slave to pride and consumed by hatred? You hate us Westerners and you hide your hatred behind your supposed prophecies, as though you wanted all the disasters therein to befall us "today before tomorrow". And why, Sheikh Sabir, do you hide what is inside you and not reveal it?' Take care, Yahya! Now you're thinking like them. You still see through the eyes of the Westerners no matter how hard you try.

All the same, I can't think of those prophecies without smiling when I remember Maleeka. She was small, perhaps about four years old. She'd barely learnt to speak but could imitate the men and women and everyone laughed when they heard her, except for her mother. Maleeka would narrow her eyes or open them to their widest, she'd pout her lips or suck in her cheeks, and she'd change the features of her beautiful face and try at the same time to change her childish voice to match the person she was imitating. My sister Khadeeja considered what Maleeka did to be scandalous and would hit and kick her to stop her speaking, so she'd run to me and take refuge behind my back, screaming, 'Save me, Uncle!' I'd rebuke my sister, of course, but at the same time I'd try to shut Maleeka up, to no avail, especially when she was imitating Sabir. She'd show the whites of her eyes and repeat in a voice that she'd try to roughen the prophecies of the horrid sheikh of which she understood not a word. I'd put my hand over her mouth so that she wouldn't repeat in front of the children and women things they shouldn't hear, but I couldn't help laughing all the same. Khadeeja reproached me for encouraging her daughter to be what she called 'shameless', but who could stop Maleeka? Beating didn't work on her and neither did leniency, not when she was a child and not when she'd grown up. It's how you were fated to be, Maleeka!

When I reached the council of the *agwad* at the house of Sheikh Sabir and saw them sitting in a circle there, I smelt once more the smell of war and my heart sank. I saw one of our *zaggala* from the West sitting on the ground with his knees drawn up to his chest away from the circle of the *agwad*. None of the *agwad* of our clan had informed me that the man would be attending, so could he have something to do with this secret council? The *zaggala* are also the troops of the *agwad* on the battlefield and they have a say in matters of war and peace. I prayed that God would disprove my fears.

No one spoke. The silence went on and on and they sat in a circle on the cushions, each evading his brother's eye. To avoid talking they picked dates from the baskets placed in front of them and busied themselves in their lengthy chewing. What were they waiting for?

Eventually, Sheikh Sabir cleared his throat and said, 'The district commissioner has summoned me to meet him.'

Eyes were raised towards him and he continued slowly, 'And the commissioner has told me that he has sent a new letter to Cairo and is expecting the answer with the next caravan.'

He fell silent again. My patience wore out and I said, 'And so, Sheikh Sabir? What did he write in his letter and what is the answer he's expecting? Why don't you speak quickly and let us go?'

After a long struggle, we got it out of Sabir that the commissioner had sent a request once again for the reduction of the tax and that the oasis's yearly liability should be one thousand camel-loads of dates instead of two, plus two hundred camel-loads of olive oil instead of five hundred. He had also requested the cancellation of the penalty for late payment.

Pandemonium broke out from the *agwad*, Easterners and Westerners alike. We'd asked for the reduction of the tax to five hundred camel-loads of dates and one hundred of olive oil. Why hadn't the commissioner asked for what we'd agreed on?

Sabir said that the commissioner had informed him that the orders he'd brought with him were for an increase in the liability, not a reduction, and that if they agreed in Cairo to what he'd asked for, we should thank God.

The angry mutterings of the *agwad* continued and Sheikh Abd el Majid of the Easterners said, 'If it were up to me, I wouldn't pay anything and let them do what they like.'

Another Eastern sheikh whom I couldn't identify responded to him in a low voice, after the commotion had calmed down, 'Every time we say that and refuse to pay the tax. Then we pay it in the end, and on top of it the late fees, when the armies and the guns come.'

Silence reigned once more. Then Sheikh Sabir said, 'You're right,' and next (like one at the end of his tether) 'and I forgot to tell you that the commissioner informed me that he will not deal himself with the families over the gathering of the tax, as used to be the case, but will hold me to account and consider me responsible for the accounts of the *agwad* and their families and the whole tax, as decided on by Cairo.'

Ah! That will not do for us Westerners, Sheikh Sabir, even if no one has said a word. At this point, however, the *zaggal* sitting at the far end of the room raised his voice and said sharply, 'God damn this commissioner and the day he came to our land. Let us be done with him, and with his wife!'

Sheikh Idrees, however, one of the sheikhs of my Western clan, raised his voice angrily and said, 'Shame on you, Mabrouk, boy! We invited you to our council so that we might hear what you have to say, not for you to offer advice to your sheikhs, so don't forget your place.'

Mabrouk shrank back into his corner, and Sheikh Sabir asked him calmly, 'And why should we be done with him and his wife?'

Mabrouk answered in a rush, 'The woman has gone into our houses and violated the decency of our womenfolk. Last Friday, she climbed to the Aghurmi ruins and treated the houses of our families there with disrespect. Since when, Sheikh Sabir, have we allowed unbelievers to desecrate our homes?'

I left them to argue and started thinking. What was new in all this that would make Sheikh Sabir move the council of the *agwad* from the lean-to to his house? No stranger would dare to pry into our council at the entrance to the town. Not to mention that if the district commissioner himself came and joined us there, he would understand nothing because he doesn't know our language. And there was nothing new in what he said about the tax. Everyone had learnt the lesson to which the other sheikh had referred: in the end, we would pay the tax whether we liked it or not. The Westerners will not, of course, accept that you, Sabir, should be in charge of collecting their share, and that is something you know as well as I do, so why did you mention it? Soon we'll find out what you're after.

I came to myself to hear him saying, 'But I heard, Sheikh Idrees, that the woman wasn't making for our houses. She wanted to see the Ruins of the Kings that are there, and on her way she passed by the houses. Did any of our women complain that she pried into the secrets of their houses and violated their decency, as you claim?'

Sheikh Idrees replied, 'If she didn't do so this time she will do so next, Sheikh Sabir. Next time she won't "cease and desist". I have learnt that today she will go with her husband to the ruins of Umm Ebeida.'

Sabir answered, 'Thank God there aren't any houses at Umm Ebeida whose privacy can be violated—' but the *zaggal* Mabrouk once again raised his voice: 'Sheikh Sabir, this woman came bringing with her the books of the foreign unbelievers that teach the magic needed to discover our treasure that is hidden in the depths of the earth. She may do as did some of those who came before her and bring up the corpses of the Abominable Ones to use in the magic.'

I smiled to myself. That treasure again? You and your grandfathers and your grandfathers' grandfathers have searched for it and you've dug in all the ruins that the kings left behind and you've rooted up the depths of the earth and dug out the mountain and still you haven't despaired?

Suppose you found it right now, what do you think you'd do with it?

Sabir surprised me, however, when he said in level tones to Mabrouk, 'Know, Mabrouk, that it is not we that guard the treasure, but it that guards us. Our treasure has a talisman that has watched over it from ancient times, since our king, Khurabeish, God rest his soul, buried it and lodged with it that infallible charm. If the woman goes anywhere near it, it will destroy her as it did those who went before her. The treasure will return – according to the prophecies – at a time that only God knows, but that can only be after we repent of our sins. Don't worry about the treasure, but do tell me, Mabrouk, what befell us when we killed the commissioner before him?'

Mabrouk responded obstinately, 'This accursed commissioner came, and with him his wife, who desecrates our houses and searches for our treasure.'

'So you see the catastrophe?' said Sheikh Sabir. 'It did us no good, then, to kill the commissioner who was before him. And what about those who died at the hands of the army that Mahir Bey brought? What about those whom they took with them to Egypt to hang, not to mention our sons who are still in prison there?'

Everyone fell silent, but the voice of Sheikh Idrees rose again and he said in frustration, 'Do you mean to tell me, Sheikh Sabir, that we should do nothing about the commissioner and his wife and tolerate dishonour!'

The clamour of the Western sheikhs in support of Idrees started up anew, but Sabir addressed to him a question I'd been waiting to hear for a while: 'Have you, Sheikh Idrees, observed anything in the new district commissioner that would require us to get rid of him? I have not heard that since he came to the oasis he has taken anything that isn't his, or flogged anyone, as was the custom of those who came before him. On the contrary, he pays for everything, even the donkeys he hires for himself and his wife to ride, and he goes about on the roads on his own, not surrounded by the guard that his predecessors used to terrorize us. His soldiers guard the town from the Bedouin robbers and he goes out himself on his horse at night at the head of the troopers to chase them into the desert.'

Despite myself, I exclaimed in bewilderment, 'And that's precisely what scares me about him, Sheikh Sabir! Why does he do all that? He does not love us.'

Sabir gave his coarse laugh and said, 'And which of the commissioners before him did love us, Sheikh Yahya? The things they did drove us to fight them. But this one, what wrong has he done that would make it lawful to spill his blood and bring ruin down upon ourselves once more?'

I said to myself, 'I'm with you in that, Sheikh Sabir, but even so this man scares me more than the rest. I don't care about the ones who flog and revile and terrorize the people with their troops in their cavalcades. Those are just like Mabrouk. I've seen them and I've had experience of them in all the wars. They strike the flint and are the first to run when the fire flares up. But I do fear this taciturn commissioner who walks our roads alone. I know that he who has no fear for his own life has no fear for others'. The hatred in his silence scorches me like fire and sears me more than the rudeness of the others. What awaits our town at his hands? And what do you find written about him in your prophecies, Sheikh Sabir?'

Did I actually utter the question, or was Sabir responding to somebody else? I heard him saying, 'I haven't found anything about him or about his wife in the prophecies. I have read them through twice since he and his wife came to us and I have found no sign that points to them, or perhaps the sign is there but I have failed to understand it. Maybe they are the harbinger of all the catastrophes in the prophecies. Have mercy upon us, O Lord!'

Sheikh Idrees said in a puzzled voice, 'So are we then to do nothing about the man and his wife, Sheikh Sabir? If we can't live in our own oasis without strangers and unbelievers humiliating us and desecrating our houses, we would do better to leave our home and wander in the desert like the Bedouin.'

With a note of sorrow in his voice, Sabir replied, 'I beseech you, don't be in a hurry to go out into the desert, Sheikh Idrees. If the British, who rule Egypt now, come to us and find our land to their liking, they may take it for themselves and indeed throw us into the desert. They have done so elsewhere.'

I nodded my head in agreement. 'You're right, Sheikh Sabir,' I said. 'They did that in the land of the Americans, and other parts of God's world.'

I was confident that the rest of the *agwad* had never heard of either the Americans or the British and had no idea what Sabir was talking about. And indeed, one of them interrupted me by saying, 'But the troops who come to our land are Egyptians, not British.'

'Let us then thank God for that,' I said. 'The Egyptians come and they kill some of us and we kill some of them but they leave us on our land.'

The other then continued, addressing Sheikh Sabir, 'Why would these British come to our land? We haven't declared war on them and we don't know them.'

Sheikh Sabir answered, 'But the district commissioner's wife is British. If we kill her, perhaps their troops will come instead of the Egyptians to take their revenge. They'll see it as an excuse, as is their custom, to take our land, and then no one will be able to save us.'

The *agwad* fell silent for a while, thinking over what had been said. Then they all started talking at once, their questions overlapping one another, but Sabir ignored them all and addressed his words in decisive tones to Mabrouk, who had raised his voice in an attempt to make himself heard:

'Mabrouk! Go back to your brothers and tell them not to harm the woman or her husband. Tell them that your sheikhs the *agwad* will think and consult with one another before they take any steps.'

Then he turned away from him and said, addressing the gathering, 'What say you to our sending a messenger to Our Master the Mahdi in Jaghboub to tell him what's happening and ask his opinion?'

I said to myself, 'Have I misjudged you, Sabir? Today you have done everything you could to turn the *zaggala* and the *agwad* from thoughts of murder and war. You frightened them with unprecedented consequences when you spoke to them of the British and you rebuked the *zaggala*, who might have incited their sheikhs to civil strife. You gained the consent of the Westerners, who place their faith in the Mahdi of the Senoussis and obey his commands, and you were able to calm their fury at the breaking of the inviolacy of Aghurmi by the commissioner's wife. You gained time until the Senoussi's answer comes from Jaghboub and the answer will, as usual, advise calm. So were my suspicions unfounded when I thought you'd invited us to a council of war? Thank God that I was wrong this time!'

Mabrouk had left the gathering, so the attendance was limited to the *agwad*, and a chatter started up to which I shut my ears. Suddenly, though, I heard my name on Sabir's tongue. He was saying, 'Why don't you say something, Sheikh Yahya? We need your opinion. Isn't she your daughter?'

Taken by surprise by the question, I asked, 'Who are you talking about, Sheikh Sabir?'

'About Maleeka, of course. Naturally, she is the daughter of us all, Easterners and Westerners, but you are her maternal uncle, so who better than you to bring her to her senses?'

I gathered my wits and resisted the urge to explode with anger. So with a passing question you'd thrust Maleeka into the cauldron of East and West? She's no longer just a wife estranged from her husband but a problem for the whole town?

I replied, my voice almost choking in my throat, 'As you said, she's the daughter of you all, so decide what you think is right.'

The divide now started to work in earnest and the voices of the sheikhs of the East began little by little to rise, the *agwad* of the West matching their cries. I forced myself to remain silent so as not to add fuel to the fire. I blocked my ears and sought refuge within myself.

'Such is your luck, Maleeka,' I said to myself. She is indeed my daughter! I love her more than any of the daughters of my loins or any of my granddaughters. But my sister married her off – Maleeka, than whom I know none more beautiful or more intelligent in our land – to the aged, feeble Mi'bid, who could be her grandfather. Keep silent, Yahya! How many girls have you married during your life whose grandfather you could have been? But I wasn't like Mi'bid! Many years ago, once I realized my business with them was done, I stopped taking wives and divorced the women I had. But Mi'bid chose Maleeka before she was fifteen years old. They selected that poor girl specifically for the experiment. Her mother, like all the Westerners, believes everything Our Master the Senoussi says, and he said, 'Let the Easterners and the Westerners marry one another that they may be one clan and the wars between them come to an end.' And of all the girls, the half-dead Mi'bid chose the fatherless Maleeka and her mother gave her consent. I did what I could but my sister dug in her heels. I know that the marriage of old men to young girls is not a matter of importance in our oasis so long as the man is rich and capable of fathering children, but I know Maleeka too, and what I expected happened. Maleeka fled her husband's house in Shali and went back to her mother in Aghurmi, asking for divorce. And now too everything I expected is taking place – Mi'bid is refusing divorce and demanding that Maleeka return to her husband's house. He didn't attend the council of the *agwad* because of his illness, but all the sheikhs of the East are taking his side and they are angrier than he. Maleeka doesn't matter to them, but how could a girl from the West refuse a sheikh of the East? Either she return or . . .

I know, however, that Maleeka will not return, and I know that the Mahdi's idea for stopping the wars will do no good. Nothing would change even if all the Easterners married Western women or the other way around. Intermarriage will not dislodge that seed which lies hidden in men's hearts. Now before us we have the marriage of one Western woman to an Easterner and it bodes no good, while for causes much less than this wars have broken out between you. If only I knew what lies behind this killing malice! If only I knew what would root it out! Just look at them consulting with one another, or pretending they are consulting with one another.

The *agwad* of the Westerners say, 'She should return the bride price and he should let her go.'

The Easterners say, 'No. She should return to her husband's house first. If he wishes to divorce her of his own free will, he may do so. But she must return first.'

'Let her go and we'll give him in marriage the most high-born of all the girls of the Westerners,' respond the Westerners.

Sheikh Sabir intervened as though he wanted to resolve the dispute, but he poured oil on the fire. He said in a reasonable tone, 'Or he could let her go and we could give him in marriage the most high-born of the Easterners, if he has no further appetite for the Western girls, or they for him.' Angry mutterings arose from Westerners and Easterners alike, and the voice of an Easterner rose above them, challengingly: 'His other wives are already of the most high-born of the Easterners, Sheikh Sabir. He's not asking for a new wife, he's asking for God's Law. Do they have no control over their daughter?'

The *agwad* of the West perceived the slight and some of them got up, waving their hands threateningly in the direction of the sheikhs of the East. I got up too and once again burst out furiously, 'Now you think of God's Law? There's nothing easier for either you or us than divorce. There's a divorcee, or more than one, in every house in this town. There are those who were divorced before even their husbands knew about it because their mothers-in-law hated the girls and concluded the divorce themselves. Why do you cling to Maleeka now?'

'Calm yourself, Sheikh Yahya,' said Sabir. 'We are consulting and will find a solution, God willing.'

I couldn't contain myself, however, and went on, 'You can go on consulting for ever! Neither your people nor the others want a solution. You are slavering to raise your rifles once again so that you can mow one another down. Enough of your lies! You have grown old, *Agwad*, and your hair has turned grey. Have your grey hairs taught you nothing?'

Sabir said, a note of anger in his voice, 'If anyone else but you had said that, Sheikh Yahya . . . And what about yourself? Haven't grey hairs taught you any patience? Who's talking about raising rifles? The *agwad* are consulting. As I said—'

'I know your consultations, Sheikh Sabir. I've known them for fifty years and more. Goodbye to you!'

'Where are you off to, Sheikh Yahya? Yahya . . . Yahya, be with us!'

'I thank God I am not with you!' I muttered to myself as I descended the slope that leads down from the gate of the fortress. So my intuition did not lie. It was indeed a council of war. Why, though, is Sabir making peace with the Egyptians and encouraging strife among his own people? Time will tell! I beg your pardon, My Master the Senoussi! Your idea's no good. It will never stop the wars. My idea, God forgive me, was better. If only they'd done it fifty years ago!

Ask forgiveness of God, Yahya! Don't return to that memory!

71

Still muttering, I had set about untying my donkey from the palm trunk when one of the boys playing in the sandy space came running to give me his shoulder while I mounted. I pushed him away gently, saying, 'Your grandfather can still get on his donkey on his own.' I pressed down with both my hands on the saddle and jumped on to the donkey, which set off of its own accord towards the east, in the direction of Aghurmi. It knows its way. I wish I could say that men know their own way. I wish I could say that even of myself!

Once more, I've been able to do nothing for you, Maleeka. Your uncle wasn't able to protect you, as a child or a woman. She was very small when she complained to me that the boys and girls cheated when they were playing in my garden, and dragged me by the hand to arbitrate between them. In front of me the children denied they had cheated but she easily lured them into revealing their lies. In the end I asked her, 'What do you want, Maleeka?' and she told me with the utmost seriousness, 'I want you to punish the cheaters, Uncle.' I made a show of rebuking them and left her to play with them, but in the end they got sick of her and me and excluded her from their games. And when she was a little older, she started coming to the garden to spend most of her time with me. She would go with me to the water troughs when I irrigated or cropped it and ask me why the plants I grew there were different from the vegetables she saw in the other gardens. I'd tell her that these plants were medicines and only a few people in the town grew them. She'd smile and ask me, her eyes roaming over the plants, 'Is there a medicine for me here?' 'A medicine for what, Maleeka?' 'A medicine to stop my devilry.' I'd smile and say, 'Now that would be a medicine, Maleeka!' 'But my mother says that a devil possesses me, and she's right. Why am I different from the other girls?'

I didn't tell her that she was this oasis's only blessing.

Or perhaps its only mistake, I don't know.

Think about something else, Yahya. Don't get yourself even more confused.

The way was long and I hadn't covered more than half the distance before I found myself bathed in sweat. The sun this early morning was hotter than the blazing heat of forenoon. I got off the donkey at Gouba Spring and went over to it. The shade of the trees surrounding it was a blessing. I took off my spectacles and carefully descended the stone steps to the spring. Then I bent down over the water and scooped it up in my hands to wash myself. It was a long time since I had seen my own face in this spring, which was as clear as a mirror. All I could see now was a shadow on the surface of the water as I bent over. What do you want, Yahya? You've become a very old man. Your sight and your body have become weak. Why then have neither my anger nor my bewilderment abated? Why do I still ask myself the same questions that tortured me in my youth? The end is near, but I still don't know peace of mind.

I sat in the shade of a palm tree next to the spring and Maleeka never left me. Why had they placed her between the grindstones of war, feuding and conflict that crush all men? And why war? Why all the suffering and misery on this earth? I can perhaps understand even Sabir's prophecies, which pour down perdition on the people as a reward for their sins, but what of those who do not commit sins? What crime, for example, did this child perpetrate?

You tormented your mother, Maleeka, and she tormented you. You tortured her first with your beauty, which put all the belles of the oasis to shame, the girls whose mothers would hang amulets on them and cense them to ward off envy. Throughout your childhood, Khadeeja would smear your face with soot and dress you in dirty clothes, but you remained the prettiest, despite it all. Adults would stop in the road to take a look at your enchanting features and say, 'God protect her!' This would make your mother even more terrified for you and she'd try to imprison you in the house, which you were not allowed to leave. But as soon as you got a little older you learnt how to escape. You'd dress in boys' clothes, hide your smooth hair under a cap, and roam the town at your leisure. And nobody could understand why the Ruins of the Kings, where the people of the town, generation after generation, have searched for treasure, attracted you. Were you looking for treasure, like them? But you'd return from the ruins with a beetle of stone in your hand or a shard of pottery bearing coloured drawings, and the moment your mother saw it, and you, she'd start yelling and wailing, smashing the things and throwing them into the fire, and then she'd summon the witches to cast the devil out of your body by beating you with sticks and reciting spells. As though a voice had told me that your mother was up to it again, I'd rush to the house and thrash them in turn with my stick, shouting that they and no one else were the devils, and they'd rush out howling while your mother beat her cheeks in despair. I'd find your body bruised and blue from the beating but you'd laugh all the same as you felt the places where it hurt and you'd say, in the midst of your moans, 'It's your fault, Uncle! You didn't find the medicine to save me from being punished.'

Indeed, you spoke like a grown-up and fashioned things such as grown-ups never made, coming to my garden and scooping up soft mud from the earth to form into the shape of beetles and birds that looked like the birds drawn on the walls of the ruins. Then you learnt how to fetch clay from which you could make small statues, which I could hardly distinguish from the tiny stone statues scattered in the ruins. I'd watch your small fingertips in amazement as they busied themselves in rounding a head and spreading out the arms and legs from balls of clay, and I'd ask myself, 'Where did she learn this craft?' No one in the town before or after her tried to do what she did. Even as a child, she realized from her experiences with her mother that the people of the oasis

74

didn't like these things either, so she'd give them to me and tell me, 'You break them, Uncle. I'll make you new ones tomorrow.' Then she'd take me by the hand and say, 'Come. Show me how to grow things.'

My heart wouldn't allow me, however, to break her beautiful little statues. I knew I mustn't keep them at my house lest any, old or young, should see them and say, 'Yahya too plays with devils.' I'd keep them for a short while and contemplate them, and the delicacy with which they were fashioned would amaze me. Then I'd dig sorrowfully in the ground after Maleeka had left me, bury the statues, and spread earth and dust over them instead of smashing them before her eyes.

Later she became my constant companion in the garden. She'd come of her own accord or her mother would bring her, to stay with me instead of running away from us in disguise to the gardens of strangers or to the Ruins of the Kings on the Mountain of the Dead, whose caves even adults fear to wander in. She was my only joy in this land of gloom and sorrows. She'd talk to me and learn from me how to cultivate plants and help me to sow and graft them. I didn't have to repeat anything to her that she'd learnt before. I became more attached to her than she to me and could no longer bear for her to be away from me for a single day. But her mother buried all that intelligence with Mi'bid and they expected Maleeka to accept that destiny, and I couldn't save her from her mother or from Mi'bid or from Sabir or from the Easterners or the Westerners. Now I see what they're planning for you, after all the hullabaloo and the threats and lies. Even if war breaks out, and irrespective of who wins, they will force you afterwards to return to the man you hate.

I know their consultations and I hate them. I know how their wars start and how they end. In my youth, this drove me to madness. So why did I go back to them? I had grown old and the wandering and loneliness had worn me out, though not as much as being close to them and living among them does now.

75

I stood up sluggishly. I had to continue my journey. Before I could leave the place, however, I heard the sound of the Crier's trumpet coming from the direction of Shali with the call that announces a death. Who, I wonder, has given up the ghost today, and passed into the mercy of Our Lord?

6

Mahmoud

I woke from sleep before dawn, as usual, drowning in sweat and the last remnants of a beautiful dream whose details dissolved into nothingness, with the exception of a face that withdrew, leaving me to wake smiling.

I washed quickly and left Catherine to go on sleeping. Then I gently opened the door of the house and sat at the top of the steps. Usually there was a breeze from the north but it didn't come today. Even so, the air was fresher than inside.

Shali, to my left, was a dark lump, quiet and sleeping, and directly in front of me was that blackish hill they call by the attractive name of the Mountain of the Dead! Couldn't they have come up with something more comforting? It's understandable why they should call it that: its caves all consist of ancient tombs of the pharaohs and others, so what do you expect them to call it, the Mountain of Joy and Celebration? The name fits well enough, so stop grumbling so early in the day! Try a little joy and celebration yourself! True, yesterday evening I received my first real threat since I came to the oasis, but I was expecting it and it added nothing to what I already knew.

In fact, I have suffered nothing from them here that I can complain about, while I have every reason to complain about Cairo. They pay no attention in the Protected City to what I write to them. I send messages and what comes back to me with the caravan is a new copy of the first letter I received – the text of the very orders that Harvey discussed with me before I left, with neither explanation nor comment; in fact without any indication that my message has even been received. All that reaches me are requests that the late taxes be collected in a hurry and sent to Cairo. They don't ask themselves, or provide me with any guidance on, how. On each occasion that the taxes have been late, it has needed an army and cannon, so what am I supposed to do with the handful of troops I have with me and our ancient rifles? Last time, two years ago, they waited until the district commissioner before me had been murdered, then sent an army that killed the mayor and collected the taxes, and thought that order had been restored.

It hadn't, my dear bashas of Cairo!

In the evening, their leader, Sheikh Sabir, came to see me. He's the only one among the *agwad* who comes. I never meet the rest except at Friday prayer at the Shali mosque. He told me the *agwad* continued to regard the reduction I'd asked for as small, and they wanted more. I reminded him forcefully – in fact I became livid as I thought of Cairo's silence – that I had promised nothing. 'I told you what I'd asked for, but it is the government in Cairo that decides,' I said. He replied, 'I understand, Mr Commissioner. But some of the *agwad* are asking what would be left for us to live on if we were to pay everything that the government is asking for.'

I replied with acerbity, 'Nevertheless, this is not the first time you've paid taxes. Sort it out.'

Sabir didn't get angry. I have never seen him angry. On the contrary, he said, as though in confirmation of my own words, 'The wiser heads know that. But what is to be done when some heads among the families, and even indeed among the *agwad*, are not so wise? No one knows what they may do. We seek God's protection.'

I understood his message well and replied to him in kind: 'In that case, Sheikh Sabir, the wiser heads should warn the others of what will happen if recklessness prevails.'

'I am not the mayor of this town,' he said, 'and I do not possess the means to impose anything on them.'

I replied, 'As far as the government is concerned, you are the leader of the *agwad*, and that is enough.'

I felt like telling him he should thank God he wasn't the mayor. It was he himself who told me the story of the mayor, who was also the owner of the house in which I now live. Mayor Hassouna built it outside the walls of Shali, on a rise. He took care to have it fortified, like all the other fortified things in this town. Then, behind it, he built a group of additional buildings that extended to the town wall. By virtue of its elevated position and the connection between his little castle and the town, he was able to resist the most recent punitive military expedition, which followed the murder of the district commissioner. He never surrendered, despite the siege, which lasted for weeks, and fought gallantly until he died, or so I heard, and I respected him for his courage.

All that's left of the castle is this raised house, which the government confiscated, and another building to the south of the wall, which it turned into a police station before demolishing everything in between. Sabir, however, told me the story of Mayor Hassouna without an ounce of sympathy for him or his fate. Could that be because he was a Westerner and Sabir's an Easterner? I need time if I'm to understand the people here, supposing fate should allow any. The calm that surrounds me does not deceive me and I understand, even without Sabir's hints and their concealed threats, that they are waiting to pounce on me. Nevertheless, I go about my work as though I have noticed nothing. Sabir and the others must not sense any weakness in my behaviour here.

But I do not like this Sheikh Sabir! He has flattered me openly from our first meeting and his impassive face resembles a mask incapable of revealing any expression.

There is something disturbing about his eyes, especially. He gazes into my face with a fixed look that never changes, so I believe nothing he says. What does he want from me exactly? To recommend him as mayor? Cairo has abandoned the idea of appointing mayors from among either the Westerners or the Easterners so that we anger neither. He ought to have worked that out for himself. Despite which, there is some truth in what he says. How indeed are these people to live if the government collects what it wants from them?

The poverty took me aback from the first moment of my entry into the oasis, and especially the poverty of the *zaggala*, just as I was taken aback by the massive amount of the taxes that the government demands I collect from them. I sent my opinion to the ministry: excessive taxation is the cause of their rebelliousness and the murder of the officials appointed by Cairo to govern them. I suggested the taxes be cut by half.

Perhaps I'm naive, though. Why am I trying to help them when I know they want to get rid of me? I sensed their deadly hatred for me and Catherine from the first day. They have walled us in with silence and avoidance. There is no communication between us but the looks of hatred in their eyes, so how can I say I have nothing to complain about with respect to them? I have a thousand causes for complaint! They are a vexation and Cairo is a vexation and I am caught in the middle. If Cairo has forgotten me, however, I shall forget them too. This will delay the moment of confrontation here. I shall deal with them as I have from the time of my arrival. I always go around without a guard of troops but my revolver holster is open the whole time. I know it's a pointless precaution, but what other measure could help me when I'm on my own in their midst?

In the desert, in the sandstorm, it all seemed easy. The faster the better, as I said to Catherine. Even now I still hope that the end will be fast and unannounced. Despite that, I feel joy at night when I'm lying in bed. A thought creeps into my mind that delights me. The day has finished and the end didn't come! I almost feel the intoxication of victory over the unknown that made the Bedouin sing for joy as they bathed in the desert spring after escaping it. So what do I want? I wish I knew what I wanted! I wish I knew who I was!

Why, for example, am I so cheerful this morning, in this heat and after the threat, which I know to be real? Is it all thanks to the dream? It must be. It can't be because of the two glasses of whisky I drank last night. I used to depend on whisky to withstand the loneliness of this oasis and I brought a sufficient supply of boxes from Cairo. Now, however, I'm drinking less and less. Why? Perhaps it's the extreme heat which prevents me from drinking, and perhaps it's not having anyone to drink with. 'No drinking without a drinking companion,' as they say. I don't have a friend in this town to drink with and my wife doesn't drink.

Catherine was of use to me, though, despite that, in our first days and weeks here. Each had only the other in the midst of this atmosphere of hostility and isolation with which the oasis took us unawares. After the working day was over we'd be alone together, me with my glass in front of me. We'd chat about any topic but something would start up, as usual, in my mind. I'd watch her, observing her body, whose every beauty I know. I'd go over its details and imagine the feel of her skin and of the embrace of our bodies and she'd blush and smile and I'd give her that long look she well understands. And the fact is we exhausted in a few weeks all the energy of our passion, after which a malaise swept over me. Catherine, however, kept searching with unceasing anxiety for something that might prolong the nights of our renewed desert passion. Some nights she would draw close to me, as I drank with a calm and a listlessness that were quite apparent to her, throw herself into my lap, and nervously and rapidly cover my face and neck with kisses until she did indeed arouse me and drag me out of my lethargy. On other nights she'd plead with me to be soft and delicate, her unseeing fingers caressing my chest with the utmost slowness. She would try to take charge herself of the intimacy, an attempt I would reject, making love the way I liked, and which she was used to, forcing her into complete submission on the bed, and I think that, despite her reproachfulness, that satisfied and pleased her, just as it has since the beginning of our relationship. In the end, however, familiarity and excess bled to death all her attempts, and mine, to invent new forms of pleasure, and we settled to a rhythm of unplanned encounters on occasional nights, rather than every night as before.

Is this the malaise of marriage that my friends in Cairo never tired of discussing, and from which I would flee to other women? And has this oasis of silence hastened this malaise? Perhaps.

The first light of dawn spreads and the outlines of Shali appear.

The town loses its grandeur when you draw close to it. It no longer displays the shape of a volcano or a pyramid. Rather, it becomes nothing more than yellowish mud houses piled on top of one another, like a dust heap pierced by holes which are the three windows of each storey. To the right, however, it stretches to the town of Aghurmi, after which, to the east, is the forest of palm trees that so please the eye after the contemplation of that upside-down funnel of dust and the gloomy Mountain of the Dead. Look, then, only to the east.

The sun's rays were really scorching my forehead, however, and I heard Catherine moving about in the house, so I rose from where I was sitting.

She greeted me with a smile. She is always more beautiful in the morning after a long, deep sleep. Insomnia is not one of her problems.

She had put the breakfast plates on the table in the spacious main room.

As we sat down, she said, 'Someone's looking refreshed this morning.'

'It's our free day. At least I shan't have to be strangled in the heat by my officer's uniform.'

'But your wicked wife is going to ruin your day off by taking you to the terrifying ruins.'

Smiling, I said, 'Precisely! Even though there's nothing better to do on our holidays, or at any other time.'

She laughed and said, 'Precisely! We're not exactly worn out by visits and social obligations.'

While we were having breakfast, however, I asked her in passing, 'What are you looking for in the ruins, Catherine? You take books with pictures of the temples with you and I see you reading them closely at home, so what exactly are you looking for?'

'I'm looking for the greatest man in the world. For Alexander.'

'I've known that for some time. You want to see the temples he visited here. But it seems you're looking for something else.'

She put down the teacup from which she'd been drinking, frowned slightly and said, 'I shall tell you a secret. I don't know what I'm looking for.'

I gave her an enquiring look and she went on, 'I came to the oasis full of dreams that I'd discover something new in the midst of these ruins, something neither the ancient historians nor the travellers who have visited the oasis had recorded. I have the capacity to do so because I know languages they did not, but I'm not finding much. With Ibraheem I visited the tombs in the Mountain of the Dead and they have all unfortunately been robbed – the mummies and the coffins and all the remains that might have been of use to any search.'

Then she sighed and said, 'And you know what happened last Friday when I visited, or tried to visit, the large temple, the Temple of the Oracle.'

'I hope you'll have better luck today, but are you aware of what the people of the oasis are saying?'

She replied indifferently, 'That I'm searching for the treasure they've been looking for everywhere among the temples, which they've dug around and beneath so much that they're ruined?'

'Exactly. Ibraheem warned me and advised me to warn you.'

'All my visits take place by day and under their eyes, so they're welcome to come and take the treasure when I find it.'

She fell silent for a moment, then looked me straight in the eyes and said, 'But of course you don't believe that nonsense, do you?'

'Frankly, I wish you would find some treasure and that we could escape with it to an unknown place.'

She laughed. 'Then you have a long time to wait! Still, I'm happy you're in a good mood this morning. Why, I wonder. If we were in another place, I'd say you'd fallen in love again but here, poor you, there aren't any women. One never ever sees them.'

'As though we ever saw the men!'

As I rose I said, 'Come on, we ought to leave early before the sun gets hot. You know we have to be back before noon.'

When she left to get dressed I said to myself, 'But you're not wrong, Catherine. The reason is indeed a woman! A woman who hasn't left me all my life long. Ni'ma visited me last night or this morning and filled me with joy. All I can remember of the dream is her beautiful face, which took me back to the days of innocence and celebration.'

'Dusky Ni'ma' got her name from the colour of her smooth, clear, golden-brown skin, which was like the colour of the Nile in flood. They couldn't think of a truer description for that unique colour and I doubt whether anyone, herself perhaps included, knew the names of her father or mother. My father bought her from the Slavers' Market as a young girl to help my mother with the housework, then gave her to me when she grew older. We were raised together and played together and were happy and she was my friend and closer to me than Suleiman my brother. I may have touched her and kissed her while we were playing, the way children do, but what I liked about her at that age were the stories she used to tell me. Where had she learnt them? From her mother, who died when she was a child? From the other girl slaves in the house or outside it? I don't know. But her stories were full of good kings and bad kings and each time she'd change the same story, so that it was as though I were hearing it for the first time, and she'd tell it as though these were things that had just taken place. Her voice would tremble as she told of how the villain cast a spell on the good king and seized his throne after turning him into an ape, and how the enchanted king saw his daughter, who was imprisoned in the palace, and how his attempts to make her recognize him with cries and dumbshow failed. Ni'ma's eyes would overflow with tears as they took the captive princess to marry the evil king, and then her face would shine with joy when the handsome prince arrived. This handsome prince would always come and release her from captivity and the hateful marriage. Then he would undo the spell on the good king, who would reward him with marriage to the princess. When I was small, I heard stories from my mother and the slave girls and other women servants in the house, but Ni'ma's were the only ones that stayed with me, along with her face as she told them, the companionship of our childhood, and the secrets we shared.

We grew up together, and Ni'ma remained in the house until my father went bankrupt.

He found homes for most of the servants and slave girls and the rest fled, and when he died the only ones left were

Ni'ma and an aged serving woman who had been with my mother all her life.

I was her first man though she wasn't my first woman, but what keeps coming back to me isn't the beginning of our affair but the memory of that feverish year that preceded my transfer to Alexandria, the memory of a young officer full of excitement in a country swept by a flood of excitement. I worked all day and most of the night with my colleague, Tal'at, and our superior, Saeed, guarding the never-ending political meetings and speech-making, and we became without realizing it part of the masses we were supposed to be watching. Ecstasy swept through us as we listened to the speeches of Abdallah el Nadeem when he attacked the Khedive, the British and the French, and to this day, bits of his high-flown rhetoric still ring in my ears. I would return to the house at the end of the night overworked to the point of exhaustion, and I'd find Ni'ma waiting for me. She would have prepared dinner, glasses of whisky and iced water. She'd give me a glass to drink and insist that I ate, no matter how much I protested I'd had enough to eat and all I wanted was to sleep. She'd feed me with her own hand as I told her what had happened to me during the preceding day and night and she'd share my excitement or anger. But when she drew close to me I'd smell the penetrating scent of Egyptian jasmine that seemed to spring from the very pores of her skin. The opening in the front of her cheap cotton *gallabiya*, which she wore over her naked body, revealed her hairless golden-brown skin, the like of whose smoothness I have never known since, and all my sleepiness would fly from my eyes and I'd hurry to finish the meal. Then I'd take her, as though kidnapping her, to my room and the night of passion would continue till it was almost dawn, when I would at last put my head on her thigh so that she could tell stories, as she had done since we were children, and fall asleep. I would sleep for barely two hours before waking and going back to work, to the meetings and the speeches. I was young and could stand it, and it was what I wanted too. I had never in my life known such pleasure with any woman, slave or free. Most of them had been greedy, wanting just to take, or acting a part to please me. Ni'ma, though, took real pleasure in love and wanted me to feel the same pleasure, to make the love complete.

She was my friend, and with her stories would make me a child again. Then, with her love, she would make me once more a man. I loved her as I had never loved anyone else, but I realized that only when it was too late – if love is the name for the fever and madness that seized me when Ni'ma fled the house. I spent days and weeks searching for her in the hospitals, the police stations and the prisons, even in the brothels. I confessed my problem to my colleague and friend Tal'at, who said quite simply, 'Buy another slave girl! Don't believe what the newspapers say about the slave trade being banned. The Slavers' Market still exists and operates beneath the eyes of our glorious khedivial police, whose pockets are capacious. Buy a Turkish girl.' Then he laughed and said, 'But you grew up rich and know all about Turkish girls and "white meat", and you're losing your mind over a slave girl you say has brown skin? Now that shows real ingratitude! You should leave that kind of thing to the likes of us!' Tal'at understood nothing, but how could he when I myself didn't? Would I have found the courage to marry her, for example, if I'd found her or if she'd come back to me? The respectable officer marry a slave of unknown parentage? What a scandal!

She asked me, as she lay next to me on the bed, 'Does My Master Mahmoud love me?' I rebuked her: 'What nonsense is that, girl? If you talk like that again, I'll throw you out on to the street!' She laughed and said, 'You're right, Master Mahmoud. Nonsense.' And she buried her head in my chest, repeating in the midst of her laughter, 'What nonsense!'

But then she went out on her own into the street and disappeared. It was my good luck, or my bad luck, to be distracted thereafter by what happened in Alexandria, and the war, and the investigations.

Ni'ma still brings back to me the child and the man, the joy and the regret. I tell myself it was just another betrayal, but then I ask myself, 'And who, my dear Major Shahriyar, was the betrayer?'

Catherine appeared, having dressed, and said, looking into my face as she passed me in the main room, 'Still in a good mood, or have we changed a little?'

I didn't answer, and she said with a smile, 'Yes, a little. I think we've changed a little!'

'Perhaps,' I said. 'I'll wait for you outside. Please be quick.'

I opened the door. The sun struck me like a blow and I closed my eyes at the brightness. Immediately I put the round hard white cork hat on my head. A dubious gift from the British! It protects from the sun but imprisons the air in its deep cavity, making the blood boil in your head. The turban made out of a broad white shawl that they wear here might be better but I can't behave like them. It would be against instructions and against my dignity!

I looked at my watch. It was ten minutes to seven. If the sun had started out with such harshness, how would it be by mid-morning? And all this for the sake of Catherine and her pharaohs! What part of their history or of that of Alexander concerns us here, buried in this remote desert? Before her renewed obsession with antiquities, she used to share my interest in the more recent past. We would talk about her wretched country and my even more wretched one. In fact, I don't know which is the more wretched. She told me of tragedies of which I was completely ignorant committed by the British in her country after they invaded it. How they had seized the best lands and farms and given them to British settlers, who had taken control of two-thirds of the island. They had banned the Catholic inhabitants from owning land and holding government positions and made these into a preserve for the British Protestant settlers. At certain periods, they had even forbidden the Irish to practise their religion, and, whenever they rose up against the oppression, savagely suppressed their uprisings. Then they dispersed them around the world, to the point that their migrants came to outnumber those who remained in the country. On one occasion, they drove off sixty thousand of them, men, women and children, and sold them into slavery in the West Indies. I thought to myself, 'At least the British didn't sell us into slavery outside Egypt. They were content to enslave us in our own country!'

A sudden braying brought me out of my reverie and when I turned round I found a boy leading two donkeys by their bridles approaching from the side that offered shade and coming to a stop at the bottom of the steps, his back to the house. He was on time but didn't say a word and didn't look in my direction. Like the others here, he was observing the law of distance and silence.

'Boy!' I called out as I made my way carefully down the steps.

He turned his head towards me without moving his body. I went up to him and asked, 'What's your name?'

'Mahmoud.'

Was he mocking me or was that really his name?

'Are you the one who was with us last Friday?'

He smiled and said nothing. Naturally! He didn't understand much Arabic, or was pretending that he didn't, and I didn't understand his language, so what was the point of the question? All the children here look like one another, however, with their wheat-coloured faces, fine features and caps, from which peeks out just one lock of hair, from whose shape the family to which the child belongs may be known. Sometimes the colour of the cap is different too. But if his head was protected from the sun by the cap, what about his bare feet on the burning sand? How could such abject poverty exist? Would one of my old pairs of shoes be of use to him? The size could never be right. Slippers, then?

'Hey, you, boy. Do you want . . .?'

I pointed to my shoes and to his naked feet and made a show of putting on shoes, raising my foot. He continued to smile but understood, for he shook his head.

Why did he refuse? Well, it was his business!

Finally the voice came loudly from the top of the steps: 'One day someone's going to have his neck broken for him coming down these stairs!'

I responded, also in a loud voice, 'There's nobody living here but you and me, so which of our necks is it that's going to be broken?'

I'm always astonished by the way she uses the passive voice even when who is doing what is perfectly clear! Yet another disaster visited by the British, this time on the language of her people? They too are very fond of the passive.

She was descending the steps with twisting movements designed to avoid the broken places where the stones had crumbled beneath the weight of people's feet. I have heard that the yellow brick that they use to build the houses here is mixed with salt that dissolves in the heat, and that this is why the bricks crumble with time. Catherine was lifting the skirt of her long grey dress with a hand from whose wrist hung a bag made of palm fronds, while with the other she gripped a folded white parasol with whose tip she probed each step before putting her weight on it. The edges of her wide hat hid her face, and when she stood upright her blue eyes shone in the light.

To be honest, Catherine, you are the only beautiful thing in this place. Without you in this oasis I'd have forgotten the meaning of women.

She sighed as she stood next to me, her face flushing with a sudden redness on the prominent curved cheekbones the moment the sun struck her. I hoped she might change her mind and call off the visit but she said, 'There's nothing funny about it, Mahmoud. Something has to be done to repair the steps, or replace them. You're the superior officer around here.'

I laughed and said, 'Superior officer, indeed! A superior officer whose instructions come to him from Cairo every few weeks with the camel caravans and whose messages and requests no one answers! The steps at the station are even worse. Some of the soldiers have almost had their necks broken in earnest coming down them.'

Catherine sighed again and said, 'All the same, something has to be done.' Then she advanced on the boy, took hold of the donkey's neck with one hand, rested the other on its worn saddle and leapt on to its back, letting her legs dangle on the same side and saying to the boy gaily, '*Siga!* Forwards!'

She knows a few words of a Libyan dialect and thinks they understand them here. Young Mahmoud didn't answer her, however, and kept looking at me till I mounted. Then he turned and went behind the donkeys and prodded them each with a thin stick. As they moved, he started jogging behind us.

'Can't we let the boy off, so that he doesn't have to run in the heat? We know the way,' said Catherine.

'We hired the donkeys and he's responsible for them, but if you know how to tell him to wait for us here, I've no objection.'

She waved at the boy a number of times to tell him to go back but he didn't halt and stopped looking at her. Then she turned her hat around on top of her head to protect her face from the sun and devoted her attention to the road.

*　　*　　*

The oasis was still free of movement and noise. The *agwad* hadn't yet appeared on their stone bench shaded by a palm-branch roof in front of the gate to the town, and the children hadn't come out to play in the large sandy space in front of my house. All the same, I was certain that many eyes were watching us from behind the dark windows, from one of which had come the bullet that killed my predecessor, inviting the arrival of the military expedition.

Cairo hadn't appointed a commissioner to succeed him. Everyone who had any influence or backing had managed to get out of the posting, until they lit on me.

The government had, however, done something new to inculcate a sense of its awe-inspiring power before the expedition troops withdrew. At the entrance of the police headquarters that had been set up on the property of the murdered mayor, it had left a large cannon. I doubt that it works or that any of my soldiers knows how to fire it, but however that may be, a show of power is important – though the cannon will not stop the bullet when the time comes. Now, though, I am thinking of Catherine. What if it's she whom the bullet strikes? What if she falls instead of me? But then who am I to tell Fate whom it should strike and whom let go?

If I can't understand myself, how can I understand Fate? So let happen what may.

Despite this, we have to be back before noon. I am always careful to pray with them on Friday at the great mosque, behind Shali's gate. I take a few of the soldiers with me but I understand only a little of the sermon, which is interspersed with Arabic phrases and verses from the Koran.

The soldiers too complained that they didn't understand anything, so I had a prayer space made for them at the police headquarters, where Sergeant Ibraheem leads them in prayer most of the time and where I sometimes pray. Still, I always go on Friday with two or three of the soldiers and we shake the hands of the *agwad* and the worshippers near us. They mumble indistinct prayers for our well-being, which we return in kind, and then all contact between us comes to an end until the next Friday.

None of them has visited me and none of them has invited me to visit his home or his garden, though from time to time they send some fruit or dishes of food to the headquarters, always taking care to mention the name of the family that sent the gift. I distribute these among the soldiers and send back a word of thanks.

Even if the truce continues in this uneasy fashion, there's no harm in it. But what of the taxes? What will happen when the critical moment comes?

We left the outskirts of Shali where the shade from the houses protected us and made our way eastward along a road that runs among the walls of the gardens, but the trees didn't soften the heat of the sun.

The sweat ran into my eyes until I could hardly see anything. Abdeen was now a distant dream, beautiful and inaccessible. The tiles of the main room, sprinkled with water, the breeze from the open north-facing window, the street vendors' cries, which would wake us in the morning and continue throughout the day, and the tuneful calls of the sellers of newspapers – *el Mu'ayyad*, which I was careful always to read, and *el Muqattam*, which I was careful always to curse, along with its writers, who defended the occupation – and, in the evening, the stroll along the banks of the river, crossing Qasr el Nil Bridge to the parties in the gardens of el Gezeera with those of my friends from the past who still keep the faith. Enough hypocrisy! Who still keeps the faith? Have I myself kept the faith?

Better not to think about that now. Let me get through my day without being pursued by those questions that will lead me I know very well where. Let me cling to the morning smile that Ni'ma bestowed on me, though I didn't deserve it.

Why, though, no matter how hard I try, is the effect of that smile fading gradually away, as Catherine noted? Why do I feel dejected and why is my heart telling me that something is about to happen – that thing which I assuredly deserve from Ni'ma and maybe from the world.

7

Catherine

Another try, on this hot day.

All I gained from the first visit was one word – one name, Maleeka – and an encounter, cut short, that I shall never forget.

I never expected this wall of silence. I told myself, 'It's a stage. It will pass and I'll manage to get close to them.' I've tried all I can. After we arrived, I wanted to go up to Shali and meet the people there. I saw panic on Ibraheem's face when I asked him to accompany me to the town market. He said to me, 'Madame, I'll buy anything you want for you.' 'But Ibraheem, what I want is to go into the town and see it!' He answered that he himself couldn't go in and see. Whatever I might want from there, he'd have to send one of the children to buy. Had I forgotten that they didn't like strangers entering their town and wandering among the houses?

I should have understood that without Ibraheem's help. Since I arrived no one has spoken to me. When I leave the house and wander around it, on my own or in Mahmoud's company, the boys and girls who play in the sandy space move away. If I approach them, smiling, they flee towards the town. I have never come across the like of it in any other place. Even the people in the small villages that I've visited in Upper Egypt and the Delta, even the Bedouin in the desert in the areas where there are antiquities, would approach and surround me out of curiosity. Before I learnt Arabic, they used to try to communicate with smiles and hand signs. Why then are they like this here? Why cannot I gain their affection, or at least get to know them? Walls around the gardens, fortifications around the town, and a wall around the fortifications – how can the world have wounded them so deeply that they have to curl up on themselves inside all these layers of shell? It's another puzzle that I shall have to try to solve as I research the puzzles of Alexander. I have to reach them before I can get to him. I need their help to get anywhere.

Also, I have to break this isolation before I turn melancholy. If I hadn't had the books and the reading and the idea of the search, I would have become completely lethargic during these last weeks. Even Mahmoud is with me and not with me. He goes to the police headquarters in the morning and comes home again in the afternoon to eat and sleep for an hour or two. Most evenings, he goes back again to the headquarters, and sometimes he mounts his horse and goes out with his cavalry on patrol in the desert, staying out until after midnight. I can't blame him for anything. I had hoped, though, that the desert journey and life here would have brought us closer together. At first, I was optimistic. There was only us and love was our only pastime. Then he started to fall victim to ennui and I too no longer experienced the pleasure to which I'd become accustomed from the start of our relationship. Let us postpone thoughts of that. I am grateful to him because he gives me the whole of his days off. We walk together or hire donkeys and wander among the closed gardens and around the lakes and sometimes we go out into the desert. Last Friday, he went with me when I decided to start by visiting the temple of Amun – the temple of the oracle who created the whole legend of Alexander.

He waited for me at the bottom of the hill on top of which stands what remains of the temple's sanctuary. He said he couldn't wander about in the midst of houses where families and women lived. I, as a woman, could do so, but he couldn't, because of their traditions and customs. He wasn't aware that it was impossible even for a woman.

I knew of course before setting off that on the ascent to the temple I would pass houses built into the mound that were

96

inhabited by some of the Aghurmi families, and I was hoping that a miracle might happen to break the silence if I met people face to face. As I climbed with difficulty the treacherous, crumbling steps, however, I saw women, as soon as I got close to any of the houses, closing their doors. Friendly smiles were of no use and neither was the 'Good morning' that I'd learnt to say in their dialect from the children who play in front of the house. Their responses were angry mutters and they slammed the doors hard.

After the tiring climb and the disappointment, all I found of the temple were ruins whose outlines were clearer from the bottom of the hill.

I was astonished at what I saw. The halls of the temple had stone gateways that were, however, blocked with yellow brick, turning them into houses, with wooden doors. I could find only one open hallway, which was preceded by a corridor, and I found traces of carvings on its entrance and walls, though I couldn't make out what any of the carvings were or read the writings inscribed on the walls. Thick soot had rendered these illegible, and I realized when I saw the primitive stone ovens scattered about the place that the women had been using the hall as a communal kitchen, which they had abandoned as soon as they'd realized I was making my way there. I tried carefully to wipe off with the palm of my hand the soot that hid the traces of a drawing of the god Amun, but my hand got dirty and the black covered over what had been visible, so I gave up the attempt.

Was it possible that this hall had been the Holy of Holies of the temple where Alexander had received Amun's oracular message? How could I find out if I couldn't see the rest of the temple? If I were the sort of woman to cry, the tears would have burst from my eyes as I compared what I'd read about Alexander's procession here as it passed between the decorated walls, surrounded by song and with the glory of the coloured images on either side, and the state it was in now. A kitchen? The Holy of Holies a kitchen?

I descended filled with sorrow and anger. I paid no attention now when the women once again closed their open doors as I groped my way down the stairs. At one of the turns on the darkened staircase, however, and among all those closed doors, I was surprised to find one door slowly and carefully opening and the whisper of a barely audible call. A girl appeared in the doorway. A face appeared whose beauty, like a light in the surrounding darkness, filled me with joy. She smiled at me and whispered something in the unknown language. I made signs to her to show that I didn't understand. She held a hand out towards my chest and gestured with the other at her own and said in a whisper, 'Maleeka.' She went on looking enquiringly at me but as I was whispering in turn 'Catherine', a shrivelled woman's hand came out and dragged Maleeka back, and the door quietly closed. I remained standing there for a while. Where had the beauty of that face come from? A smooth white skin and fine, well-proportioned features – grey eyes and full rosy lips, chestnut hair, of which a single thick lock fell across her brow, and the rest of which hung down on either side of her face in hundreds of fine plaits with silver decorations to form a frame from which emerged the radiant face. Perhaps her features were not out of the ordinary for a beautiful face. If so, why did I find myself nailed to the spot because of it? Was it the shock of friendliness in the midst of all this incomprehensible hostility? Maybe.

Let me forget about that too and think about what awaits me today. Like Mahmoud, I hope I have better luck when we visit the temple that they call here Umm Ma'bad, or Umm Ebeida. This too is a temple to Amun and its style points to its having been built in the age of the Egyptian awakening that preceded the Persian invasion. I've seen it many times from the outside during my walks in the oasis and I hope it's been spared the vandalizing of the carvings and inscriptions whose forms were recorded by the German traveller Von Minutoli at the beginning of the century. He, as I realized merely by looking at them, had erred frequently and obviously by copying the hieroglyphs as though they were simply pictures. The book is with me, and if the carvings have remained intact, I shall endeavour to correct those mistakes.

The heat today is fiercer than usual, even though we're almost at the end of autumn. The scent of lemon blossom steals from the gardens, but all we can see over the tops of the walls is the fans of the palm fronds, whose pointed ends gleam in the sun like arrows.

Mahmoud rode his donkey with his head bowed and eyes closed. He was still in a better mood than on many days. I hoped he would hold on and not suddenly change, as he usually did.

'Why are you silent, Mahmoud?' I called out.

He lifted his head towards me and laughed in an irritated way, pointing to his legs, as though to say, 'What can I say when I'm like this?'

He's right. He isn't at ease on his donkey. His feet are almost touching the ground so he has to bend his long legs. He's been embarrassed to ride a donkey comfortably, with his legs dangling on either side, since we were told that they allow that method here only for women. Why? Especially when the opposite would be the more logical! As though this was the only thing I don't understand here!

As we drew close to Gouba Spring, I shouted, 'We're almost there. Alexander the Great and his entourage passed this way and were entranced by this spring. They knew it as the "Spring of the Sun", perhaps because of the many suns that multiply on its surface, as you can see.'

Mahmoud shouted back, 'I've been by it and seen it often before. Now I can't see a thing, though. The sun is blinding me.'

We said nothing more until we reached the temple and Ibraheem, who had preceded us there, came towards us. Mahmoud shouted to him as he got down from his donkey

99

and helped me to alight, 'Quick, Ibraheem. Bring us water to drink,' and Ibraheem ran off in the direction of the spring.

I followed with my eye the boy who had been running behind us and saw him take the halters of the two donkeys and move towards the nearest palm tree in front of the temple.

Mahmoud took off his round helmet and started wiping the sweat off his face and head with a large handkerchief. His eyes roamed over the temple, in the midst of whose ruins were piled large stones that had fallen during the earthquake at the beginning of the century, as I had read in the books. With a wan smile, he said, 'Here's the whole site laid out before you. Try to make up for what you couldn't do last Friday.'

He couldn't wait, however. He said, 'Excuse me,' and ran off in the same direction as Ibraheem.

I raised the parasol over my head and stood, contemplating the little temple, or what remained of it. There was the stone gateway, or outer portal, which the earthquake had split in two halves that were still joined by the stones of the ceiling, most of which had also collapsed. Inside, the remains of walls divided the temple into halls, of which little evidence remained except ruined pillars and floors paved with white stones among which sprouted weeds.

However dilapidated the temple, it was in a much better state than the Temple of the Oracle, which had been converted into dwellings and kitchens. The drawings and hieroglyphs were still visible on the walls.

The parasol wasn't helping me at all, so I went into the temple and sat on one of the stones in the shade of the lofty portal. No call to be stubborn about it – the heat today was insupportable, but what was to be done when Mahmoud insisted that I not wander about in the heart of the oasis on my own and that my morning outings be with him, on his day of rest? Perhaps I could start today by reading the inscriptions written on the fallen stones, for there was no means for me to read what was written at the top of the gateway. On the other hand, how was this ancient ruin supposed to help me in my search for something that had happened centuries after it had been built? I hung my hope on the custom of the Egyptians, in which they were imitated by the Greeks, of adding elements to the temples of their ancestors and, even more importantly, of adding writings and inscriptions. And I would depend even more on luck.

If only someone would guide me to something, anything! Who? For example, that boy who was sitting opposite me under the shade of a palm tree guarding the two donkeys. I could teach him and make him my friend, and he could guide me to places I didn't know about. His bright eyes spoke of intelligence, but he himself didn't utter a word. And that other boy, the one with his face covered, who was hovering around the temple with his donkey, coming a little closer as though he were watching me and then moving away again; when he came next to the temple gate I waved to him but he turned his donkey's neck to one side and hurried off, as though in flight, in the direction of Aghurmi. Why did he approach and why did he flee? What made him fear me?

I had to try something!

I gestured to the boy who was sitting under the palm and called out in a loud voice, 'Boy!' He got up and started looking around him. Then he came hesitantly towards me. When he stood in front of me, I noticed profuse sweat dripping from his brow and saw the pallor and exhaustion in his face. Of course! How could he be strong enough to run the whole way in this heat, which Mahmoud and I could barely stand when mounted? But it was he who had insisted.

'Good morning!' I said to him. 'Good morning,' he responded, with a forced smile. Not bad! Even if he was making fun of me, we had broken a barrier. And now, how to proceed?

I made a circular movement with my hand to indicate the remains of the temple and asked him in Arabic, 'Have you gone inside?' He stood looking at my face with astonishment and incomprehension, so I got up and led him to a wall that still retained lovely carvings of the ancient gods. I pointed to a beautifully shaped image of the goddess Isis coloured in blue and red and asked him in the simplest Arabic possible, 'Nice?' His face darkened and he snatched his hand violently from mine. Then he spat on the image, saying angrily, 'Unbelievers!', turned around quickly and, almost falling over, ran away from the temple and sat down again in his original place.

I continued to stand there, overwhelmed by frustration and embarrassment at myself, but still made a mental note: 'So "unbelievers" is another word that's common to both languages.'

I too went back to my place in the shade of the gate.

It was hopeless. No one was going to extend a hand to me. I apologize, my dear Isis, for this indignity. I apologize, Alexander. I don't know where or how to begin.

I had lost all my enthusiasm for work and the search and for the visit itself. Mahmoud would be happy to go home early, so why not?

'Haven't you started your rounds yet?'

I was startled to find Mahmoud in front of me with Ibraheem beside him, holding out to me an earthenware pot brimming with water, which I drank to the last drop. He had washed his face and put a large white handkerchief, which he had soaked in water, on his head.

He turned to address Ibraheem and said, 'Go back and sit in the shade.'

Looking at me, and with the sweat running in the wrinkles of his lined brown face, Ibraheem said, 'Perhaps you or the madame will need me for something, Excellency.'

'Thank you, Ibraheem,' I said. 'If I need you, I'll call you.' Then I pointed to the boy sitting with his legs drawn up to his chest opposite me under the palm tree and watching me.

'And tell that boy to go with you too and rest over there. I don't want him in my view all the time!'

I saw Ibraheem bend over the boy and speak to him, but the boy shook his head and didn't get up and go off with him. In fact, he stretched out on the ground and lay on his side, putting his hand under his head, while Ibraheem went back on his own in the direction of the spring.

Mahmoud said, 'The air's a lot fresher there, near the water and in the shade of the trees,' and he started looking for a place to sit in the shade, which he found on a stone at the bottom of a wall that stood close by me. He sat, rested his back against the wall, and repeated his question.

'When will you begin, Catherine, so that we can get back to the house before . . .'

'Before your Friday prayer appointment. I know.'

I took a deep breath and made an effort to control myself. Then I said, 'I'm working now, in fact. I'm thinking and reviewing the information I have before looking at these remains, which time, earthquakes and the search for treasure have ruined.'

Taking my books from my bag, I went on, 'But wouldn't you like first to hear what Herodotus said about the "Spring of the Sun", whose air you like so much? Do you know Herodotus?'

'Of course. We learnt in school that he said, "Egypt is the gift of the Nile."'

'Correct. He was the world's first historian, and he visited Egypt before writing his book. They call him the "Father of History".'

'And he really mentions this small spring in his book?'

Smiling, I said, 'In no uncertain terms! He says, my dear, that the water of this spring is warm in the morning, then cools gradually and becomes very cold at noon, when the gardens are being watered, and then the coldness disappears during the day and at midnight the water in the spring boils fiercely. Then the wonder is reversed and it slowly gets cooler again as dawn approaches.'

Mahmoud looked at me, amazement growing in his eyes. He let out a loud laugh and said, 'Did he really write that?'

I waved the book in my hand. 'Do you want me to read it to you?'

'No,' he answered, still laughing. 'Now that's what I call historical scholarship! I've been past the spring at night, at dawn and in the afternoon, and I've drunk from the well and washed in it, and I've never seen the water "boiling fiercely", or even slightly, at any of those times.'

To provoke him, I said, 'Perhaps that's how it was in Herodotus's day.'

He continued as though he hadn't heard me, 'The Father of History, indeed! Why not, when things I saw with my own eyes only a few years ago are now being recounted in the history books exactly the wrong way round? Father of History! History, it seems, truly is a bastard!'

I looked at him as he bent his head, the water dripping from the handkerchief with which he'd covered his head. His tone was sad. His mood had turned gloomy, as I'd feared.

My eyes roamed over the temple and fell on the boy lying on the ground opposite me, who had spat on the image of Isis, and I said to Mahmoud with a little laugh, 'Poor history! It has no friends today.'

I thought, there may well be lies. Certainly there are lies. But by what method are we to know the truth if not that of searching for it?

Suddenly we heard loud clamouring and shouting from the direction of the spring. Ibraheem appeared, hurrying as usual, bent down to speak to Mahmoud and said something to him in a low voice. Mahmoud replied by asking, 'After the Friday prayer? We'll be there.'

Then he got ready to leave with Ibraheem, telling me, 'I'll leave you to hasten your work a little and go back to the spring with the boiling water. Ibraheem says we have to give our condolences to the *agwad* because one of them has died.'

Ibraheem continued, 'It's Sheikh Mi'bid, God rest his soul and those of all our dead. Still, his death has spared the oasis a war that was just about to break out between the Easterners and the Westerners. God, glory be to Him, has His wisdom.'

They went off together, so I took out all the old pictures I had with me and compared them with what I could see around me. The pictures of the nearby wall and its writings didn't concern me. Most of them showed the ceremonies to make the dead speak the truth on the Day of Judgement that some call the Book of the Dead. Usually they're found in tombs, rarely in temples. Anyway, they were an indication that this was a funerary temple, made for the final orations over and immortalization of a king or other important person who worshipped the god Amun. There was nothing here to do with any search for Alexander, whose visit occurred after the building of the temple. Since we were here, however, we might as well work. I would begin by copying what was on the walls and correcting the mistakes to be found in the books. Luck might be mine, and I'd chance on a more recent text. Who knew?

Alexander's successors, in the shape of the Greek Ptolemies, ruled Egypt for centuries, and many of their nobility lived in the Oasis of Amun and were buried there. Could they really have left no trace that would be of use to us? A small temple, a shrine, or even a commemorative plaque inside a temple that spoke of their divine Alexander and might add to the sum of our knowledge about him?

Would that the spirit of Alexander might help me! I have that book on conjuring up spirits with me. Should I use it? On the other hand, I don't believe in the conjuring of spirits, and I even have questions about the spirits themselves. Enough silliness. To work!

I went towards the wall, then suddenly stopped.

Wait a moment, Catherine! What do all these signs mean?

The conjuring up of spirits, the funerary temple and the Book of the Dead on the wall. Isn't it all leading you to something? Think for a moment. Perhaps what you should be looking for is Alexander's death, not his life! Something that has to do with his death. Yes!

The only person who could have understood me at that moment was my father. He could have helped me too.

But he was helping me!

Everything around me brought to my mind a discussion we had that had ended with a passing phrase that now seemed like a message. It was as though I'd been going round and round this message without realizing. That evening he was talking to me about Alexander and reading to me from Plutarch's book on his final days, and I interrupted him to ask with some bewilderment, 'Isn't it strange that all talk of Alexander's mausoleum in Alexandria, which was the most famous of its landmarks and the objective of all who visited the city, comes to a sudden halt after the fourth century?' My father answered, 'You are right. The question has often bothered me too. What might have happened? Did the sepulchre sink into the sea? Was it destroyed in an earthquake? Was it demolished by the Romans, who demolished so many pagan monuments after embracing Christianity?' He was silent for a moment. Then, thinking out loud, he said, 'Or did some of them take the sepulchre to another place? Did the worship of Alexander continue and did he still have faithful devotees who might have considered how to save the mortal remains of their divinity?'

Why not? If my father were alive, I would persuade him that if his supposition were true there could be no more suitable place than the Oasis of Amun to which to remove the embalmed corpse and sepulchre. Wasn't Alexander's last request that he be buried here, in this oasis, next to his father Amun?

If his supposition were true and *if* my interpretation were correct. Mere guesswork, there being no indication in history that the sepulchre was moved. No evidence, not the slightest sign.

It was an insane idea, an insane intuition. But every discovery ever made began with this kindness of insanity, didn't it? I would hold my tongue, then, and let my goal be to prove my intuition, to find some evidence, even the slightest evidence, that might lead others to search and dig, and then I'd have some credit for the greatest discovery in the history of the world.

If I succeeded, it would make up for everything I'd had to endure in this oasis. It would give my life the meaning I've been searching for. The important thing, though, was to be patient.

I had less than three hours remaining now in the temple, so I must try to do something useful.

The time passed quickly and made me forget even the heat.

As I was gathering my papers and books together, I said to myself, 'Not a bad harvest. I've corrected some of the mistakes of the books and copied down a prayer to Amun in late Egyptian. However, the miracle of stumbling across a text written in Greek that might lead me to Alexander, alive or dead, did not materialize. No matter. We spoke of patience.'

I finished at the right moment. I heard Mahmoud's voice approaching and with him Ibraheem, and saw them as they came closer.

Then, all of a sudden, there was a slight shaking under my feet and at the same time the sound of stone breaking reached me. Instinctively I raised my head and saw the capstones that held together the two halves of the sundered gateway slowly coming apart. Then I saw them fly and screamed and ran to get away.

A large stone was falling from the ceiling like a missile, making for the boy sleeping under the palm tree.

I ran towards him screaming and he roused himself and sat watching the falling stone.

I would never reach him. It was a matter of seconds!

I saw Mahmoud and Ibraheem shouting and flinging themselves at the boy, who was sitting paralysed, staring upwards.

Then I saw the three of them throwing themselves to the ground, but couldn't tell which of them the stone, which was now rolling near by, had struck.

I went on running towards them and suddenly there were children and adults everywhere, all yelling and all rushing towards the three persons lying in a heap.

8

Alexander the Great

The snake bit my mother with the bite of love, and I came into this world. The Divine Ram appeared to her as a snake, and I was the fruit of that holy conception. My earthly father, Philip, King of Macedon, was about to go in unto my mother, Olympias, when he witnessed through the half-open door her intercourse with the slithery god. He saw the huge black snake slithering over her marble-white belly as she embraced it in love and he saw it enter into her. So he withdrew, closing the door behind him in reverence and holy awe. Then he sent an offering to the temple of Amun-Zeus, the Snake God, the Ram, the Hawk of Hidden Names.

Such am I and such is my ancestry. Who, then, are you, you stranger to my country and to the land of Amun? Are you a man or a woman? I have no certain knowledge but I think you are a woman. I will think of you as a woman. That kind of unceasing insistence I have known since I was a boy from my mother, and then from every woman after her. Why, then, do you disturb my spirit, which has chosen this wild land in which to wander? You are insistent in your calls to me from your world and you seek something of which I have no knowledge.

It is your reckoning that I know more than you. No. Our spirits after death roam in the darkness, and now I am like a blind fish that knows of the vast ocean only that it is swimming in black water beyond which follows more of the same. Thus do I grope aimlessly in darkness beyond which lies darkness. Is this the hell of Hades that the Greeks held to be the resting place of evildoers, while the spirits of the good floated in light with their lords? Or is it the sinners' void described by the priests of the Egyptians? I do not know. I cannot say. From the moment I departed life, I could see you mortals for forty days, no more. After that, the darkness fell and it has lasted for a time I cannot calculate. Is it a day, or an aeon?

I see no one from your world. I hear no voice and I do not speak. I do not encounter good spirits or evil and I do not believe that I can reach you or inspire you with anything. Nevertheless, from time to time, someone like you comes and calls to me, and wakens my spirit without my being able to understand what it is that it wants. I know nothing here beyond what I knew on Earth. I go over it time after time, and each time the picture of my life that I see is at odds with what I saw the time before.

Is this a limbo that will open up in the end to reveal mercy and ease, or a new torment? I do not know. I cannot say.

I do not know even the nature of Amun, with whom I seek refuge. Was he a divinity, or a delusion?

And was the priest who conveyed to me the oracle's message a guide who could pass through the veil of the unseen or an impostor concocting lies? All the same, my spirit followed behind my corpse for weeks and I made haste to reach here before the forty days so that I might see the temple of Amun for a final time. I want it to be the first thing I see when the light shines again, should it ever shine, so that I can know the truth.

From the moment that I became conscious of the world, my mother sowed in my soul the certainty that I was the son of the god. And how could I deny Olympias's claims when she had been raised as a priestess in the temples of the gods? She had penetrated the worlds of the hidden secrets and in my childhood I saw her pass through into those worlds unknown to mankind. A spellbinding gleam would light up in her green eyes. Then, little by little, her look would cloud over as she gazed on what we cannot see, and finally her body would go rigid and she would fall to the ground, speaking in a language unlike any we know. After a while, she would return to us, a limpid gaze in her bewitching eyes and her face clear and beautiful. The oracles of the gods would come to her from the rustling of the leaves of the trees, from the whispering of the breeze, from the singing of the birds, from the scintillating of the stars, and from a world we do not know. Then she would declare to us what had passed and what was to come.

When I was ten years old, in the palace of her royal brother, she revived after one of her journeys to the unknown and said, as one who brings glad and certain tidings, 'I saw you as a white eagle hovering in the sky with silver wings that reached out and grew and grew until their shadow covered the whole world. You will be the shadow and the light. You will be the sun and you will be all that is and all that will be. You will rule the earth and no one shall defeat you and you will be blessed with the immortality of the gods.'

I was a sad child then, and an angry one too, because my father had married another woman and divorced my mother, so that she accompanied me to the palace of her brother the king, far from Philip and Macedonia. She told me, 'Do not be sad. Philip is not your father. You are the son of Amun-Zeus. And yet we shall return to Macedonia before months have passed. You will spend ten years with your earthly father before inheriting from him the throne. Then you shall rule the world and all who are upon it.' None of her earthly prophecies had ever lied, so how could I doubt that I was the son of a god? But how could I have two fathers, Philip on Earth and Amun in Heaven? Who was I and what was demanded of me in this world?

No one was more capable of helping me to understand these mysteries than Aristotle, the greatest philosopher of the Greeks, whom Philip had summoned to teach me since I was a child and heir to the throne, but he did not guide me easily to the answers. He was accustomed to delivering his wisdom in short, obscure utterances. He venerated the gods of the Greeks, or made a show of venerating them, and had nothing to say about the gods of the Egyptians. He must certainly have been scared of meeting the fate of his predecessor Socrates, who talked so much about the gods that Athens punished him, seeing in him a blasphemer and an unbeliever, and forced him to swallow poison. I, though, was thirsty for knowledge and to understand the strange happenings that had accompanied my life from birth. Aristotle wanted me for philosophy and politics, but I was preparing for other lessons.

On some, rare, occasions, I was able to apply my teacher's most important lesson, which was to hold in check the raging passions of the appetite and master my mind, but his greatest gifts to me were poetry and music. I read Homer's epic the Iliad to him and the copy of it that he himself had corrected stayed with me all through my life. It was always beneath my pillow, in peace and in war. And one of his puzzling sayings – that tragic verse, with the feelings of pity and fear that it provokes, serves to purge us – stuck in my mind.

What taught me the meaning of the saying, as I read poetry or listened to music, was the experience of life itself. How often during my life did the ecstasy of poetry take me to worlds that lay far beyond all that was tangible and visible, so that I felt that the veil between me and the unknown was about to fall, and that my spirit was about to hover outside my body and pass through the solid obstacles of the cold, dumb world to the world of eternal secrets glittering with the lights of immortal realities! How many a time did I wake up at night, even in the midst of the battles of my ceaseless wars, to read from the Iliad and plead with its writer that he might release in me the very fountain from which he himself had drunk! Many times the call would continue for whole days and nights, during which the recitation of poetry and the playing of music would never cease at court, until my troops thought that their commander had lost his mind.

Perhaps, in fact, I did yearn that madness would descend on me, for in the midst of that ecstasy I would forget Aristotle and remember my mother, who had taught me that no one may enter the kingdom of holy secrets unless they be in the grip of an ecstasy that violates the familiar in order to break through to the unknown.

I told myself, 'Even if I don't attain that, the joys of this world are scarce enough!'

I tried to stretch out that joy, to wrest it from the world so that it might last, but there was always another Alexander, the one who wrested me from joy, the Alexander of blood who chased away the Alexander of song. Throughout my short life, there was always an Alexander against an Alexander.

But the songs are also associated in my mind with my meeting with Amun in His oasis. I entered Egypt as a conqueror and the Egyptians received me as a liberator and a saviour because I freed them from occupation by the Persians, who humiliated them and ruined the temples of their gods.

I showered their priests with gifts and made offerings to their gods, so they loved me. I didn't worship those gods or know them, and in the beginning I recoiled from their frightful images. What could the Greek gods, with their noble, beautiful, human faces, have in common with the scowling animal faces of those Egyptian gods, which evoke terror? They are not to be compared. The divinities of the Greeks take the worshipper to the peak of Olympus, their refuge, so that man may share with them their sublimity and joy. The gods of the Egyptians, though, scared me and gave me to think that man was a stranger to them, a cipher in a world ruled by the frightening gods. They also cast into my soul a new doubt. They created a third Alexander, who asked, 'Which is more proper for the life of man on Earth – delight or fear? Which of them is more conducive to right conduct and the good?' And I did not arrive in my depths at an answer, but I tried to impose the answer.

113

Despite this, I showed every respect towards those gods, and it wasn't all hypocrisy. It was also a way of getting closer to their great one, Amun, whom I hoped would show me the secret of my birth and destiny. Since my youth, I had heard that the seeker of knowledge must make his way to Egypt and that Plato, my master Aristotle's teacher, had said that the Greeks, despite all that they prided themselves on by way of practice and philosophy, were mere infants when compared with the Egyptians. Would the oracle of Amun fulfil my hope? His fame had spread to Greece in the distant past and reached such heights that they had made Him one with Zeus, the leader of their gods. It was said too that every prediction of the oracle of His oasis had come true, so that many Greeks came to him to seek his counsel.

Did I, though, believe that? I did. One Alexander believed and another Alexander refused to believe and I hoped for a miracle at Amun's hands that would make the two of them one.

In those days there were only two of them.

I laid the foundation for my city Alexandria on the shores of the sea. Then I decided to make my way to the oasis. The court was upset. They warned me of the desert that had destroyed an army of the Persian Cambyses, and that it was then midwinter, the season of storms. And I heard their mutterings that I was going there to receive the title 'Son of the God' from the priests, even though the Greeks and Macedonians hate those Eastern beliefs. The utmost pinnacle a man can reach in our belief is to become a hero like Hercules, which is to say 'immortal' but lower than the gods. It's only in Egypt, where they deify their kings, that the gods adopt a man and make him one of them. Some men of my entourage said it was just another caprice of Alexander's, a challenge to those before him who had failed to cross that trackless waste.

I listened to it all but said nothing, and I rode my horse westwards along the shore, and the thought came to me that, as I had tamed this raging black stallion when I was a boy and all the knights of Macedonia had failed to subdue it, so would I tame this desert.

I headed south towards the oasis, accompanied by a small number of soldiers and friends, and every disaster did indeed befall us on the way. The water stored in leather bags ran out two days into our journey, seeping into the sand or evaporating into the air, and the caravan was stricken with panic. Suddenly, though, rains fell from the sky, and they refilled the water skins and one of the soldiers said in excitement, 'See how the gods' concern guards Alexander from harm!', though another muttered that, on the contrary, it was the season of the rains and there was no miracle in it. I smiled to myself, thinking, 'Which of them is right?' Then the violent storm arose and the wind and sand scattered our cavalcade east and west, and when the wind abated and the whirlwinds moved away, we had lost our path, fatigue had ground us down, and we no longer knew which track to take.

Later in my life I read that certain writers said it was a flock of crows which saved the caravan and set it on the right course. They said that this flock had continued to hover above us by day and its cawing had guided us by night till the end of the journey. Others wrote that, no, a sacred Egyptian cobra had appeared before the caravan and led us to the oasis of Amun.

And what of it if it was the stars which guided the riders? Mortals, though, are entranced by stories of crows and snakes, and the Greeks are no different to the rest, and nor was I, despite all the teachings of Aristotle. How I wished, though, that I might be different!

I reached the oasis of Amun early in the morning after a week, and a large golden sun flooded the temple of the oracle with its light. I saw a procession of pilgrims proceeding on foot up the hill. I, though, spurred my horse in quick bounds to the top of the rise and arrived before them all. My heart quickened as I looked around me. Everything was new and unfamiliar to my eyes. Below me, in the middle of the desert, I saw a green sea of palms and another large sun, exactly like the sun in the sky, shining from a spring at the foot of the temple, and yet others flashing among the blue lakes that dotted the sands. In front of the entrance to the temple with its decorations of brightly coloured painting, I saw the priestesses of Amun, the breeze moving their diaphanous robes so that they undulated about their slender, dancing bodies like white wings, as though they were about to fly away, high in the air, towards that sun to which they waved their arms in supplication. They were singing a low song whose words I could not understand, but their voices, quavering as they chanted, had the ring to my ears not of a prayer of entreaty but of a lover's whispered plea. To whom? To the gods? To Amun alone? To me?

I dismounted, my heart still beating hard in my chest at what I had seen and heard and all that awaited me in this place, but despite that I moved with the dignity of a king, and directed my steps towards the high priest, who stepped out from among the chanting priestesses and came forwards to receive me. His head was completely shaven and he too was wearing a flowing white robe. He bowed at length before me, then, extending his hand, welcomed me in Greek: 'He has been waiting for you, Son of the God and Master of the World.'

I gestured to the entourage who were following me and they presented him with gifts and offerings. He accepted these and then led me towards the entrance of the temple. My companions were about to enter with me when he stopped them with a wave of his hand. It was not permitted to any but me to penetrate the sanctuary. We went forwards together through the door of the Holy of Holies, the singing and the dancing stopping in the outer courtyard. A sudden, thick silence fell, and a white cloud of incense the like of whose fragrance had never before caressed my nostrils gusted from the interior of the temple. A dread such as I had never known in all the battles in which I had faced death swept over me.

I entered the place where the statue of the god sits on its gilded throne so that His priest might announce the oracle, for the priest does not speak of his own volition. And in the darkened Holy of Holies and amidst the clouds of incense came the voice, deep and calm and slow, emerging through the walls from nowhere and everywhere.

Finally, Amun revealed what he wanted me to hear, and left it to me to understand.

I left the temple once more in the company of the priest and he raised his hands for all to be silent. I was afraid lest he proclaim something of what the oracle had said before the crowds, but he contented himself with saying that the gods had chosen me as Pharaoh of Egypt and that their god Horus was incarnate in my body from that moment. The second he announced this, the throngs of priests and priestesses, and the Egyptian pilgrims, started cheering and waving with convulsive enthusiasm as they exclaimed the name of the new pharaoh, the voices of the men and women tremulous with tears of joy.

My companions and soldiers gathered around me, their eyes enquiring as to what had taken place at my encounter with the god, but I contented myself with a smile. Philotas, however, that brave warrior and my close friend, asked me in something like reproach, 'So you're a god, then?', and when he failed to hear a reply from me he muttered, as he looked sadly around, 'We were happy for a mere hero to lead us to victory.'

I understood the import of his words, even if the unceasing roaring by the crowds of the beloved name of pharaoh, of my name, of Alexander, God-Pharaoh of Egypt, drowned them, and I asked myself at that instant what the Greeks had done with that freedom of which they were so proud. They would never have stopped dividing and fighting until their cities had destroyed each other, had not my father, Philip, united them at the last by the sword under the rule of Macedonia. Here, on the other hand, were the Egyptians, whose state had lasted undisturbed for thousands of years under the authority of their divinities, pharaohs and priests by virtue of that tyranny the Greeks hated. Why, then, should I not take my lessons from Egypt? And why should I not try to combine them with those of Aristotle?

As I pondered, I was gazing at Hephaestion, my dearest friend. I saw neither reproach nor doubt in his limpid eyes. He believed. Then I removed my glance to the angry Philotas. It didn't matter. I would kill him later.

Later on, I told everyone I would never reveal anything of what happened between Amun and me in the Holy of Holies except to my mother Olympias when I met her. My life came to an end, however, before we could meet again, and the secret of that encounter died with me.

And you, woman, who calls to me and disturbs my spirit, do you wish me to reveal the secret to you now?

As though you were Olympias!

The visit to Amun provided me for a period with the inner peace that I had spent my whole life looking for, torn as I was between the severity of my father Philip, the ecstatic visions of my mother and the wisdom of Aristotle. I had found this peace in war, and had chased the Persians from Anatolia, Syria, Palestine and Egypt. I had defeated their king Darius in every battle he had waged against me. After my encounter with Amun, however, I did not continue the war with the Persians as enemies whom I wished to rival in the occupation of lands. No, I waged war now as a god of justice, which I was to spread throughout the universe. It was not just another battle, as their poor king thought, but a war to the end, a war to end all wars, a war of good versus evil, that peace might reign upon Earth for ever.

Darius prepared himself well during my stay in Egypt. From what was left of his empire he gathered an army that outnumbered mine ten times over. He didn't understand that numbers mean nothing, or the lesson I had learnt from my father Philip – that you may rule men by repression and fear, but the fearful can never be victorious in war; on the field of battle they must be free men, they must conquer their fear by their own will and not by order of their commanders. I learnt that bravery is not an instinct; rather it is precisely the conquest of the fear that lurks in every soul. So I made myself the example for my soldiers. I didn't issue orders, but would stand at the forefront in every battle, brandishing my sword, thrusting and being thrust at, the blood running from every limb, but confident of victory. The boldness, the thrusting and the blood infected my troops and they would charge behind me, to victory or to death, it mattered not. I knew how to inspire the troops so that they became drunk on the ecstasy of war and forgot themselves, and that is how I made an army out of them. Darius was never able to do such a thing. And this even though in peace I ruled them with a fist of iron harder than his own, the fist of a god-pharaoh.

Again I defeated him in two great battles and his troops fled, with him in their footsteps. He sent envoys with offers to divide the world between us and give me anything I wanted of the heaped treasures and wealth of his empire, but why should I accept half the world when I was certain that I held it whole in my right hand? And how could his wealth, which was destined anyway to be spoils for me to distribute to my soldiers, tempt me? His offer to wed me to his daughter made me laugh too – she who had been a captive in my camp along with her mother and the women of his family since my first battle with him. I replied to his offer by setting the captives free, including his mother, and I entertained them as honoured guests in a palace of his that I had taken on my march. Nevertheless, he failed to understand my message and waited for me again with a huge army at the capital of his ruined kingdom, Persepolis, glory of the empire, home of the throne of the King of Kings and his sceptre. For the third and last time he was defeated and fled in search of a new army, though I knew, as did my troops, that this was the end of the war with the Persians and the end of their state.

It was only justice, after this, that I should destroy his capital, burning it to the ground. Had not the Persians burnt beautiful Athens, the pearl of the Greeks, two centuries before? I paid no attention to the counsels of my troops and courtiers who opposed the destruction of Persepolis. They asked me why I had made pacts with the other Persian cities that I had taken, restored their temples, and won over the hearts of their inhabitants, and why I wanted to destroy the capital, whose palaces and wealth had become my possession. I let them talk and then lifted a brand, which I threw at the palace of the King of Kings, signalled to my troops to do the same, and the fires blazed in the palace until it became a ball of smoke and flame. Then why not another offering? Why not the whole city as a flaming offering?

This was not the justice of a god but the revenge of a man possessed by hatred. The crackling and hissing of the fires filled me with an intoxication like that of wine and I became afraid of myself. Yet again I asked, 'Who can I really be? Who am I?' And there was a question I would ask many times from then on: 'Why do I do the thing and its opposite?'

After Persepolis, however, I destroyed no more cities. Rather, I built new ones, more Alexandrias. I pardoned the commanders in the lands I had liberated and made them rulers of provinces of my Macedonian empire. I reconciled their hearts and restored the temples of their gods, though I also erected temples to a new god whom they had to come to know well and to whom they had to make offerings too. His name was 'the God Alexander, son of Amun'.

I paid no attention to the restlessness of my Greek and Macedonian troops. They too had to worship the god who had led them to a victory no man before had achieved and of which no man thereafter could ever dream. Who but a god could have achieved such conquests?

The Earth was at my feet. I annexed to Macedonia all the empire of the Persians, then set off with my army and conquered all the lands to the east. I swept through valleys and deserts and passed across the rugged mountains that had defeated all who had tried to cross them until I reached the continent of India itself, and I subdued it. I conquered Asia up to its farthest shores and seas and I made good the prophecy of Olympias and Amun concerning me that I should be victorious wherever I set foot. Then it was left to me to go back, having conquered the East, and conquer the West.

Not, however, before succeeding at something at which no man or god had succeeded before me. I was going to fashion a new world without peer. A world in which the races of man would become one and speak one language, which would be Greek, the most sublime of languages, the language of the Iliad, and whose peoples would marry one another, so that there would be only one race throughout the world.

I caught up with the Persians whom I had defeated with my army and tried to foster brotherhood between them and my soldiers. The Macedonians and the Greeks, however, recoiled in disgust at the idea of considering their enemies of yesterday, the barbarians, equals as companions-in-arms. This did not turn me aside from my plan. I married the daughter of Darius, who had been my captive since the beginning of the war, and the night of my marriage to her I married eighty of the commanders of my army to noble Persian women and encouraged my Macedonian troops to do the same, and there were thousands of marriages.

I dreamt of filling the world with a new strain, from the loins of the Europeans and the Asians, after which there could be no ill will among them or wars. Alexander wanted to bring about what the other gods had failed to do – to create a world in which there was neither blond nor brown and in which there was no difference between those who worshipped Zeus and those who worshipped the fire of the Persians or the gods of the Indians.

Alexander asked himself, 'Must I, for the sake of this dream, wade through a sea of blood – the blood of the defeated and the blood of my soldiers?'

And another Alexander answered, 'Yes, so long as that is for their good in the end. No one understands the wisdom of the gods, so why should it be necessary for them to understand my wisdom?'

The members of my entourage whispered that Alexander had become a tyrant like the tyrants of the East. He wore the robes of the barbarian Persians and sat on the throne of Darius, holding Darius's sceptre. It seemed he had forgotten the freedom of the Greeks, for he allowed none to argue with him and wanted to make the entire world his subjects.

Some of the troops wanted to return to their homelands after their mission in Asia was finished, so I dismissed those soldiers who wanted to go back to Greece and was left with only the faithful among my commanders, at their head Hephaestion, my lifelong friend, and the soldiers of my people the Macedonians, who stood alone, as an army that had never been defeated. It was no longer in their power, now that they had become addicted to the wine of victory, to retreat, even had their souls told them to respond to the call of the mind, or of family or offspring.

Yet despite this, the plots against my life among my remaining troops went on and this stirred up my anger and sorrow, so I turned my attention more to drink. I held banquets and evening parties at which the tuns of wine were emptied without reckoning. No one could keep pace with me in my drinking, and it may be that I drank more than any other because I had greater need than the rest of the wine, in whose forgetfulness the scattered shards of Alexander came together and were made one. Or perhaps, quite the opposite, it scattered those shards, and I could observe my severed parts and give voice to what I could not reveal when sober.

At such times I would not hesitate to kill anyone who wanted to wake me so that I could become the Alexander he wanted me to be.

Which of my sins exceeds that which I committed at one of those banquets against the brave soldier who had once saved my life – Clytus, who threw himself on top of me when I fell wounded from my horse at the start of one of my battles with the Persians and took in his body the arrows that were meant for me? But at that banquet, Alexander was settling scores with Philip, his earthly father.

I used to boast to my soldiers that all the wars and victories of Philip in the lands of the Greeks were as nothing compared with what I had achieved in Asia. Indeed, Philip would have been able to achieve none of his Greek victories had not I been the true leader of his armies in the wars he embarked on. Why should Clytus interfere in this business between me and Philip? He dared to say that, were it not for the victories of my father in the lands of the Greeks, I would have done nothing, and that there Philip had been fighting real men, while I, in Asia, was fighting women. When he said that, I became blind to everything. I didn't see Clytus, to whom I owed my life, in front of me, but an enemy taking Philip's side against Alexander. Then he committed the great sin. He denied that I was the son of the Mighty God! He said sarcastically that this frankness of his with me was more honest than the prophecies of my 'father'. In a fit of madness, I snatched a spear from one of the guards and thrust it into his side, screaming in his face, 'Go, then, and join Philip, if you love him so much!'

The fountain of blood that spouted from his wound before my eyes and drenched me brought back the Alexander whom the wine had splintered into so many people and gods and made him one Alexander again, an Alexander lost and terrified. I continued to stare at the corpse of Clytus for a second as it released its blood, the spear still stuck in it. I thought, 'That is my friend. The companion of my pleasures and in battle the bravest of my men. Were it not for him I would not now be alive. He who now lies murdered, I have struck down with my own hand.' And with a weeping scream I yanked the spear from his body and turned it towards my breast.

Had my drunken hand reached my heart at that instant and delivered the thrust that I desired, I would have spared myself days and years that brought nothing new but further bewilderment. The guards, however, were faster than I and they wrested the spear from my hand and I fell to the ground despite myself. I spent the whole night stretched out next to the corpse, crying for Clytus and crying in terror at the monster that dwelt beneath my divine skin.

Amun had not granted me the right to make human sacrifices. That came from my mother Olympias, who never shrank from killing and didn't know remorse. As for me, though, when the guards came to remove the body from my tent, I gave orders that no one was to come in to me again. I lay in the corpse's place for three days during which I tasted no food and never moved. I stayed with my eyes fixed skywards, imploring Amun and the gods to gather my scattered parts once and for all, though it be as a corpse.

My guards and companions realized that I had surrendered myself to death, so they burst into my tent and started to beg me to rise and live. I obeyed them because I wanted to obey them, for the moment of true yearning for death had not yet come.

Among them that day was Callisthenes, the companion of my studies with Aristotle and the nephew of my teacher the philosopher. He was the historian of my campaigns who immortalized my military glories. He pleaded with me to live, not for myself but so that the glory of Macedonia should not be lost.

He was unaware at the time that he was pleading for the life of his executioner. He begged me to live, so I lived, only to kill him a few months later. They seized him as a suspect in a plot to assassinate me and he defended himself eloquently, as was his custom and as he had learnt to do from his uncle. It was, however, his eloquence which confirmed my suspicions. The truth is simple and doesn't need to be adorned with words. On that basis, I ordered his death along with the others, after torture. Then I repented again after he was dead and locked myself up once more, weeping for him and for myself. In my loneliness it occurred to me that when I killed him I was killing, for ever, whatever remained inside me of Aristotle, and the echo of his lessons on the happiness that comes with wisdom and rationality.

It occurred to me that everything I had done in life flew in the face of what he had taught me. He had dreamt of a middling country, neither too large nor too small, so that its governance would be easy. I, though, had built an empire as big as the world. He had wanted too a middling government, composed neither of the rich nor of the common people but of wise middling people. What would he have made of the government of the god-hero who united the whole world under his rule? And he had wanted a middling happiness, between excess and renunciation, the arbiter of whose boundaries is the rational mind. I used to ask myself, 'Where in the world, my old teacher, can one find this well-governed life, other than in the garden of your Academy, where you can enjoy talking about it with your students as you walk in the shade of the trees, back and forth?'

All these lessons were swept aside by my visit to Amun and my meeting with the Egyptian priests who spoke in the name of their divinities.

There, I learnt that fear, not wisdom, is the basis of rule. I learnt that one must make the common people live in constant fear of punishment and torment on Earth and in Heaven so that they may know obedience and righteousness. I learnt that the ruler must not allow freedom or pleasure for the common people but must teach them to find pleasure in fear. They must worship me in fear and through fear. That was the most valuable lesson I learnt from Amun and the Egyptians. I applied it and it worked, not just in Egypt but everywhere. I could hear the echo of the insane shouts of the Egyptians, their voices tremulous with tears, for their pharaoh Alexander, in other shouts in other parts of Asia for the new conquering god.

And naturally I also found that small group of rebels who dreamt of freedom, and these were generally taken care of by the common people themselves before I had to take care of them, the commoners uncovering their plots and rejoicing at their fall because those dreamers would have robbed them of the luxury of their peace-of-mind-in-fear.

I will never forget one of those rebels, a youth of sixteen, one of the Macedonian noblemen's sons who used to guard my tent, the last from whom I expected betrayal, and yet they did it. One of them denounced the others for plotting against my life, so I ordered them all seized.

This boy, their leader, dared to stand up in front of me and challenge me as I interrogated him.

He said, 'You ask as though you didn't know! Yes, we plotted against you, because you no longer conduct yourself as a king with subjects who were born free men but as a tyrant with slaves. You want the Macedonians to kneel before you and worship you as a god and you even deny your own father, Philip. So how can it astonish you that we cannot stand your conceit?'

As though the child were my teacher! How could a boy like him comprehend my divine plan for the glory of Macedonia and the peace of the world? He may have thought that he would move me when he said, 'Take us straight away to the execution field, that we may gain by our death what we sought to gain by yours!'

Naturally, I sentenced him to be killed, along with the rest of his rebellious companions, after torture on the wheel, where their bones were crushed and broken.

Then, after the execution, came, as usual, the seclusion and the regret. Alexander the God-Emperor disappeared and a pitiful Alexander took his place.

In my seclusion, the image of that courageous youth would not leave me. I realized that he had spoken only the truth. Yes, of course, I was a tyrant, no matter what justifications I might find for my tyranny. I ruled my subjects by fear, and fear gave birth to obedience as I wanted, but also to betrayal. Those closest to me betrayed me and plotted against me time after time. Not one of them found the courage of that boy when he confronted me with his words, perhaps because they were not betraying me for a principle but out of greed to inherit my power. Why, though, did that other boy, his companion, betray him and denounce him and the rest of his companions when he knew he was delivering them to torture and death? Was that fear too, or greed?

I thought long but could not discern the starting point in the chain of tyranny, fear and betrayal. Which gave birth to which? And was I truly the one who fashioned it, or one of its victims?

In my seclusion, during which the image of the murdered young man was my constant companion, the many images of Alexander disappeared and all that remained was one Alexander, who realized that he had reached the end of his path. I had experienced everything – victory and glory such as had blessed no one before me and the gratification of governance and power, pardoning as a god and killing as a man – and I had experienced the ecstasy of poetry and music, the indulgence of women and wine. So why hadn't I achieved happiness?

For what remained of my life, I tried to live the happiness of men, not that of the gods. During my life I had known women and loved them; Roxana, my Persian wife, was the closest of them to my heart. I didn't live with her that transcendent love for which a man may sacrifice the whole world, like the love of Paris for Helen in the Iliad, which ignited the Trojan War, but my love for Roxana was calm and deep. I also lived true friendship with Hephaestion, and this was my consolation in what remained of my life. It was a friendship that meant that the two of us were one. Once, the mother of Darius, when she had become our captive, mistakenly fell on her knees before him, entreating him to spare her life, for she thought he was the king. When they indicated that she should direct her words to me, I told her not to be ashamed for he too was Alexander.

I wasn't lying. I truly felt that Hephaestion was the best of all those Alexanders who lived inside me. Aristotle would probably have liked him. He lived quietly and moderately and didn't get angry, and he knew nothing of the madness that pursued me throughout my life. He was, however, able to understand that madness and forgive. When I looked into his eyes, I knew that he understood all my contradictory actions and understood the bewilderment that pushed me to perform them, which I myself never understood.

But he departed before his time. The sickness came upon him at the start of the return march from Asia to the West, when we stopped at the city of Babel, and there he met his end.

His death left me certain that Alexander the Man had gone for ever, and that the other broken pieces that jostled within me and whose presence terrified me were biding their time. So I decided that I would not live with these distorted creatures, now that Hephaestion had taken with him the peace that he had been unable to pass on to me, and so bring these severed limbs together into a harmonious mortal whole. I tried to take care of it myself by throwing myself in the river, but my faithful Roxana saved me.

I found myself utterly alone, but while in Babel I had to oversee my last campaigns before the return to Europe. I determined to explore the last unknown land of Asia, that vast desert where the Arabs dwell. I readied the fleet that was to discover their peninsula, but an inner voice told me that I would not complete even this last task in Asia.

After Hephaestion, I contemplated the meaning of the things that had determined my life.

Amun inducted me into the ranks of the immortal gods and I believed in that, so I behaved as a god and tried to recreate the world and mankind. From time to time I would remember the lessons of Aristotle and a wave of self-doubt would sweep over me regarding what I was doing; the wounds of the immortal gods do not bleed, they know no pain, and they do not attempt suicide out of regret or despair – and I tried to end my life at least twice.

That may have been the third time, when I drank to excess at a banquet put on by some garrulous friend in Babel. He kept urging me to continue drinking, even after I had become fatigued and sick. Why would I have obeyed him had I not wanted in the depths of my soul to be done? Following the banquet I was stricken by the fever that put an end to my life in days.

My whole adventure in Asia lasted seven years and my entire life on Earth thirty-three years, during which I never knew peace of mind.

What, then, have you understood, you who call to me to waken my spirit? Are you listening to me? And are you now any the wiser?

Here, in the world of death, I know for sure that I am not a god. The immortal life of the gods does not take place in blind darkness and impotence. I am confident now that I did not understand the oracle of Amun, if his oracle was speaking the truth in any case and if Amun was a god. Why, then, have I been afflicted by this retribution?

Of the prophecies of the Egyptian priests, the only one that turned out to be true was the one concerning the afterlife. I learnt from them that the spirit hovers around the body and goes on living after its departure for forty days. It can see everything that it could before it left its owner. And indeed there was another Alexander, a final Alexander, who let out a breath like a sigh of relief at the disappearance of an intolerable burden as he lightly rose, like a feather in space, and watched himself, watched his dead, laid-out body.

What my spirit saw thereafter made me not greatly regret departing the world.

They left my body forgotten on its deathbed in the palace for seven whole days, during which my faithful friends and the commanders of my army argued over who should inherit my dominions. They excluded the foetus Roxana was carrying and another son of mine, whom they said was a bastard and therefore unworthy of inheriting the throne. None of these excuses was anything but a means to get to what all of them were striving for without openly saying so. In the end they appointed my half-witted half-brother to rule so that the commanders of my army could divide up the empire among themselves.

Only after all this did they remember Alexander and embalm him and anoint him with perfumes. They also decided to construct a wagon to transport me to the oasis of Amun, which I had designated in my will as my burial place. It was not given to me to see that wondrous vehicle over whose description I have heard them waxing lyrical, saying that it was like a huge temple with statues and images on either side, where my relics were held in a golden coffin.

And I saw who wept for me too.

Roxana and others of my women wept for me. The only woman, though, who was destroyed by grief was the mother of Darius, my most dogged opponent, who had been my prisoner for years and who I had often in my moments of anger treated slightingly. Following my death, she didn't think of how ill I had treated her; she remembered only that I had spared her life when I could have killed her, and that I had truly loved her and told her once that she was my second mother.

She alone wept for me till her death. She alone said she couldn't bear life without me and refused to eat or drink until she died, five days after I did, while my closest companions were struggling with one another over who should succeed me.

How did the depth of that love manage to escape me during my entire life? And what else in the world escaped me?

My spirit saw her and kept her company and screamed at her in an attempt to talk to her, but without a voice. It screamed at her not to die for my sake because, in truth, I wasn't worth it.

Part Two

9

Mahmoud

My crisis? Catherine asks me about my crisis? I ask *myself* about it?

There was my crisis. In one instant, the crisis of Mahmoud Abd el Zahir was made plain.

In a few seconds, the false image of the past that I'd drawn for myself fell away and with it all my hypocritical thoughts on life and death.

I boast to myself of a heroic past and deliberately forget the moment of ignominy. I think of myself as being unfairly treated and a martyr in the police, when I may be the worst of them all. The mutinous officer! I liked the role, so I believed myself. Perhaps I also deliberately passed this legend on to Catherine from the first days of our relationship and in our sentimental conversations mixed anguish over what the British had done to Ireland and Egypt and what I specifically had suffered at their hands.

But let's face things now; the time for deception is over. What precisely did I do during the revolution? I ran from the beach to the hospital transporting the wounded and the dead, did I? No, men of the native population, wearing *gallabiyas*, not military uniform, climbed up to the forts and fired the guns alongside the artillerymen. They picked up the wounded and the dead, soldiers and relatives who had fallen in the fighting, and carried them on their shoulders to the carts which it was your role to gallop in front of. Women from Alexandria did the same and climbed up to the forts and were wounded and never thought of themselves as heroines or martyrs. They lived saying nothing and died saying nothing. And what did you do exactly?

You fired on the Bedouin after they opened fire on you? What else would anyone have done to defend himself? The war in which thousands died left you with an injury as a result of a bullet in your shoulder that neither ended your life nor threatened it. You didn't even receive the bullet while fighting the enemy who were invading your country. No, it was like a wound received in some fleeting accident on the road, yet you lived your life thinking of your wound as a medal worn under the skin and a badge of glory. Now all that's gone, so what's left of your image?

There remains the betrayal by Tal'at, your colleague and old friend, which you have likewise continued to carry inside you as an emblem of the way the world has let you down and betrayed you. You were summoned to appear before the commission of inquiry at the ministry the day they interrogated the officers accused of working for the revolution and sympathizing with the revolutionaries. They had found the old complaint against me by the Italian officer and reopened the investigation.

I felt happy when I saw Tal'at at the commission. I wanted to ask him about his health and how his wounds were faring but contented myself by smiling and nodding in greeting. He nodded too but then looked away. Then the Circassian head of the commission began his interrogation of me and addressed to me questions I didn't understand and found laughable.

'Did the breaking of the photograph depicting the August Khedivial Presence in front of the Labban police station take place in your presence?'

'No, it did not.'

'Did you observe, during the burning of Alexandria, individuals from the army distributing quarterstaves to members of the civilian population and inciting them to smash and rob stores?'

'No. On the contrary, the opposite occurred, as I mentioned

at the first investigation. I saw soldiers from the army arresting looters and executing them.'

'Does it follow from the previous statement that you defend the actions of the mutineers in Alexandria?'

'No.'

The head of the commission turned his attention from me to Tal'at, reading to him the statement of the Italian station chief in Alexandria and asking for his testimony, and what he said left me speechless.

He confirmed before me and without the slightest hesitation every word the station chief had written: I was the one who had opened fire on the Bedouin for no reason and he had tried to stop me. He said that I'd received a bullet because of my reckless provocation of the Bedouin but didn't mention that I had visited him in hospital after he was injured.

And that was enough to support the station chief's accusation against me that I had been absent without leave while on duty during the fire. When the interrogator asked him whether he had heard anything to confirm my support for the Urabist mutineers, he tried to appear truthful, and said that, no, he had heard nothing from me that pointed to my supporting the actions of the mutineers but it was also true that he had heard nothing from me that would point to my support for the August Presence!

At that moment, I couldn't believe he would say all that to my face. I told myself that, however bad things were, there were limits to how much one could lie. Not while looking me in the eye! But he did precisely that, and they believed him and declared everything I'd said at the first investigation to be lies. I realized that he must have come to an understanding with the Italian station chief and his superior officers in Alexandria.

I couldn't forgive him and I didn't understand the secret of why he'd turned against me until Captain Saeed explained it to me later, in a whispered confidence. Now, though, what

I think is, even if I don't forgive him, why should I blame him? In those days everybody was looking for something that would save him from prison or expulsion from his position. A traitor, but honest with himself. He lied about me but not to himself, as though all his enthusiasm for the revolution in Alexandria had been just a whim. And indeed, my enthusiasm too and the enthusiasm of the whole country passed like a frivolous whim from whose spell we were woken by defeat.

In what way am I better than Tal'at? Why do I deliberately not think of the moment of ignominy and betrayal? It was two short answers I gave during the commission's interrogation, which I constantly push aside in my memory but which continue to lurk inside me like embers.

Question: 'Did you support Ahmad Urabi and his followers?'

Answer: 'On the contrary, I was one of those who most bitterly condemned the actions of those miscreants.'

Question: 'What do you know of the activities of His Excellency Umar Basha Lutfi, Governor of Alexandria, during the civil strife of 11 June?'

Answer: 'I know that His Excellency ordered the police companies to suppress the civil strife but that those assisting the mutineers failed to carry out his orders. I misunderstood what the Bedouin said, however, because of my ignorance of their dialect.'

It was Captain Saeed who suggested these answers to me. He himself never underwent investigation. His caution, which made him always remain silent and move carefully, even when helping the revolutionaries, protected him. He was always advising me in those days to keep my mouth shut. He'd tell me, 'Be aware that the Protected City has more informers than inhabitants.'

But he knew that I knew his past at the time of the revolution and he also wanted to protect me, so he pointed out the weakness in my statements to the first investigation, which he had conducted himself, which was the charge that Umar Basha had enlisted the Bedouin to carry out the massacre. He advised me to withdraw that statement, saying, 'As you see, Umar Basha is now the minister for the army, and yesterday's revolutionaries are now "mutineers".' I added my own contribution at the investigation and described them as 'miscreants'!

Saeed said, 'We shelved the first investigation and circumstances may help you this time. The ministry may shelve this one too and then, after a little while, destroy all the papers. It may be that they are anxious that no trace remain among the official papers of the charge against Umar Basha.'

Circumstances did indeed help me and they kept me on active service, after reducing my salary and issuing a reprimand. The price was small – to deny the truth, to betray and save my skin. So I too accepted the bargain.

Then, however, I had to accept my situation in the police as someone who had been found guilty and remained under observation. My promotions were frozen and they entrusted me with missions such as guarding installations, accompanying delegations on official visits, and unimportant clerical work. Tal'at, who chose to remain in Alexandria, or on whom this choice was imposed, far outdistanced me in promotions. This persecution served my interests, however: by degrees I created for myself the image of the forgotten victim, the man with a cause.

Following the investigation I lived for months in a state of self-disgust. I drank like one running after death. Then came the blessing of forgetfulness and I pushed out of my memory the disgrace of cowardice and betrayal. An entire life during which my main concern has been to chase away the memory every time it raises its head, and to deny it.

This time, however, it's not a memory, it's real.

Yes, I saw the stone falling on the boy and I rushed forwards with Ibraheem to save the young Mahmoud. At the last instant, however, in the final seconds during which I saw that the large stone would hit me too, I stopped. I went rigid with fear where I stood. I was the one closest to him but Ibraheem passed me with a single bound and flung himself forwards, taking the boy in his arms, pushing him away, and throwing himself on top of him. Coming to my senses, I flung myself on top of Ibraheem as well but it came too late – after I'd made sure my own life was safe and after the stone had smashed Ibraheem's leg.

Young Mahmoud didn't receive a scratch but Ibraheem was screaming and Catherine too was screaming from a distance and there was a great crowd of children and adults milling around and yelling. I saw the blood spreading over Ibraheem's ripped trousers so I picked him up carefully and laid him down on the ground, the blood gushing from his leg, which a sliver of rock had sliced through like a knife. My mind was completely paralysed but I moved as though someone else was dictating to me what to do. Catherine handed me a large handkerchief, which I used to bind the wound, and Ibraheem moaned with pain, thanking me through his moans. When I tried to make him stand, though, his moans turned into suppressed screams and tears burst from his eyes in spite of himself.

I must have spent entire days standing next to Ibraheem's bed. We treated him with the disinfectants and bandages in the keeping of the soldier charged with nursing at the police station. Ibraheem's leg, however, continued to swell and, with the fever that struck him, his pain became unbearable and he started to rave. He would raise his torso and say he could see the cholera but was going to throttle it with his own hands before it could attack Zahran and Darwish, and that he was going to complain unto his Lord against the honourable officer Abd el Rahman because he'd refused to give him leave. And beware, beware, Your Excellency, of the snakes on the wall. Then his eyes would fall on me and he'd yell that he didn't want to die in a strange place and we had to get him back so that he could sleep next to the tomb of his father and mother and children.

I watched him impotently, aware that all that pain would have been mine if I had gone forwards instead of back. All I could do for him now, though, was to stay with him. Sometimes his mind would be clear and he'd recognize me and apologize to His Excellency for the trouble he was causing me, but begging me too to bury him in his own village. I would try to comfort him and say that he had a long life ahead of him, God willing, and that he'd recover soon from this minor wound and be as strong as a horse again. What was this wound compared to all the things that had happened to him in the wars?

I'd rattle on with these and similar words but the terror of his impending death never left me. There was no doctor in the oasis and he was in no condition to be moved by caravan to Marsa Matrouh or anywhere else.

After two days of fever, the nursing soldier asked for a word with me on our own. He said that Ibraheem was indeed dying and he had blood poisoning. He'd put therapeutic worms on his leg close to the bandaged wound but they weren't sucking the blood any more because it had become poisoned. He knew such cases. When the blood turned poisonous, the end was near. He said that the bone was broken and the only solution that might save his life was to amputate the leg and leave the rest to God. I asked him, 'And who will amputate it? You?'

He fell silent.

The same day, Sheikh Sabir visited me for the second time since Ibraheem's injury. The first time he came to thank him and me for saving young Mahmoud, and this time he came in the company of some of the other sheikhs and the boy's relatives, who were Easterners, to call on Ibraheem. I couldn't concentrate enough to hear what he was saying and I couldn't understand what they were discussing in their own language as they surrounded the unconscious Ibraheem's bed, his pale face bathed in sweat. I was in almost as bad a state as he, and scarcely able to take anything in.

Sabir noticed my condition, however, pulled me aside by the hand, and started talking volubly, though I could barely see him. I replied despairingly to what he had said by exclaiming, 'Sheikh Sabir, Ibraheem is dying,' but then I realized that he was saying, 'No. He will live, God willing.' He was talking and I tried to concentrate. He was saying, 'This is not the first time someone's leg has been broken in the oasis, or someone has had a fever, and they have people who can treat such conditions.' 'Who are they?' I asked. 'The people who treat our own sick and wounded,' he replied. 'Don't we too get sick? And those leeches that you put on his leg will do him no good and may harm him. They draw off the blood in cases of headache but do not cure wounds. Whoever told you to apply them was wrong. Let the man I was telling you about take care of him.'

So he'd also been talking about a man? I said, 'And what if he dies, Sheikh Sabir?' and he replied, 'That too would be the will of God.'

I had no other solution.

The nurse told me that 'with Your Excellency's permission' he'd take no responsibility for what might happen. They were making Ibraheem drink things he knew nothing about and they'd torn the bandage off his leg and were putting oils and ointments on the wound that might increase the putrefaction. I asked him again, 'Are you capable of amputating his leg?' and he answered, 'I couldn't take that responsibility, Excellency.'

Catherine followed the news of Ibraheem's condition with concern and would ask me about him in the brief moments when I went home to change my clothes. When she heard I'd handed his treatment over to the Siwans, she protested. 'I agree with the nurse's opinion,' she said. 'What can primitive medicine do in a case like this? It really is blood poisoning, in the leg and the body, and there's no treatment except surgery and amputation.'

Exasperated, I said, to make her shut up, 'Would you like to do the operation, Catherine?' and she astounded me by replying, 'I have no objection to trying. Perhaps I could help the nurse. I have some idea of nursing too.' Preparing to leave, I said, 'The nurse has relinquished his responsibility,' and she said, 'Then you shouldn't implicate yourself in the killing of poor Ibraheem either.'

I didn't tell her I was already implicated. There was no witness but me to those seconds and perhaps even Ibraheem hadn't noticed them and if he lived would never mention them, but I am the one who always holds myself to account. It astonishes me that Catherine doesn't feel any regret or pangs of conscience. It never occurs to her that everything that happened did so because of her visit to that ill-omened temple on the day of that ominous heat. If only she'd understood what the heat was saying and given up the visit! If only I myself had understood it and insisted we stay at home! But we went and we let young Mahmoud run behind us in the killing heat. It's not surprising he was so exhausted he slept too deeply to notice the danger when it occurred. Our voices woke him when it was too late for him to run away and save himself, he was paralysed by terror, and that led to Ibraheem's saving him and sending me to hell.

Catherine, however, goes on reading her books and reviewing her drawings as though nothing at all has happened, and she seems amazed at my insistence on staying by Ibraheem's side all the time. What right does she have to think she knows what's going on in my mind – that constant interrogation of past and present? I say to myself, 'Right there I faced the death which I philosophized about in the desert, talking about its seductive qualities and the voice that called to me. But when I saw it descending, in the shape of a stone, from the sky, I was terrified. Even when it was a duty that

I had absolutely to obey, I behaved like a coward and let another perform it. Is this then my reality?'

I wasn't born a coward, though. Whatever I've said about myself in Alexandria, I faced death at every moment there without thought of flight. I acted without hesitation in the midst of the shrapnel and the fires, the bullets of the Bedouin and the gangs of looters, as though I were indeed looking for death. When did I change? At the moment when I took Saeed's advice and denied everything at the investigation? But I obeyed Saeed only because I would have wanted in the depths of my heart to do what he advised even if he'd never spoken.

I could have chosen the truth. Others did. Admittedly, they weren't the majority, but there were thousands of them. They bore prison, expulsion from their positions and exile. I could have done as they did. Found other work, or even gone to Damascus and joined my brother Suleiman. He wouldn't have refused to help me and might have made me a partner in his business. I am the one who chose, of my own free will, to betray and abandon, just as I abandoned Ibraheem and left him to run the risk of getting killed.

And now I'm pinning all my hope on the Siwans saving him, and saving me.

I permitted them to start the treatment that the nurse and Catherine protested at, and which I agreed to out of despair. The soldiers said nothing but I could see in their eyes too looks of objection and reproach at my allowing this hocus-pocus.

A few days after Ibraheem started taking the various drinks of whose composition we were ignorant and following the anointment of his leg with the various oils, however, the blue colour that had appeared on his injured leg disappeared, though it remained swollen. Then the fever started slowly to abate. Rashid, the Siwan curer, would come to see Ibraheem several times a day, entering silently and leaving without a word. Sometimes Sheikh Sabir would come with him and they'd stand either side of the patient's bed and deliberate with grim faces, which would make my anxiety increase, and I'd ask Sheikh Sabir how he was and what they were doing and hear nothing from him to reassure me. With frowning face he'd say, 'Everything is in God's hands, Your Excellency.'

When the fever was gone and Ibraheem woke from his long delirium, he looked emaciated and weak, so his fellows gave him soup and boiled rice, which he gobbled up straight away. Then, however, his condition deteriorated again. When Sabir heard what had happened, he said they'd made a grave mistake and that nothing must enter his stomach but sugar water till God had decided what He willed.

One time Rashid surprised me by blocking my path when I was on my way to Ibraheem's room and addressing me in Arabic, which I'd thought he didn't know. He said he was doing what he could but that Ibraheem's cure would be complete only when the swelling in his leg had disappeared. 'So what is to be done?' I asked. He said the only remaining hope was cauterization, which only a few knew how to do, the best person to carry out the treatment being a Bedouin who lived outside Shali and had no fixed abode. I would have to ask Sheikh Sabir to look for him and summon him because this Bedouin charged a lot. I said I'd pay the Bedouin whatever he wanted and I'd pay him too for his treatment of Ibraheem, to which Rashid replied, 'My reward is that God cure this man. He and you saved my son from death.'

I asked in astonishment, 'Mahmoud's your son? Why didn't you mention this earlier?'

He said, 'I didn't want to say anything until I was sure that I had done for the sergeant everything I could, and I shall pray to God that his cure is completed.'

Days passed before Sheikh Sabir managed to find the Bedouin, and he brought him himself. He was a giant and he wore a wide abaya with red stripes and spoke in coarse, commanding tones. I hated him from the moment I saw him and wanted to send him away, but Sheikh Sabir and Rashid treated him with the utmost respect as they spoke of his powers, so I backed down and grudgingly gave the order for him to do what he wanted.

The Bedouin asked for fire, and placed in it a large iron nail with a wooden handle, leaving it there until it glowed red hot, and he ordered us to secure Ibraheem well and stretch his swollen leg out all the way so that it couldn't move. Ibraheem, in terror, begged us to excuse him from this treatment, saying he was getting better, thank God, and didn't need anything more, his eye never leaving the nail as it heated in the fire.

I also saw looks of disgust in the eyes of the soldiers surrounding Ibraheem, and one of them, perhaps the nurse, said in a loud voice, 'May the Lord protect him!' which I was also whispering myself. I had heard about cauterization before but had never seen it and I had no idea what use it could be in a case like Ibraheem's. Still, we did what the Bedouin asked. We sat Ibraheem on a chair and two of the soldiers took hold of him by his upper arms and armpits and two others by his extended legs.

The Bedouin spent some time feeling the injured leg below the knee but far from the site of the wound. Ibraheem's moans increased as the man felt these places slowly with his thick fingers, and at a certain moment he stopped and pressed with his index finger on a particular spot, causing Ibraheem to let out a sudden scream of pain. The Bedouin shouted at the soldiers not to let Ibraheem make any movement and then snatched the nail from the fire and with it cauterized for a few seconds the place that he had chosen, and then for a few more seconds another place next to it, to the accompaniment of Ibraheem's screams and wails. With some amazement, the Bedouin said, 'All the men weep and scream! What is this fire compared to the fire of Hell?'

But was I dreaming? Had I gone mad? Fire burnt the skin of my leg in the very place where Ibraheem's was being cauterized. I shuddered and turned my face away, placing my hand over my mouth so that I wouldn't scream like him.

The smell of burnt flesh filled the place, and then the Bedouin extracted from his robes a flask in a leather holder from which he poured a liquid onto the site of the cauterization. I heard a repeated sizzling sound and saw what looked like white foam at the place where he'd been burnt, and at that same moment a shiver of cold passed through my leg and my whole body and I had to make an effort to control myself in front of my men.

The Bedouin waited for a moment, holding Ibraheem's leg, the patient's screams having changed into a continuous moan of pain, and when the liquid had dried, he started tying up the place he had cauterized with a bandage, replying to a question from Sheikh Sabir by saying, 'No. I won't come again. Rashid knows what has to be done now to clean the wound, and the sergeant will be on his feet in two days.'

Then he went on, with a loud laugh, 'But he'll limp for the rest of his life!'

'You didn't have to say that!' I muttered.

Nevertheless I remained standing where I was, certain that if I moved, I'd limp.

For two days at the police station and at home I walked with slow steps so that no one would notice anything. Then the pain in my leg improved. After the same two days, Ibraheem indeed got up from his bed and started walking, limping on the leg for which the nurse and Catherine had seen no solution but amputation.

When Sheikh Sabir came to enquire about Ibraheem's health, after he was back on his feet, I thanked him and Rashid and the Bedouin, whose name I didn't know.

The only reward that I could offer Sheikh Sabir, though, was to tell him that the ministry had refused my request for the reduction of the tax and sent a warning that if the collected taxes did not arrive with the next caravan, the fine would be doubled and other measures would be taken.

The attitude of the local people towards me had improved following my supposed role in the saving of the young Mahmoud, but, after they heard what I had to say, I read in Sabir's and Rashid's eyes the old hatred, peering out anew.

The period of forgiveness was over.

10

Catherine

I know I'm doing something wrong. Mahmoud will be very angry, but I have to do it.

I can't see any other solution. Many weeks have passed here and I've made no progress with anything. I've taught myself many dead languages but I still don't know a single sentence of the language of these real people whom I'm living among and whose help I need. I no longer do any work and my search for evidence that might lead me to Alexander has come to a halt. But I've had enough. Today I'm going to go to them myself and on my own. I'll apologize to Mahmoud later – not just for what I'm going to do now but for having encouraged him to come to this place at all.

He's got much worse since Ibraheem's accident. He was with him from the time he was hurt until he could stand. He behaves as though he were responsible for what happened to the poor soldier. Stranger still, he talks about my visit to the temple almost reproachfully, as though that were the reason for Ibraheem's leg getting broken! He ought to understand it was just an accident and that no one's responsible for fate. And anyway, it can't have been that grave an accident, since it was possible to treat it with primitive medicine. Mahmoud, though, is always panting after reasons to be miserable.

His worries are the last thing I need now. This morning he is not himself.

Since yesterday things have been unsettling. Fiona's letter, which reached me with the latest caravan, upset me greatly. It's not her usual long letter full of news. She just says she'll be arriving in Alexandria soon on one of the steamers and she's coming here to visit us in Siwa. Just like that, without preamble or explanation. Maybe she thinks the journey from Alexandria to Siwa is like travelling from our province of Connaught to Dublin by train! I've asked Mahmoud to write to one of his officer friends in Alexandria and ask him to wait for her and arrange accommodation for her there until we can decide what to do. Should I go there and take her to Cairo, or should we really arrange a way for her to come to Siwa? Why, though? Even her writing was disturbed and messy, unlike her normal hand. What problem are you hiding from me, Fiona?

She visits me often in my dreams. Last night I saw her beautiful face disappearing behind a transparent silk mask, which she was trying to tear off with both her hands. Every time that she tried, though, she'd tear off the face itself, which would turn to rubber as she pulled at the mask.

I woke up in a panic, but she visited me once again, and she wasn't alone. She came bringing Alexander. He often comes to me these days in my sleep, but it's my fault. Last night he came to me with an angry face. Then I saw Fiona carrying him and holding him like a weeping child in her arms. I approached them and discovered that the child was made out of marble and that there were copious tears in its stone eyes. Mahmoud woke me, asking, 'Why are you screaming?' I said, gasping for breath, 'There's something frightful in this desert.' Patting me, he said, 'It's only a nightmare. Go to sleep, Catherine.' I fell silent, clinging on to him in the bed, but my eyes stayed open. I was afraid that drowsiness would return, and remained restless till morning.

This isn't like me. I'm not afraid of the desert, or dreams, and I'm not superstitious, in spite of which I carried out a stupid experiment to talk to the spirit of Alexander. Naturally, I didn't believe that his spirit would appear to me or visit me but I told myself that I'd play the game to pass the time while I was a prisoner in the house after Ibraheem's accident. I did what it said in the book. I closed the windows and doors so that the room was completely dark and lit a candle and put it on the table, with an upturned water glass next to it. I did change the book's instructions, though: I didn't put pieces of paper with the letters of the alphabet round the glass. Why would I need them? I just put next to the glass the three letters YES and, on the other side, NO. That's all I want to know. I closed my eyes, concentrated all my thoughts on Alexander, and murmured his name many times over while at the same time extending the tips of my fingers towards the glass. Then I stated my question: Will I find you here? My voice came out shakily and I was breathing hard, despite myself. Of course I was afraid. Of course, I'm human. Of course my hand that was touching the glass had to tremble, making it move with a low ringing sound, so I got scared and stood up straight away and opened the doors and windows.

I will not repeat the experiment. I still believe that this business of spirits is mere superstition. My fear proved, however, that, like all people, I am afraid of the unknown that cannot be understood. An inherited horror, so there's no need to be ashamed of myself.

There's no need to be ashamed either of the dreams that pursue me, for they are a part of my fear and I'm the one that summoned them. Alexander came to me twice after my stupid call.

On the first night, he came to me in the form that I know from books. He came riding a black horse that flew fast through the sky on its white wings. Then he suddenly swooped towards me and pounced on me, brandishing a sword longer than any I'd ever seen, and I screamed.

The second night, he terrified me again when he came, but this time he had the features of Maleeka and his blond hair was twisted into the same multiple braids as hers. I asked him, 'Why did you do that?' and he laughed and at the same time the braids began to move and twist and change into snakes which started to slither towards me and wrap themselves around my body, and I woke up screaming again.

No, my state is not normal and I have to recover my old self. The first step is to forget all that and start work, the real work that drives out fears and delusions.

I shall confront their leaders themselves and let happen what may.

I set off from our house, which is situated at the bottom of the hill, and climbed towards the entrance to the fortified town. I saw the *agwad* sitting as usual on their palm-frond-shaded bench in front of the great door.

I had prepared in my head what to say to them. I would repeat what I'd explained to Mahmoud: that I wasn't looking for their wretched treasure in excavating for which they'd destroyed the temples. I didn't want the mummies or the small stone antiquities that the Europeans were so set on finding. Perhaps these words would reassure them and they'd help me. I took with me the big sketchbook so they could understand my request and I ascended the narrow path leading to their gathering place with determined steps.

As soon as they realized I was making for them, they all jumped up and started waving their hands at me to go back. I paid no attention but quickened my step. Their leader, Sheikh Sabir, whom I'd met with Mahmoud on our arrival at the oasis, and who had introduced himself to me, came forwards. He speaks an elevated Arabic which shows that he is well educated, and he expresses himself with extreme refinement, but I find him repulsive. I saw cunning in his narrow eyes. For all that, I may be mistaken, though. Mahmoud told me that this sheikh concerned himself greatly with Sergeant Ibraheem's treatment, in which case he isn't evil. And also, since when has it been enough to judge people by their faces? I should learn from the lesson of Michael and his angelic face.

He came down the slope a few paces while the rest of the *agwad* continued to yell and wave their hands at me to go back. Despite this, I continued my ascent and Sheikh Sabir continued his descent and when we met he said to me calmly in his classical Arabic, indicating his fellows, 'Your pardon, madame. Are you aware that this gate is that of the *agwad*?'

He pointed behind him to the thick gate made from the conjoined trunks of palm trees and I replied irritably, despite myself, 'I know, but are you aware that—'

He interrupted me, pointing his forefinger to the left, and saying, 'There is another gate for the women. In our tradition, women cannot enter by the gate of the *agwad*.'

I tried to control myself. 'I know that too. I know the Qaddouma Gate that is set aside for women. However, you have not had the patience to find out what I want. I have not come here in order to enter the town by your gate, or by the women's gate. What point would there be in entering it when you . . .? Never mind. I have come to meet the *agwad* themselves. I want to tell them—'

Once again he interrupted me with his false politeness. 'The *agwad* may come to you themselves, if His Excellency the district commissioner commands. We are at his service and yours. However, as you can see, the *agwad* are not at all accustomed to having women approach their gathering. It makes them angry, and His Excellency the district commissioner knows that.'

His repeated and deliberate references to Mahmoud annoyed me. Nevertheless, I opened the sketchbook, saying, 'All I wanted was to ask . . .'

When I saw him standing unmoving before me, however, as though prepared to prevent me by force from going any farther up, and when I saw his cold eyes and his face, empty of all expression, my enthusiasm suddenly evaporated, and I slammed the sketchbook shut, turned my back on him and set off again without a word. While I was descending the slope, I heard behind me a quavering voice saying in Arabic, 'Madame, wait. Wait.'

I turned round and saw an extremely elderly member of the *agwad* leaning on a stick and attempting to control his steps as he carefully descended the slope. I waited for him watchfully as he approached and was surprised to see that he was wearing a pair of spectacles secured on his ears with a piece of string. He was the first person I'd seen wearing spectacles in this oasis.

He approached me and said with an Egyptian accent, 'Don't be upset. The *agwad* don't mean you any harm. It's just that this gate . . .'

'Is not to be approached by women! I told Sheikh Sabir I didn't want to go into the town anyway.'

'What do you want, then?'

I could hear Sheikh Sabir and the other *agwad* calling, 'Sheikh Yahya! Sheikh Yahya!'

They continued to gesture to him with their hands, shouting in angry tones, but the aged sheikh didn't look at them and asked me again, 'What do you want? Can we help you?'

I opened the sketchbook and stammered to him, 'I wanted the *agwad* to understand that I'm not looking for . . . what I'm more interested in is . . . What I mean is, can anyone help me to find out if there are any drawings like this in the Great Temple in Aghurmi or anywhere else?'

Then I continued in a rush, 'I swear what I'm looking for has nothing to do with your treasure or any gold. On the contrary, what I'm looking for may bring your oasis lots of gold and treasure. I mean . . .'

The sheikh said, smiling, the wrinkles on his brown face multiplying, 'Why do you swear? I believe you.'

He suddenly let out a low laugh as he went on, 'I believe that you're sensible and know that there isn't really any treasure, underneath the temples or on top of them!'

Then he put his finger to his lips as though to swear me to secrecy, and I smiled at him as I brought the sketchbook close to his face and asked, 'And so?'

The shouts of the *agwad* continued and some had leapt up as though they too were about to come down to us. At this point, I was taken aback to see Sheikh Yahya's face turn dark, and in a strong, loud voice out of keeping with his age and the emaciation of his body he shouted and roared at them at great length in an angry tone, turning only his head in their direction. Some of them continued their shouting and muttering but they sat down again in their places.

The sheikh took hold of the sketchbook that I held out to him, holding it with difficulty as he screwed up his eyes. Then he told me in bewilderment, 'I can read Arabic but I don't know the language of the pharaohs.'

Realizing that he could make nothing of it, I said, 'This isn't the language of the pharaohs, it's the language of the Ancient Greeks.'

The man's bewilderment increased and he looked into my face and said, 'There's no one in our town who knows the languages of the ancients. Wait and maybe some foreigners from your country will come.'

Then he thrust the sketchbook into my hands and said, laughing again and pointing to his glasses, 'As for me, I can barely see you now, and you expect me to distinguish between different scripts that I don't know?'

All the same, I said again, with an irritation I did not intend, 'But perhaps you could help me with something. All I want to know is whether there are carvings of characters like these in the Great Temple or elsewhere. I have been to the temple at Aghurmi, but I wasn't able to wander around or see anything. The houses have closed off the remains.'

Sheikh Yahya said slowly, in a different tone of voice, 'Then leave them closed off! I said that you were sensible, and a sensible person doesn't enter a house whose door is closed to him.'

He stood there looking straight into my eyes and I understood that he was giving me a warning, so I asked him, 'What, then, is to be done?'

'There are antiquities far from houses and there are carvings and writing everywhere in the open, and there are villages in the oasis other than Shali and Aghurmi and many temples. Look among those if you wish.'

'Have I finished searching here that I should try somewhere else? Have I started even?'

'Listen. I do not understand what it is you are looking for. However, if I were in your place, I'd think twice, after the stone that fell . . .'

Then he stopped for a moment before saying quietly to himself, 'No one but me will understand that you are not looking for the treasure and for gold. They see the falling of the stone as a punishment and a warning from the owner of the treasure, who has cast a spell to keep people away from it until the appointed time for it to be uncovered has come.'

I didn't understand everything he said, so I asked him, 'But you don't believe these myths yourself?'

Suddenly he grew angry again and said, pointing to the *agwad*, who still kept up their clamour, 'What does it matter what I believe or don't believe? What matters is what they believe. They aren't evil. On the contrary, they have good hearts, but they're afraid.' Then his face darkened further and he said, 'All people have good hearts, but they're stupid! You too, why can't you understand after everything I've told you? Goodbye! Watch out for yourself and watch out for your husband.'

He turned to go back, supporting himself on his stick and repeating in agitation, 'Goodbye!'

I almost smiled, even though he'd been rude to me. Like Sheikh Sabir before him, he'd urged me to go away, but I really believed that he wanted to help me, and that he was sending me a message.

*   *   *

On my way home, it occurred to me that the old man might be right to warn me. Indeed, why shouldn't I abandon everything? I could think of my whole affair with the desert, Alexander and this oasis as an adventure that failed but whose failure wouldn't be the end of the world. It wouldn't be my first failure and I've always been able to start anew, whatever happened to me. They hate me roaming among the temples and complain that I want to rob them, and my insistence on searching may increase the dangers to Mahmoud.

I've heard from him that he has enough problems with them these days. From the time he started collecting the taxes, or trying to collect them, there have been daily quarrels with one or other of the families. He told me he'd charged Sabir with collecting the various shares but they were refusing to pay, and Mahmoud has been obliged to go himself or send police troops, though it's made no difference. He says that what he's collected so far is very little and that the whole oasis is on the verge of exploding again. Would it not then be better if I were to pull back and behave inconspicuously until this crisis is over? In that case, though, what would be the point of my staying here? The best thing now might be for us to leave together. Mahmoud, though, will never consent to abandoning his duty and fleeing, for to do so would be to expose himself to disgrace, and perhaps to prison. What to do?

I reached the house and sat on the front steps. The sun today is bearable and I started watching children who were playing in the open space, stealing timid glances at me and ready to run away if I approached. I long ago gave up showing friendliness and smiling at them or trying to talk to them. There's no point. An ingrate oasis. Didn't Mahmoud expose himself to danger to save one of their children? They ought to be showing him gratitude instead of subjecting him to all these tribulations. What's more, everything that is happening now is corrupting our relationship.

He's gone back to drinking heavily since the accident at the temple, and I can't bear him when he's drunk. I can put up with him up to two glasses. That's tolerable. But I avoid him when intoxication takes over. The fact is, we've taken to avoiding one another, and we sleep in the bed like strangers most of the time. I no longer mind very much. On the contrary, it's a relief for me, especially after the night he tried to make love to me when he was drunk and failed. He became livid with fury. He kept on trying, in indignation and anger. He was muttering and cursing himself and kept getting out of bed to storm around and bang his head on the wall. Then he'd come staggering back and throw himself on top of me and try again and become even more furious. It was the first time he'd failed since I'd known him and I tried, despite my disgust with both him and myself, to offer him comfort: maybe it had been one glass too many; maybe he was more exhausted than usual. It was no good. He kept on trying till fatigue demolished us both and horrible memories of Michael returned to me.

What happened during the following days revolted me even more. The moment he came home at the end of the morning on the following day, and before having lunch, he dragged me to the bed and succeeded. Then he tried again that evening, and succeeded, and was more than usually violent, even though he knows that I hate violence. It was as though he were taking revenge on himself and on me. He went on like that for days and nights on end.

Perhaps he believed that our passion and true harmony continued as before and that my protests were a kind of coquetry or play. No, we aren't as we were. And he's like me. I felt that there wasn't an ounce of true desire or passionate enjoyment in what he did. All he wanted was to reassure himself as to his virility, and when he was so reassured, he started avoiding me again, and I was overcome by relief. In my heart, I thanked him.

It had never before occurred to me for an instant that I would be happy to see him distance himself from me, but that is what the oasis has done to us.

Perhaps I am being unfair to the oasis. Mahmoud's Mahmoud and he'll never change. Or, as is his wont, he changes all the time from mood to mood, drinking the alcohol that his religion forbids him and attending the Friday prayer in the mosque as a social obligation, so that he won't lose people's respect, though at the same time I see him some evenings jump out of bed in the darkness, wash and then, weeping, devote himself wholeheartedly to lengthy prayer. This doesn't happen often and makes me very surprised. I don't know whether to feel pity for him or to laugh at him. But I do ask myself, 'What does Mahmoud really believe?' And what do I believe too? I gave up thinking about that long ago. I no longer go to church and I no longer pray on my own. Perhaps I believe that the Divinity will reveal Himself to me one day, but the subject no longer bothers me.

I happened to glance at the children playing. How comfortable to be a child! How comfortable to be ignorant! The boys had dug channels in the ground and were pouring water into them and putting small green twigs along the length of them so that they could irrigate gardens like those of their fathers. The most important thing, though, was that they weren't forgetting to build high walls of sand around their gardens. They had been taught about the walls since they were little. The girls were playing on their own far from the boys. More walls!

I love, though, the sight of the little girls at play. The only place I see cheerful colours is in their long-sleeved embroidered dresses. I would also love to know how the girls make those long thin braids that frame their heads like decorated crowns. Who, though, will show me? Their mothers? They travel on the road only in groups going to funerals or weddings, and all that one can see of them is their wide blue cloaks –

dumb lumps, moving slowly and silently like a warning of ill tidings, so that I want to scream when I see them, 'Where are the people?'

Eventually I got up, feeling giddy from the sun in which I'd been sitting too long, and I had to climb the remaining steps slowly and carefully.

The hot, dark house was much better. I closed the door and was looking forward to taking a cold bath, stretching myself out on the bed, and chasing away all thought – of Mahmoud, Alexander, the sheikhs, the women, the children and the whole oasis – and then sleeping a dreamless sleep, but before I could enter the bathroom I heard rapid knocks in quick succession on the door.

Who could it be? No one knocked on our door, and these weren't the familiar knocks that Mahmoud would make before inserting the key in the lock.

Who could it be?

'Who is it?' I asked fearfully. 'Who is it?'

A tense voice, sounding as though the speaker's mouth were pressed close to the door, responded, 'Maleeka!'

I I

Mahmoud

As though I need more problems!

What's this business about Fiona coming, in the midst of this oppressive atmosphere in which we're living? I hope my letter reaches Alexandria before she arrives on her steamer and before she makes up her mind to come to Siwa. She may be insane, but she won't find a caravan guide insane enough to agree to bring her here unaccompanied. The true problem, though, is that she may actually find someone to agree, and have things end in catastrophe. I'll be the one held responsible, naturally. I'll have to protect her, when I don't even know how to protect Catherine or myself.

I looked out of my office at the forecourt of the station, where crouches the great cannon that the army left behind. I think it's wonderful! A short gun mounted on two wooden wheels like those of a horse-drawn cart. Of what use is it here, in the absence of any soldiers trained in how to fire artillery? I imagine they left it as a reminder of the awe-inspiring dignity of the state. How we need that dignity now!

The oasis is seething. Every day quarrels and protests from the families.

I returned to sit at my desk with the latest correspondence from the ministry before me. Reproaches, reproaches, reproaches. Then advice on how to do things. I am to use determination and strength with the native population because leniency will not work, as experience has demonstrated. Excellent, my dear ministry, but where are the additional troops and weaponry?

Sergeant Ibraheem, who knew the oasis before me, also gives me his advice: I have to do as my predecessors did and select some of those who were refusing to pay and flog them in the forecourt of the station, or imprison them along with their families. This would be a lesson to the rest. One day, I said, 'Ibraheem, those people saved your life. Does it really please you to see them being treated like that?' 'No, Excellency, it doesn't please me, but what else can one do? We and they both belong to the government and the government shows mercy to none until it gets what it wants. You may excuse them, but then it will send a new military expedition, which will not be content with flogging and imprisonment. It's the lesser of two evils.'

I couldn't argue with Ibraheem's logic. I proposed to him, when he was back on his feet, that I should send him back to the Protected City and ask Saeed Bey to have him pensioned. I thought I was helping him, but a sad look appeared in his eyes and it seemed as though he was about to cry as he said, 'I can still serve Your Excellency with my limp.'

I asked him in amazement, 'When did I ever charge you with anything that was beyond your powers to perform, Ibraheem?'

'Right now, Excellency,' he said, 'it is beyond my powers to return to Cairo. I need the money I'm putting aside here. I have a pack of children to look after in the village. Saeed Bey, God protect him, knows my case. He told me, "Go with His Excellency the district commissioner. You'll get a raise there and you may be able to save something." He knows my situation because he's from my village and he's the head of our Sufi order and one of the righteous. He likes to help people. He saw how things were with me when they pensioned me off from the army that they disbanded after the British war. The children and I were starving, and if it hadn't been for Saeed Bey using his good offices to get me a job in the police, I'd have been done for, and the children along with me.'

'But I'm thinking now about your interests and your health after the accident.'

'The accident was God's doing. It might have hit you, God forbid, or I might have died, but God, glory be to Him, granted me a new life. So don't deprive me, Excellency, of the chance to benefit from it.'

'As you wish, Ibraheem,' I said.

To myself I said, 'Maybe I wanted him to go away so that I could forget once more the moment of ignominy that he never noticed. It's better, though, that he remain to remind me of it. There's no new life left for me to flee to.'

I did not, however, take his advice about flogging and imprisoning the local population. I went with Sheikh Sabir to meet the *agwad* of the families that were refusing to pay. I tried to take advantage of the good feeling that followed my 'heroic act' in saving their son, tried to convince them that it was in their interest to pay so that the government wouldn't punish them as it always had. Some responded with words of anger and protest at the excessive demands of the government and others replied with sweet words, but payment continued to be delayed.

It was my counsellor Ibraheem too who drew my attention to the fact that most of the families whom Sheikh Sabir complained were not paying were Westerners. I said, 'Perhaps he's better at persuading his own clan of the Easterners,' but Ibraheem replied, 'God only knows, but I don't see many Easterners paying.'

On my way home from the station I was thinking, 'What is Sheikh Sabir trying to get? If what Ibraheem is hinting at is true, he wants to bring about the downfall of the Westerners, but the government cares only that the taxes are collected, and if it decides to send a military expedition, as usual, it won't discriminate between Easterners and Westerners. He's too intelligent not to know that, so what does he want? Anyway, it doesn't matter.'

What does matter is how I'm to get out of this dilemma the ministry has put me in. I came to this oasis hating it and its people and I have come to hate them even more because of their hostility towards me, Catherine and even the troops. Nevertheless, the more I think about what we've done to them since we came as rulers, the more I find their behaviour perfectly natural.

We didn't come to them as brothers, but as conquerors. We didn't treat them as though they were fellow citizens but as though they were a colonized people who had to pay their taxes to the conquerors, like it or not. Why then should we get angry at what the British were doing to us, or why should Catherine get angry at what they were doing in Ireland? We practise the law of might here just as the British practise it there. When they saw an example of good treatment from Ibraheem, or what they thought was goodness from me, they changed the way they treated us. Can't they, though, see that I am truly different from the others? Why all this obstinacy and stupidity? Why do they want to destroy themselves, and me along with them? There's no point in thinking about it. The wheel has started turning and nothing can stop it.

When I neared home I found the children who play on the empty space standing silently and staring in the direction of the house, and a donkey standing at the bottom of the steps.

When the children saw me approaching, they fled, as usual, but continued looking curiously and warily in the direction of the house.

Hearing a yell come from inside, I too felt foreboding.

The children froze where they were and, as the yell repeated itself, I recognized Catherine's voice, so I pulled out my revolver and raced up the stairs, shouting, 'Catherine! What's happening! I'm here! I'm coming!'

I burst into the house brandishing my revolver. Then I came

164

to a stop, unable to take in what I saw in the half-darkened room.

I saw Catherine standing holding a palm rib and clutching in her other hand the buttons of her blouse, which was torn. Then I noticed that she was gently striking with the rib a girl, who was kneeling on the ground embracing Catherine's feet and making a noise like an injured cat.

'What's happening?' I repeated.

Without thinking, I pointed the revolver at the kneeling girl, but as I pulled the trigger the rib that Catherine was holding struck my hand and the bullet went wide and I yelled with pain. The revolver flew from my hand and Catherine kicked it with her foot, which she had pulled free, into a distant corner. I was letting out a stream of curses and holding my injured hand, my mind racing as I tried to piece together what I saw in front of me. Had they sent someone to kill Catherine? Had they decided to begin with her instead of me? What did the children's gathering in front of the house and their fearful looks mean? This girl had attacked Catherine, torn her clothes, and perhaps tried to kill her. So why, then, was she clinging on to her legs and kissing them? I could understand nothing except that Catherine was defending herself with the palm rib.

I threw myself on the girl and wrested away her hands, which were gripping my wife's legs. Then I kicked her, as she screamed, towards the door, intending to push her down the steps. Catherine, however, hurried towards me, pushing the palm rib into my chest this time and shouting in a breathless voice, 'You didn't kill her with your revolver and now you want them to kill her in the road when they see her half naked?'

Catherine threw a *gallabiya* that had been in a heap on the floor over the girl where she lay moaning and gestured to her angrily to put it on.

The girl, who was wearing a dirty white robe, got up and

165

quickly shoved herself into the man's *gallabiya* and pulled a scarf over her face. Looking as slight as a young boy, she set off at a run towards the door while I asked Catherine, my thoughts in disarray, who she was, how she had got in, and what she'd done.

The girl herself, though, turned suddenly before going out through the door and pulled the covering from her face, whose radiant beauty I took note of, despite everything, as she rushed towards Catherine, her grey eyes flashing, and pointed to her own breast, to my wife and to the revolver which lay on the floor, screaming as she did so in her own language, the tears streaming from her eyes. Then she rushed forwards again and knelt on the ground at Catherine's feet, embracing them and kissing them and making a low sobbing noise like a moan, while all the time she talked through her tears.

I was paralysed by astonishment, and Catherine too stood rigid where she was, leaving her torn garment open to reveal the two perfectly matched globes of her breasts, the upper halves pressed together and extremely white.

As the girl's weeping and moaning changed to something more like a death rattle, I asked Catherine in amazement, 'Do you understand anything?'

Like one under a spell, she replied, 'Not a word, but I think she's angry because she wants us to understand something that we can't, and that's why she wants you to shoot her with the revolver.'

'And that's what I want too!'

An overwhelming anger swept aside the moment of astonishment and I jumped up, intending to reach the gun, but Catherine extended her free arm and placed her hand on my chest, making an attempt to speak calmly amid her gasps.

'Look. She really is insane, so don't act like a madman yourself.'

The girl, however, suddenly jumped up and stretched her hands out as though she wanted to grab Catherine's chest, or embrace her, or throttle her – I don't know. I flung myself on her from behind and took hold of her neck, and she started screaming as I almost did strangle her, possessed by a crazy jealousy and a feeling that she would desecrate my wife if she touched her body with her hands one more time. Catherine's blue eyes flashed and she started firing off rapid phrases with an Irish accent I couldn't understand. Then, suddenly, she raised the palm rib and brought it down on the head of the girl, who was trying to wriggle out of my grip, and the girl let out a loud scream and a trickle of blood ran across her brow. Catherine then picked up the scarf and threw it over the girl's head, trying at the same time to get free of the girl's hands. She pushed her out of the door and closed it hard behind her.

When the girl had left, I noticed the complete silence that had overtaken the place. Despite everything that was happening in the house, I had been hearing loud noises outside – screams of adults, shouts of children, and repeated cries of apprehension – but now the silence was total. I opened the door, but all I could see was the girl mounted on her donkey, still wailing, and heading east, her back to the town, over which hung the silence of death. Out of all the children who had been thronging the open space, I now found only one, aged about four, sitting on the ground and crying. Then a man came running and picked the child up without looking towards the house and without raising his head and returned quickly with the child in the direction of the town. I was puzzled by what I saw and my anger redoubled as I looked at the empty square. I rushed back inside the house, shouting furiously, 'The grown-ups and children have disappeared from the square. There isn't a soul there.'

Catherine was sitting on a chair, glowering, and after a moment she said, 'So they must have discovered who she is.'

'You know her, then?'

'Yes. It's Maleeka, the only girl to speak to me the day I went to the Temple of the Oracle. She told me her name then and that was all and today she came disguised as a boy, as you saw. But they must certainly have discovered afterwards that she's the ghoul-woman, and she's escaped from her house.'

'The ghoul-woman? You mean she's one of the witches of the oasis they talk about?'

'No. I mean she's the ghoul-woman. She dared to leave her house before the months of imprisonment were over.'

I understood nothing of what Catherine was saying. She started trying to close the buttons on her dress, and then she said suddenly, almost shuddering, 'The ghoul-woman kissed my breast!'

I shouted in agitation, 'Don't play with me, Catherine! Why did you let her do that? Has she entered our house before? And what does it mean that she's the ghoul-woman?'

With greater anger, Catherine replied, straightening her back in the chair, 'And you ... and in this oasis ... Tell me why the women are required to be more intelligent than their menfolk? And how can you be the ruler of this oasis and not know who the ghoul-woman is?'

'Is that part of my official duties too?'

'Of course! Since I've studied and read every book and every word written by every scholar or visitor who passed by this oasis, it should have been your duty too to study and learn. How can you govern people you don't know? When you calm down, you'll regret that you thought of killing her, and I too shall be sorry, for I was on the verge of killing her too. Why did I do that?'

She was silent for a moment. Then she said, 'But the girl is dead in any case. Her family will certainly kill her.'

I sat down on a chair facing Catherine and said, defeated, 'Please, then, help me to calm down. I asked you, please, who is this Maleeka, and what does it mean that she's the ghoul-woman, and what happened in this house?'

She laughed irritably and said, 'Just wait a little till I calm down myself!'

She slumped once more in her chair and took a deep breath before saying, in an exhausted voice, 'I don't know Maleeka. I saw her for one minute in Aghurmi.'

Then she paused once more and corrected herself. 'I think I saw her another time. There was a boy watching me when I went to the Umm Ebeida temple. I think it was her too. She'd come in disguise, as she did today.'

'So she's been spying on you for a while? We'll come back to that. But I asked you, please, what does it mean that she's the ghoul-woman?'

Catherine spoke and I tried to concentrate but I couldn't take in what she was saying. She asked me first, 'Did you notice that Maleeka's dress was white? Did you notice that her hair wasn't braided or combed? Did you notice that she wasn't wearing any jewellery and that her face was without any make-up, even the kohl that all the girls put on their eyes?'

'Are you making fun of me, Catherine? Of course I didn't notice any of that, and even if I had, I wouldn't have given it any thought. The only girls I see here are the very young ones when they play in the road, and I don't know what they wear or how they make themselves up when they get older. What can it matter?'

She answered that she didn't see women either but it was all recorded in the books that she'd read about the oasis. The white robe was mourning dress for widows here. When Maleeka took off her man's outer robe and removed the cloth over her mouth and she saw her dirty white robe and her face without any make-up, she'd realized at once that she was a widow, and she knew that she would be living under the punishment that they impose on widows in this oasis.

Perhaps it wasn't a punishment but just a manifestation of an ancestral fear of death. Or rather, not of death but of the woman herself, because they didn't impose this punishment on the widower; he was free to remarry even before a single month had passed after the death of his wife. The widow, though, had to wait for a long period so that she could become cleansed of the spirit that had possessed her and brought death to her husband. She remained a prisoner for four months and ten days. She was not allowed to change her mourning dress no matter how dirty it got. She could not bathe and she could not put on make-up. She couldn't wear any of her jewellery or comb her hair. Before all this, and more important than all this, however, was that she could not leave her house lest anyone's eye might fall on her, for whoever saw the ghoul-woman, as the widow was called, during that period was destined to perish because she was inhabited by the angel of death. During the period of cleansing, she was forbidden to speak to anyone and no one was allowed to speak to her, other than those of her closest relatives who had the courage, and even they had to do so from behind a wall. All this was kept up throughout the months needed for the widow to rid herself of the evil that had taken up residence in her body simply by virtue of the death of her husband, and only at the end of that period was she allowed to bathe in one of the springs of the oasis and resume her jewellery and make-up. On that day, however, the danger was extreme. The crier would go around the roads of the town crying in warning, 'The ghoul-woman is coming to you! Beware the evil destiny!' Then all would keep to their houses, because the evil powers of the ghoul-woman were strongest during the moments preceding her purification from the spirit of death, and any who saw her were doomed to perish.

I listened and couldn't believe my ears, and I asked Catherine to stop and made her repeat what she'd said over and over again so that I could understand, despite which many details escaped me. When she'd finished I said to her without reflecting, 'I often hear the crier moving between Shali and Aghurmi but of course I didn't understand a word of what he was saying.'

That wasn't what I wanted to say, so I asked her, when I'd pulled myself together, 'What, then, is the punishment for the widow who rebels against this imprisonment?'

'You mean, what will Maleeka's punishment be? I don't know. I didn't see anything about that in the books. I didn't read that a widow had ever rebelled against these practices.'

'But you said that they'd kill her.'

'I was just guessing.'

She paused for a moment. Then she said, 'I hope I'm wrong. I hope they don't do it and that Maleeka is unharmed! But I fear for her because she has broken many of their taboos. She left the house when she was a ghoul-woman who had not yet been cleansed, and she dared to come from Aghurmi to Shali, thus spreading the fatal curse over the whole community, as they see it.'

As I stood up, I shouted, 'And she dared to assault you. Don't forget that.'

Catherine gestured to show her indifference and said, 'She's a child and may be genuinely insane as well and we've punished her enough. More than enough, perhaps. I shall never forgive myself for what I did.'

I could not, however, join Catherine in her sudden forgiveness. Many thoughts were mixed up in my mind. I had to take revenge! I had to take vengeance on the one who'd broken into my house and assaulted my wife – child or grown-up, deranged or rational, ghoul-woman or angel, I could not forgive that!

Angrily I said, 'And why did this ghoul-woman choose our house of all houses?'

Catherine looked at me in amazement and said, 'Can you really not have understood yet?' Then she shouted, 'Where are you going now?'

And I left without replying.

12

Sheikh Sabir

A fear worse than any in my prophecies has come upon you now, people of my land! You mocked the prophecies and now you are visited with something beside which they are as nothing – the terror that 'none but He can remove' and that entered your houses the day the ghoul-woman went out against you. You summoned the sheikhs and the witches to find out what might release you from the curse that is abroad in the oasis.

The ghoul-woman only came out yesterday afternoon, yet by night the wailing filled the oasis, from Shali to Aghurmi. Women aborted and children who had never been sick were stricken with fever! Palm trees on the road to Aghurmi that had been healthy fell over dead when the ghoul-woman passed by them! Fires started in houses where not an ember burnt! Every minute, word of a new disaster would come from some house or garden and weeping and screaming arose from every house that the ghoul-woman passed in front of and from every house that contained anyone, man or child, whose eyes had fallen upon her. They expect a catastrophe at any second and have no idea how to prevent it.

Now, people of my land, you have what you deserve. I am not safe either from that bird of ill-omen that hovers over all our heads, but I weep neither for you nor for myself. May retribution spare none, and though I should perish with you, I shall try before the end to savour the taste of revenge for which all my life I have longed!

Here I am, waiting for you, *Agwad*, with the keenest curiosity, sitting in your lean-to, before the sun has even risen.

173

I will forgive no one, not the Westerners, nor the Egyptians, nor even the Easterners. I will never forget what I have suffered at your hands. The moment for which I have been waiting so long has come and all of you together will be the willing instrument in my hand. I never imagined that the moment would come in this form or for this reason, but so be it. All roads are good.

The terror that you are experiencing now came to me when I was five years old, when Yousif the Westerner set a trap for my father and the sheikhs of the Easterners. He is the Westerner I hate most, yet I concede that he laid his trap well. I understood it only after I had grown up and the chance of taking revenge on him had passed. Nevertheless, I studied every step he took that I might learn.

I think it over, I contemplate it and I memorize it so that none of its lessons or details may escape me. He started by deliberately spreading anarchy in the oasis at a time when the Egyptians had insufficient troops here. He provoked the *zaggala* of the Easterners into laying siege to the tent of one of the accursed Europeans who had come to steal the antiquities from the temples and tombs, and he put into their heads the idea of killing him and burning his tent and belongings. Before they could carry out what he had put them up to, however, he sent for the man and informed him he had heard that his life was in danger. He then invited him into his home to protect him. When the Eastern *zaggala* arrived and didn't find him, they plundered his belongings and burnt his tent.

Yousif was aware that the Egyptians gave the highest priority to the safety of those foreigners, more than to that of their own children, so he kept the man in his house for a few days and then took him by stealth to Cairo. And in Cairo, the hoodwinked foreigner said that were it not for Yousif he would have lost his life and been burnt with his tent, so the dupes there rewarded Yousif by appointing him mayor of the oasis and sent with him a large force of Egyptian troops and Bedouin, and this was the cause of my calamity.

The new mayor, with his Egyptian troops, made camp on the outskirts of the town and sent a messenger to the sheikhs of my clan, who had fortified themselves inside the town and prepared their weapons to defend themselves. He informed them that the Egyptians had not come to fight and that if the Easterners were to send a delegation of their sheikhs, they would draw up a settlement with them that would bring peace to the oasis. My people too were taken in by Yousif's trap and a group of them went to the Egyptian camp. As soon as they arrived, however, the Egyptians bound them all with chains and announced that they would hang them if the rest of those who had walled themselves up in Shali did not throw down their weapons and hand over their leaders. When they came to take my father, I cried and clung to him and one of the soldiers hit me with a big stick that cracked my skull and half blinded me.

I remember nothing of my childhood other than those few moments of terror. Even now, in my dreams, countless thick sticks rain down on my head, reminding me of those people, just as my left eye, with which I can now see only shadows, reminds me of them in my waking moments, and just as do my memories of being an orphan and of my helplessness as a child and a boy. But when I was young I learnt my lesson, which was to say nothing and reveal nothing of what I was thinking. At first, this silence was the child of the fear that made me turn in on myself and flee from the company of others. Later it became a useful habit, reminding me of Yousif, who relied on secrecy and trickery to achieve his goals. I made it my aim to be like him so that I could take revenge on his people.

I didn't even let anyone know that I could see only shadows with my left eye. So long as it looked sound, let them think it was sound. And when, after I had memorized the Koran here, my uncles wanted to send me to el Azhar to study, I didn't say that I had no love for Egypt and its people. Rather, I begged them to allow me to study in Tunisia. I have no regret that I studied at the Zeitouna mosque. There I met sheikhs from the south of the country whom I could understand and who understood my language, and who knew my country and its tribes.

There too I met the man who provided me with the book of prophecies. I saw him in the mosque staring at my face so hard that the brilliance of his eyes scared me. He was old and fading but he caught up with me when I went outside and grabbed hold of me so hard I almost fell over. He spoke to me in our language without the accent of the Tunisians and said to me, 'You're the one I've been waiting for!' I realized at once that he was from my clan, but I asked him fearfully, 'And who may you be?' He contented himself by pulling the sleeve of his *gallabiya* up from his other hand, revealing to me an arm amputated at the elbow. Then he raised his head and I saw a deep scar running from one side of his neck to the other, revealing white flesh not covered by skin, and he said to me, 'You are he to whom the stars have pointed me. You are the one who will take revenge for me and for us all on the Westerners.'

I was afraid of him but did not trust him and wanted to test him. I said, 'There are Westerners who have been wounded as badly as you, or maybe worse, in our wars.' He paid no attention to what I had said but continued his speech. 'I have spent my life here observing the stars and the calculus of the planets and I have read the horoscope of our oasis as though it were an open book. There will be no peace in the oasis until the face of the land has become an unimpeded domain for either us or them.'

His words reminded me of something and I said, 'One of the sheikhs of the Westerners once tried to clear the land of everyone but them and didn't succeed.' 'I know,' he replied, 'but you will. It is written that you will succeed, and if not, then all these prophecies will come to pass. Until we put paid to our enemies, the fate of those of you who survive will be mine. Warn your people!' Then he provided me with another piece of advice, one of which I was in no need – that I should be ever alert and silent because my clan listened to neither counsel nor warning. Their way was stubbornness and that was the way of the Westerners too, but I would be able to achieve by guile what I could not achieve by fighting. I had learnt this lesson before he told it to me and my thirst for revenge on our enemies exceeded his: I do not remember even the features of my father's face but I remember my hatred for those who killed him. Is it not just that I should seek revenge for him and myself?

I do not know how true the prophecies of this self-exiled Easterner are but I repeat them in the hope that they will come true and I also repeat them to terrorize them with. It is only through fear that I can rule them.

All that my clan has done so far has not assuaged my rancour. True, they killed Mayor Yousif in a battle before he could be congratulated on holding the office for one year, and we were victorious over the Westerners thereafter in other wars. But our victory wasn't what I'd been dreaming of. It wasn't final enough to clear the Earth of all but us, as the writer of the prophecies had wanted. On the contrary, we would beat them and they would beat us. We would make alliances and then break our alliances, and this will continue until God knows when so long as we haven't learnt how to plan even better than Mayor Yousif.

In the past, I thought that the solution was all-out war between the Westerners and the Egyptians, without it appearing that we had any hand in it. That is why I humour both in exactly the same way. I appear to them as the angel of peace and am hoping for the moment when I shall become their angel of destruction, and I try to gain the trust of this

177

disdainful district commissioner who has descended on us, he and his accursed wife, like destiny.

By my enthusiasm for curing Sergeant Ibraheem I also put on a show of solidarity with the family of the child whom he saved, who are from our clan, though I wouldn't have felt sorry for the sergeant if the stone had broken his neck in two. And I seized another great opportunity that my people had, as usual, squandered, when I encouraged them to pay the tax, unlike the Westerners. I know that the holding back by our opponents and the shortfall in the tax will hasten the dispatch of another military expedition, and this time we shall be the innocent party and the war will be between the Westerners and the Egyptians only. I may be able to light its spark from a distance, as did Yousif. I explained to my people, albeit with the greatest caution, what we might gain if we fulfilled our tax commitments and left the rebellion and disobedience to our opponents, but competitiveness took possession of them. 'We shall never pay as long as they don't! How can we take the initiative to pay before they do?'

Never mind. If that opportunity has passed, welcome now to the tempest of the ghoul-woman. And this time I will work to make sure it engulfs them.

What can you say or do now, Yahya, to defend Maleeka? I know you will be, as usual, one of the first to arrive, but I have been waiting for you here under the lean-to for a long time. You are always spoiling things for me with your spurious goodness and your spurious history. You convince the gullible that you are above discord and difference, that you are neither with your own people nor with us, but I do not believe you. I find you to be the most devious of all the people of the oasis, but I will bide my time with you as I bide it with them. God help me today to hide my joy at their misfortune. The death of Mi'bid saved you, you Westerners, from fighting, but what can save you today from what Maleeka did? Today I don't even need to speak; indeed, it will be better if I don't open my mouth. Up to now everything has gone as I would wish. I hear the bray of your donkey coming from Aghurmi and I shall embrace you, Yahya, as I always do, dreaming that you may crumble into dust in my arms.

The cluster of *agwad* assembled earlier than usual. On the faces of the leaders of the sheikhs of the West – Idrees, Abd el Majid, Yahya – was anxiety and gloom, and I could see in the faces of the sheikhs of my clan – Sallam, Nafi', Abdallah – repressed anger. Greater than all of that, however, was the terror that could be seen in the eyes of all. I would, then, add to their grief.

In a sad voice, and with my head bowed, I said, 'The district commissioner asked for me yesterday but I couldn't fathom exactly what he wanted. He says he wants us to punish Maleeka and her family and those who allowed her to leave her house or he will exact his own revenge.'

The voices of the *agwad* rose as one, cursing the commissioner, his wife and the day they'd alighted in our land, to which I added a silent 'Amen!'

Sheikh Abdallah said, 'Wouldn't it have been better if we'd acted on what the boy Mabrouk said and killed him along with his wife the moment they descended on our land as harbingers of ill-omen?'

Sheikh Nafi' said, 'We sought to escape disaster that day and we fell into a greater disaster . . .'

Sheikh Abdallah interrupted him and said, 'Don't waste our time on what will not help us. What is to be done now about the calamity that has befallen our land? What is to be done about the defilement of the ghoul-woman that has spread ruin everywhere?'

A heavy silence reigned that was ended only by the voice of Sheikh Yahya, which sounded weaker than usual, as though he himself did not believe what he was saying. 'I have heard,' he said, 'of the disasters that have occurred and on my way from Aghurmi I saw a fallen palm tree. But I know it had been rotten for a while . . .'

The sheikhs interrupted him angrily and some of them jumped to their feet shouting, 'What do you mean? In my neighbour's house, the children were struck by fever. Black scorpions crawled out from beneath the earth and filled the houses like ants. With my own eyes I saw an olive tree burning. We shall all die if things go on this way. Do you not hear the weeping in every house?'

I smiled to myself as I watched them almost come to blows, but Yahya waited for them to fall silent and turned to Sheikh Sallam, whose family has for generations recorded the noteworthy events of our oasis in a written ledger, and asked him what our ancestors used to do when such a catastrophe befell them.

Sallam answered, 'No disaster of this sort has befallen our land before. I know that for certain. Nevertheless, yesterday I reviewed the manuscript where all the news is gathered and I could find no allusion to such a thing.'

Sheikh Idrees said, sorrow almost preventing him from speaking, 'If we were to kill our daughter, would that erase the pollution of the ghoul-woman?'

Everyone fell silent. I know they were waiting to hear that but I couldn't prevent myself from saying, 'That would make His Excellency the district commissioner happy and relieve us of his wrath.'

Sheikh Idrees burst out hotly, 'God's wrath upon him and his wife, the bringers of disasters! I'm not thinking about what will please or displease him. As far as I'm concerned, he's far easier to deal with than the disaster of the ghoul-woman, and we'll take care of him soon, God willing.'

The rest of the Western sheikhs looked at him in reproof and some gestured at him to put him off, but Yahya was oblivious to it all.

Sheikh Nafi' said, 'Calm down, Idrees, and let us think. Didn't you hear Sallam say that this is the first time such a catastrophe has befallen the oasis? The people are waiting for the sheikhs to find a solution.'

As though he'd seen a road to salvation open before him, Yahya raised his voice, which was still, however, weak and hesitant, and asked, looking at Sallam, 'What says the manuscript, Sheikh Sallam, of what we used to do to women afflicted by insanity?'

Sallam replied in amazement, 'What kind of a question is that, Sheikh Yahya? We did with them as we do now – summon a sheikh who has memorized the Koran and knows the prayers that expel the jinn from the woman's body. Then we imprison the madwoman till she is cured or dies. But this is no jinn whose harm is confined to the one he possesses. This is a terrifying evil against which our ancestors took every possible precaution. What possesses the ghoul-woman is a reaper of souls and spreader of ruin. Our ancestors knew how dangerous it was and imposed imprisonment on widows till the spirit of perdition should leave them . . .'

Sheikh Abdallah said simply, 'So let us do what Sheikh Idrees has said and leave the rest to God. Let us kill her quickly so that she be gone from us and her evil with her.'

Suddenly Sheikh Yahya's voice arose, restored to its usual wrath. 'Are we here to find a solution or so that each of you can repeat, one after the other, "Kill, kill, kill," as though the one that possesses you all is the angel of death. God grant me patience.'

I saw Yahya flailing around like prey in a trap and thought it a good opportunity to let fly my arrow, so I said quietly, 'Whatever Maleeka may have done, *Agwad*, she's not just the concern of her family any longer . . .'

Sheikh Abdallah seized the thread I'd thrown out and said, 'You're right, Sheikh Sabir. Maleeka is the daughter of us all and the evil she is spreading injures us all. It isn't up to the Westerners now to decide on their own what to do.'

Yahya continued to flail around furiously. 'Have you heard me or any of the *agwad* of the West express a unilateral opinion? Or have we been "consulting", as you call it, and asking Sheikh Sallam what our ancestors used to do when disasters befell us?'

Sheikh Sallam replied, a note of anger in his voice too, 'To be frank, Sheikh Yahya, you don't want any solution that harms this girl who's at the root of the calamity.'

Unable to control either himself or his voice, Sheikh Yahya said, 'And do you too want to kill her? Yes, Sheikh Abdallah, Maleeka is like a daughter to me and I love her, but if I knew, *Agwad*, that her death would rid the land of the ruination you speak of . . . If you swore that you knew that killing her is what will remove the defilement from our community, I would not stand in your way. But what if she dies and everything goes on as before?'

The *agwad* exchanged glances, but they weren't listening now to what Yahya was saying. They were straining to hear a noise that was coming from the direction of the gardens of Aghurmi, filling my heart with joy.

A few *zaggala* passed by running along the road below us, carrying their rifles and not raising their heads to look at us. Then dozens more carrying rifles, spears and sticks joined them below the town, shouting, 'Death to the district commissioner and the unbelievers!' and some of them fired shots into the air as they proceeded in the direction of the police station.

Sheikh Yahya realized what was going on and stopped his speech, screaming to make himself heard above the din on the road, 'Sheikh Sabir, stop those madmen! They're the ones who'll bring ruin on us!'

I raised my voice too so that he could hear me and shouted, 'Could any ruin greater than that which we are in now afflict us, Sheikh Yahya? They're your men, so stop them yourself.'

Yahya went up to Sheikh Abd el Majid and, bending over him, started shaking him by the shoulders and saying, 'You know I can't run and catch up with them. You're a young man, Abd el Majid. Run and stop them! Tell them that we've tried that before and all it brought us was war, the gallows and prison.'

Abd el Majid bowed his head so that he wouldn't have to look Yahya in the eye and said in a voice I could barely hear, 'It's too late, Sheikh Yahya.'

Yahya straightened himself and stood, his eyes roaming over the assembled sheikhs. In a tremulous voice, he said, 'So you agreed on this before we came here. Am I the only one not to know? You decided to start with the district commissioner and then turn to Maleeka? All your consultations were, as usual, nothing but lies?'

He tried to shout but his voice failed him as he said, 'Even if I have to fight you on my own!'

No one answered him, and if they had, he wouldn't have heard them over the rifle shots and the shouts of the *zaggala*. He hurried, staggering along on his stick, trying to set off down the hill, but as he was preparing to descend, a sudden silence fell.

The firing and the shouts stopped and we all looked in the direction of the police station.

I stood up to look and I saw terror in the faces of the *zaggala*. Some of them came up the slope towards us waving in warning towards the south, in the direction of the police station, but before they could say anything a ball of fire burst in the air, distributing a shower of flaming sparks, quickly followed by a roar of thunder. The sheikhs leapt up shouting, the earth shook, the lean-to shuddered, its palm branches falling on our heads in fragments and dust, the shouting of the women rose louder even than the roar of the explosion, and the *zaggala* who had gone to attack the police station returned in chaos, pushing one another out of the way, not stopping to pick up those who fell, though some found the time during their flight to turn towards us and yell, as though we hadn't yet understood, 'The gun!'

The sheikhs were running around brushing the dust off themselves and coughing. When the row made by the *zaggala* had faded away and they had dispersed, and the screams of the women had turned to sobs, the sheikhs' terror subsided, though they remained dumbfounded as they looked at the round white cloud of smoke that remained unmoving between earth and sky in the place where the ball of fire had been, all eyes hanging on it as though enquiring what would happen next, while the smell of the gunpowder filled the air.

The answer was not long in coming. District Commissioner Mahmoud Abd el Zahir appeared at the bottom of the hill, riding his white horse and surrounded by a number of mounted policemen.

He paused for an instant at a point below the lean-to, put his horse to the rise, mounting it in two large bounds as though charging us, and then paused again and looked at us.

Without dismounting from his horse he said in a loud voice but in calm tones, pointing to the white cloud, 'That was just a warning, *Agwad*. Next time, the cannon will pound the walls of your town and your houses, with the results you experienced during the army's last expedition.'

He twisted his horse's reins to go back the way he had come but paused once more and shouted, 'Sheikh Sabir, I want the tax in full within a week. Inform me of the names of the families that refuse. And I want Sheikh Idrees and Sheikh Abdallah to come to me together at the police station tomorrow, after the dawn prayer.'

Then he left with his soldiers, the sheikhs remaining silent and I myself standing in bemusement. After I'd arranged everything! After fate had helped me with the disaster of the ghoul-woman! Even when this time it was between just the Egyptians and the Westerners!

184

My eye fell on Yahya, who had frozen where he was at the top of the slope, his back towards us as it had been when he left the group. He turned his head towards me all of a sudden, shaking it sorrowfully, before slowly continuing his descent.

As though addressing him, I muttered, 'It doesn't matter, Yahya. There'll be another chance!'

13

Catherine, Mahmoud, Sheikh Yahya

Catherine

Have all these things really happened since yesterday?

Maleeka came and we embraced and quarrelled and I almost killed her, and cannon fire resounded through the oasis, and then I became the ghoul-woman in her prison instead of Maleeka? Was that whole nightmare real?

An hour ago, Mahmoud issued his order that I was to stay in the house, not to leave it, and not even to open the door. He was in a hurry and wanted to go and I could hear the neighing of horses below our house, where his soldiers were waiting for him so that they could return to the police station after having fired the cannon. I took a grip on his arm, stopped him forcibly, and asked him to explain to me the reason. At the end of his tether and trying to free his arm from my grip, he said my life was in danger. The people considered me responsible for all that had happened since the ghoul-woman had left her house. I asked angrily, 'Was it I that asked her to come or was it she who broke into the house?' In fact, the original mistake was his. He was the one who threw Maleeka out of the house and made the whole thing public, and he was the one who threatened the people of the oasis, demanding a vengeance neither they nor I could understand.

He replied that what had happened had happened and I had to understand that the calm prevailing in the oasis after the firing of the cannon was not to be trusted. They were undoubtedly planning something now, so I was to stay in the house until he could find a solution. I screamed, 'I don't care about their threats and I'd rather be dead than live as a prisoner,' and he screamed in his turn as he pulled his arm away that I could die when I pleased but not here and not because of him or while under his responsibility. He left angrily, saying that he'd put soldiers in front of the house to stop me by force if I thought up any rash deeds, and I heard him lock the door from the outside.

Not an hour has passed, but the forcible imprisonment is choking me. I spend many days in the house, never leaving it – reading, or writing – but of my own choice. Now I have been deprived of my will. Mahmoud has become another Michael! And me? What have I become?

I couldn't summon up the slightest desire to do anything, so I gave up and lay on the bed, staring at the bedroom ceiling. What exactly was happening to me? Since yesterday I'd been blaming myself, and the image of Maleeka had never left me. If Mahmoud had hit her and kicked her, I had been on the verge of killing her. A bad end to a beautiful beginning.

I was delighted when I opened the door to her and my heart beat with joy when I saw her beautiful face, after she took off the cloth that was wound around it. She came forwards awkwardly into the room and started pointing at me and then herself. Then she took two small stone statues of women that had been wrapped and tied in a cloth and showed them to me, smiling.

I contemplated them with astonishment. Two statues, primitive but displaying in their sculpting a feminine suavity and flow most appropriate to a woman's form. Where had she come across them, and why was she offering them to me? I looked at her for my part, smiling enquiringly, and she approached me and pointed to the heads of the two statues, so I started examining them in amazement. One of them had features resembling my own, while the other's had hers. I asked her in Arabic, holding the statues out to her, 'Who?'

I wanted to ask her who had sculpted them but I didn't know how to get what I wanted to say across to her, and she took hold of the statues and brought them towards one another so that they touched, then pointed at me and herself once again. Then she raised the statues in front of my face and brought them together as though they were embracing. I kept on looking at her. She seemed to be thirsty, for she kept licking her full lips with her tongue. I did not, however, offer her anything to drink – my mind seemed suddenly to have stopped working – but stood there, my eyes fastened on her scarlet lips and her bewitching grey eyes.

My silence and smile must have encouraged her, for she placed the statues on the table and came hesitantly towards me. She approached until she was almost touching me and her heavy breathing was hot on my neck. Then she slowly raised her hands, put them around my shoulders and embraced me with extreme delicacy. I put my arms around her and hugged her too, but suddenly I screamed, 'No!' and pushed her away from me while she clung on to my shoulders and my dress tore and I kept pushing her away and repeating, 'No! No! I'm not Sappho!' Maleeka didn't understand anything but stood at a distance from me, looking at me with a wounded glance, tears gathering in her eyes. Then she started talking fast in her own language as I repeated, 'I'm not Sappho!' She went back to her statues and held them together while I shook my head saying 'No! No!' with determination and anger, and she threw the statues violently to the ground, where they smashed, and approached me again, and I realized from her tone of voice that she was pleading with me to understand what she was saying, despite my ignorance of her language. Kneeling on the ground in front of me, she embraced my legs with trembling fingers, weeping softly. Then she rose slowly to her feet, her fingers never leaving first my legs, then my thighs, then my waist until finally she buried her head between my exposed breasts and kissed them with her lips, which were wet with her tears and saliva. From that instant to this, the question keeps coming back to me – was the shudder that swept over me then one of revulsion or one of pleasure? Did I snatch up the palm rib and strike her with it when she sank back to her kneeling position beneath my feet in order to punish her or to confirm that this seduction could never touch me?

I kept repeating to myself, 'I am not Sappho!' True, I have memorized her poetry about her pupils and lovers but I am not like her. In agitation, I kept muttering to myself the same sentence, 'I am not Sappho! I am not Sappho!' while at the same time resisting the temptation to stretch out my hand once more and raise her from the ground and clasp her face to my bosom. Instead of doing that, however, I snatched up the palm rib and started beating her, and in the end I nearly killed her. Was I really angry with her or with myself? Was I angry because she kissed me or because of the shudder that swept over me when she kissed me? And since yesterday I have been asking myself the question. Why had her image never left me since I first saw her? Why did I become excited and my heart beat with joy when she knocked on my door? And why have I memorized the poetry of Sappho if I want nothing of her feminine love? I answer myself that I have memorized much ancient Greek poetry, from Homer to the verses of Alcaeus, Sappho's male lover!

After Maleeka left, I started trying to gather the bits of the two statues that she had smashed and put them together again, without success. They had broken into shards that could no longer be mended. What delicate fingertips, though, had sculpted this torso and formed these tiny hands and this cheekbone? Could it possibly be that it was she, Maleeka?

And while I fondled the smashed pieces in my hand, I kept turning over in my mind, in spite of myself, these lines by Sappho:

I have heard no word from her!
When she left me she was weeping.
I wished that I might die.
Before, she had revealed much to me, spoken much.
She had said, 'This parting had to happen, Sappho.
I leave you in spite of myself.'
'Go, then,' I said, 'and be happy!'

But it wasn't in my power to say to Maleeka, 'Go, then, and be happy!', knowing what awaited her at the hands of her family. If she should escape unharmed, if she should return . . . !

I was never like that in any way! I am not like that in any way!

Catherine, how many times have you said this phrase recently? You said it when you tried to conjure the spirit of Alexander, and when you were happy that Mahmoud was keeping away from you, and now when you submitted to Maleeka's seduction. Who are you, then? There's something here that changes people. In this isolated oasis in the centre of the vast desert, there is something that changes us. There's no call for me to be astonished that Mahmoud should fire the cannon to repulse a barefoot army after having been miraculously changed from a hater of the oasis to one who feels for its people. Enough of Mahmoud now. What about yourself? I would like to say that both of us have changed in this oasis, but what if it's the other way around? Why shouldn't it be that each of us has found his truth in this oasis?

No, this is not my truth!

But *I have heard no word from her* since she left me.

Mahmoud

There can be no stopping or going back now. I am henceforth responsible only for these soldiers who gallop behind me

190

on their horses. Each has a family, a home and loved ones far from here. We were very close to death an hour ago. We needed a miracle to escape a massacre. Now we need more miracles. They are not deceived by this calm and nor am I.

We have reached the station and I have distributed them in defensible positions ready with their rifles – behind windows, on the roof, behind the surrounding wall – and we await what events may bring.

If they renew the attack we will not be able to do the same thing again. I hardly believed it myself anyway when the shell actually fired. I had pinned my hopes on the rust, sand and humidity not having ruined the gun and its ammunition alike. When I primed the gun and fired the charge myself towards the sky, aimed far from the town, I was certain that these were the seconds that would make the difference between life and death. I had distributed the soldiers in the best places I could think of for the defence of the building and ordered them to return the *zaggala*'s fire if they charged the station, fully aware that there would be many dead on both sides.

Ibraheem warned me the moment I arrived at the station early in the morning. He said the atmosphere among the people was dangerous. There were people mobilizing the Westerners against me and Catherine, saying that we were the reason for all the disasters that had befallen them. They accused Catherine of having cast a spell to release the ghoul-woman from her prison and they were encouraging them to take revenge on us so that the curse that was destroying human, beast and tree might be removed from their land. He alerted me to today's expected attack and reminded me that they were fearless fighters. When it came to fighting outsiders in defence of their community, they would fling themselves at death as though they couldn't see the weapons of their opponents, rushing at them in droves and killing whoever was in front of them without caring how many of their own might fall.

I immediately sent Ibraheem to the house to warn Catherine against going out and thought of sending two soldiers to guard it, but then I realized that they would have no choice but to start with me before attacking Catherine. Her salvation would depend on mine.

That was when it occurred to me to scare them with the cannon, whose might the town had had a taste of before. I decided to use it just to terrorize them and the miracle was achieved. I don't know whether it can be repeated or not, but that miracle saved them and us from massacre and gained us some time. Now I have to keep going down the same road, maintaining the threat with the utmost confidence, even though I don't feel confident about anything whatsoever! They have understood, certainly, that tomorrow I intend to arrest Idrees the Westerner and Abd el Majid the Easterner to force the two clans to pay the taxes. Whether they come tomorrow will be a crucial test of my success in imposing my authority on the oasis. If tomorrow ever comes!

Of course, I realize now – too late, as usual – that I was wrong from the beginning. I shouldn't have threatened Sheikh Sabir or insisted on taking revenge on Maleeka and her family. She is indeed, as Catherine said, a child, and insane. What sane man takes revenge on children and lunatics? And what could her family do given that she had fled without their permission and forced her way into the house in disguise behind their backs? Shouldn't all those blows and kicks, as well as the cut that Catherine gave her, have sufficed?

Now Ibraheem has assured me that, having failed to kill me and Catherine, they will shift to killing Maleeka to save themselves from the curse of the ghoul-woman. How can I or any person understand such customs? There is nothing I can do now to save Maleeka. If they are going to kill her, the cause is their superstitions about widows – even if I hadn't fired the cannon, even if I hadn't said one word to Sheikh Sabir.

If I'm convinced by all that, then why don't I feel in the depths of my soul that I'm innocent? It would be better, instead of thinking about things that I can't change, if I were to think about how to save that other madwoman, Catherine. If we survive, I will have to send her away from the oasis as soon as possible and make sure she arrives safely in Cairo. How, though?

As for myself, I will continue down the road that has been laid out for me and which I tried to avoid. I shall imprison, and possibly flog, to collect the taxes, as did my predecessors. Perhaps I shall try also to pit the Easterners against the Westerners or vice versa, following the advice, which I despised, of Mr Harvey, whom I despised for giving it.

And to what other wretched destiny shall I lower myself here?

Sheikh Yahya

Did I say I'd fight you on my own? You're raving, Yahya! You must think that time runs backwards. Even if time doesn't run backwards, for your sake, Maleeka, I'll make it start over again by force! I promise you, my child.

But the donkey refuses to move. He brays as though he were weeping and stops more than he walks, which is not his way. He hasn't yet become ancient, like me. Even I, donkey, can still run, so get a move on! Perhaps the miserable cannon shell has struck terror into you as it did the sheikhs, or the smell of gunpowder is suffocating you as it is me.

Suffocating or not, I'm coming, Maleeka!

I could smell the rottenness in this fallen palm tree every time I passed it, and the black scorpions come and go, so what fault are these things of Maleeka's?

I understand you, my child. I understand that you can't bear to be locked up now that you're divorced. You're the lone free bird among us crippled corpses. Perhaps once I was like you. No. You're better!

Move, donkey, for yesterday I was not able to see her. I went to my sister's house when I heard what had happened. It was crowded with women I didn't know, who had thrown their abayas in front of the door so that no man would enter. Maybe Khadeeja had planned it that way so that I wouldn't see Maleeka or interfere in what they were planning for her.

Hurry, donkey, for I must see her today, even if all the women of the oasis and their menfolk come to stop me!

How can you expect Maleeka to understand your customs, when I myself have reached old age without being able to fathom them? Maleeka the Beautiful, the angel of death? Black scorpions and fires in houses and trees, and sick children? You're the ones who are sick! It's just like the prophecies of Sheikh Sabir that you always used to make fun of, Maleeka. You don't understand what sin you've committed to be imprisoned, and all my life long I've never understood this superstition either.

It sends me wild, just like the wars – those celebrations of blood that begin again the moment they're finished. They live to start them for the slightest of reasons or for no reason at all. The *agwad* consult each clan and then they all consult together, and the outcome is war! What is that? What does it mean? Parties with ululations and singing and drums and presents, whose bride and groom are corpses and severed limbs, but they prepare for them in high spirits. They agree on the time and choose the place and the judge. Everything has to be done according to the rules. At the appointed time, the ranks of our clan draw themselves up opposite the ranks of their clan. Each family has a place that has been set since time immemorial opposite a particular enemy family. And behind the ranks stand the women. They ululate and chant their chants and when the judge strikes his drum, the party begins. All the fighters fire one shot, no more. Then they pause so that the bodies of the slain can be removed. Then it's the drum and the shot again and the party goes on for days on end until one side is victorious over the other.

How, Maleeka, could you have wanted your uncle to restrain his anger at these insane celebrations with their chants and their ululations, their screams and their wails, their blood and their drums? It was because of these that I fought them all on my own, and for your sake too I will fight them again on my own. I still know how to use my rifle.

They didn't tell you my story. My clan ceased telling it to the young ones a long time ago, but I know they whisper to one another in secret of how Yahya went mad in his youth. Don't believe them, my child. I wasn't mad. I was trying to stop the madness.

Today I shall tell you something I've told no one else so that you can understand and so that together we can stop this insanity in our land. In my youth they considered me the champion of the Westerners and the bravest of their men, because I had never been defeated in battle and never retreated before the enemy. Day by day and war by war, though, I became more and more unhappy at these butcheries, and my conscience tortured me over all the blood I'd spilt in them. I refused to take part with my people in a certain unjust battle in which they were in the wrong. I secluded myself from them, and my brothers and my uncles came to me. How could I abandon them in the hour of war, when I was their champion? How could I accept such a disgrace? I lost my patience and told them, 'If you want it to be war, then let it be the last war of all!' 'What do you mean, Yahya?' 'I mean that we should fight them not as we always do, so that we or they are awarded the victory. We should fight them until either they or we are obliterated!' They laughed. 'Are you joking, Yahya?' 'No. But that is my condition. This business has to come to an end once and for all.' 'Your condition is strange, Yahya, but we will accept it so long as you are with us.' 'To the last man?' 'Yes, to the last man.' 'Do you swear on the Koran?' 'Yes, we swear.'

After they had sworn this oath, I went with them to the war. On the first day, I would fire and look around to seek out the weak spots in the ranks of our enemies, thinking how we might benefit from these gaps in the next day's fighting and the fighting of the day after, until the promise that one of our clans would be obliterated was made good. Before midday, however, I saw that some or our men were defeated and withdrawing. My shouts to them reminding them of the oath did no good, and neither did the slights of the women or their insults against those who fled. By the afternoon, I found myself among a minority of my people. Then I found myself alone. I would emerge from my position and fire one drum's-worth with great precision at the serried ranks of the Easterners. Their bullets, however, always went wide. They could have killed me with the greatest of ease but they didn't do so. Then suddenly, after one of their shots, they rushed towards me, threw their weapons at my feet, and started kissing my hands and kissing my head and saying I was the bravest man the Earth had ever borne. They proposed that I stay with them and live among the Easterners as their honoured guest, but I mounted my donkey and returned neither to my house nor to my people. Instead I proceeded towards the labyrinth of the desert, determined never to return.

This is the story of my madness, Maleeka, which they don't like to tell. I know I was wrong, my child, but believe me it was because I loved my people that I'd hoped they might be obliterated so that someone at least might live in peace, and believe me, I am ready to do the same now. At this age of mine, I will fight them on my own to give you life. Who, in this land, cursed in its people and its superstitions, is worthier of life than you?

If only it were my life that were the price, Maleeka!

If only this donkey would hurry!

*   *   *

At Gouba Spring I saw people coming from the direction of Aghurmi.

One of them took hold of the donkey's halter, stopped it in the middle of the path, and spoke to me. He spoke at length and I did not respond.

I remained where I was, in the sun, for I don't know how long, and eventually the donkey moved on of its own accord, with slow steps, towards the house.

I entered without saying anything. My sister Khadeeja spoke and her sons spoke. They interrupted one another in their noisy determination to get the story straight. I, however, neither interrupted nor questioned. I just listened to the men with their oaths and the screaming women and said nothing. They said that Maleeka had locked herself up in her room as soon as she returned from the commissioner's. She didn't content herself with simply locking her door but piled all the chests and furniture that were in the room behind it. She screamed abuse at anyone who knocked on the door or addressed a word to her. At the top of her lungs she insulted her mother and her brothers and she made a special point of cursing the late Mi'bid. Why did they consider her a widow when Mi'bid wasn't a man? She was still a virgin and the blood that Mi'bid had brought them after his first night with her was faked. She'd never been a wife or a widow, so how could she be a ghoul-woman? She repeated what she said many times and laughed and wept, saying the ghoul-woman must be Mi'bid because he wasn't a man. But she also challenged anyone who knocked on her door to enter and let her heap all the curses of the ghoul-woman on their heads and afflict them with every one of her catastrophes and burn up every man, woman, rock and tree in the oasis. But first, they had to tell her why she was a ghoul-woman. She complained to her mother that the man with whom she'd lived for two years had never come near her and would beat her for no reason, which made her mother beat her too and

197

forbid her to say such things again, for it was enough that she had the shadow of a man in which to shelter. But she hated Mi'bid's shadow and because of him hated all the men and all the women of the oasis. She hated them all, so why wouldn't they let her, after God had sent her the mercy of Mi'bid's death, seek a beautiful friendship far from them? She wasn't like them and there was no one else like her in the oasis and she loved the woman more than her mother. Where's my uncle Yahya? Where's my uncle? He's the only one I want to talk to. Why didn't he come and why doesn't God make the Earth swallow up the rest of you?

I listened in silence to what they said. In the end they had succeeded in breaking down the door and left her mother to enter alone. They said, 'Maleeka received her standing in the middle of the room holding a large knife in her hand, her hair dishevelled and spattered with blood. Khadeeja tried to calm her down and held her hand out to her with a plate of food, but Maleeka spat at her and asked her, weeping, why had she sold her? Why had she thrown her to Mi'bid? Then she turned the knife on herself and buried it in her breast, cursing all the men and women, and a fountain of blood spurted from her towards her mother.

My sister, weeping, pointed to her bloodstained clothes, then started slapping her cheeks again, but I left without a word.

Khadeeja ran after me. The funeral, Sheikh Yahya? When is the funeral?

I didn't look back.

On the road to my garden I was thinking over what I'd heard and asking myself, where lay the truth? Did Maleeka indeed plunge the knife into her breast, or was it you who buried it in her heart to remove, as your *agwad* claimed, the defilement of the ghoul-woman from the land? Where was the truth and what difference would it make if I knew, now that Maleeka was lost? Lost to men's lies and women's terror and the conceit of that district commissioner who was consumed with hatred. Lost, so what was the point of anything?

I don't want to see her dead body. In the days that remain to me I don't want to remember that child as a corpse. I want her to remain a living creature to me as I used to know her. The loveliest shoot this land ever put forth.

She needed shade and protection and to have us keep the evil weeds away from her but . . . Yahya, O Yahya, how much death has come your way during your life! With these two hands, I've buried brothers and sisters, wives, children and grandchildren. How is it, then, that now that I am old and failing I cannot bear your death, my child? I weep for you and for myself. Now I despair of this land of theirs.

I have not been able to bring it out of its darkness, either as a young man or as an old one. I tried and I failed. The Lord didn't guide me to the right path, but now I know my way. I shall seclude myself from them all. I no longer have the strength to go out into the desert as I did in my youth. I shall keep to the small hut in my garden and never set eyes on you again.

I renounce you now, oasis, not, this time, to find myself, but to bid her farewell.

14

Mahmoud

I don't know which did the trick. Was it the shot from the cannon, which was just a deafening bang and a few flying sparks, or the imprisonment of the two sheikhs? After that, I haven't needed to imprison or flog anyone. I kept Idrees and Abd el Majid as guests in a room at the station and ordered the soldiers to treat them well and allow their relatives to visit them and bring them whatever they wanted from their houses. In any case, the message got through and after a few days I let them go.

From the first day, loads of dates and tuns of olive oil started to arrive, filling the stores to overflowing, so that we had to put some of them in the station forecourt. Sheikh Sabir comes himself or sends a representative to say this is the quota of such and such a family and ask for a receipt to the effect that they have paid their share of the taxes. The greater part of the tax in kind has been received, plus the fine in cash, and I stay in the station almost all day to monitor the collection of the shares and their inventorying.

Sitting in my office on the second floor, I heard a hubbub from the station, accompanied by the shouts of children. I'd become accustomed to hearing this noise when the family shares arrived, or, I thought, it might be the return of the troops sent to meet the Matrouh caravan. But no. Here was the sound of many horses' hoofs.

I went to look out of the window and was surprised to see a young officer getting off his horse. With him were six cavalry troopers who also dismounted and quickly formed a single line, which the soldiers I had sent to meet the caravan joined.

The officer stood for a moment as though reviewing them and they gave him a salute. Then he left them standing where they were and pointed to one of the soldiers from the station, who had surrounded the incoming company in silence and apprehension. He said something to the soldier, then walked ahead of him to the stairs.

I was standing when he entered my office. He raised his hand in salute and clicked his heels hard. Then he came towards me with measured steps and held out to me a yellow envelope, saying in an official tone of voice, 'Captain Wasfi Himmat Niyazi at Your Excellency's command, sir!'

Captain? At his age? I didn't make his rank till I was a few years past thirty and he looked barely twenty-five. What was going on?

Indicating a chair in front of the desk, I said, 'Welcome, Captain. Be seated.'

I contemplated him as I sat at my desk. Blond, with a boyish face, of middling build but on the short side. The most noticeable thing about him was his honey-coloured eyes, which were always on the move.

Wasfi didn't sit until I'd resumed my seat behind the desk. Laughing, I said, 'The ministry promised me these reinforcements months ago, but they didn't inform me as to the time of their arrival or we would have prepared a welcome for you.'

I didn't say that I'd been expecting a larger number of both troops and officers. While casting a quick glance at a letter he'd brought with him to the oasis, which was covered with signatures and official seals, I said, 'However, I certainly need you and your horses. The only horses left in the station are worn out.'

I clapped and Sergeant Ibraheem, who minded the door, entered, and I asked Wasfi whether he wanted tea or coffee. He replied he'd be grateful if I could offer him a glass of water because he didn't drink either.

I said, smiling, 'You mean a tin mug of water. We don't have glasses at the station.'

When the soldier had left, I said to Wasfi, 'You will rest now from your journey. Then tomorrow we shall talk about work. The first order of business, though, is to find you a place to stay.'

He said that they'd told him about that in Cairo and explained to him the traditions of the oasis and that it was better for him to stay at the station. Things would be no different from when he was in military college.

I said, 'Life may be a little more difficult than at military college. You will discover that—'

But Wasfi suddenly set down the mug of water from which he'd been drinking in large gulps, and interrupted me to say, 'Excuse me, Your Excellency. Perhaps I should have informed you before anything else. I took Miss Fiona to Your Excellency's house before coming here. They showed me the place so I took her there before reporting for duty.'

At first, I didn't take it in. I had in fact forgotten the business of Fiona in the rush of events that had overtaken us. Wasfi, however, went on to tell me with a certain zeal that the chief of police of Alexandria had recommended Miss Fiona to his keeping until she reached the oasis and that His Excellency the Basha had come himself with his deputy to bid her farewell before the caravan left. Wasfi was dazzled by this and ended his speech by saying that His Excellency the deputy chief of police had sent me his greetings.

I asked him, 'Who is that?' and he replied that it was His Excellency Brigadier General Tal'at Abd el Aziz.

'My thanks to you and to the brigadier general.'

My spirits sank and I postponed my return to the house. So now there were two problems. I would have to send the two sisters back together and in the shortest time possible. Perhaps with the very same caravan. I would see.

Somewhat distracted, I asked Wasfi how it was that the journey hadn't affected the smartness of his turnout or soiled his uniform or tarboosh. He replied earnestly that he'd changed his clothes that morning in preparation for meeting me and assuming his duties.

I explained to him the circumstances in which we worked in the oasis, without referring to recent events, and said that his first task would be to help with the collection of the remaining taxes and arrange for the dispatch of the first consignment with the caravan that had just arrived. Then I made a brief tour of the station with him. I picked out a suitable room for him to move his things into and asked Sergeant Ibraheem to find places for the new troops and give them lunch. Then, before I left, I told Wasfi that I had to pass by the house briefly and that if he wasn't too tired he could come with me for lunch later on.

I knocked a number of times on the door and waited a little before opening it. I found Catherine and Fiona standing in the main room on either side of the table, ready to greet me. I had prepared myself to say, with false jocularity, 'Welcome to our desert, Fiona,' but I stood at the door and couldn't get a word out after 'Welcome'. I saw identical twins, two copies of Catherine.

I went towards them with slow steps and stammered out the same 'Welcome . . .' and Catherine gave a soft laugh and said, 'You've already said that, Mahmoud. What do you think of this surprise?' I responded, out of politeness, 'A pleasant one indeed. You have the same eye colour and high cheekbones.' Then Catherine said, 'But Fiona is much prettier.'

I drew nearer to them. Catherine wasn't lying. Her sister was svelte and her features were more symmetrical – a gloriously beautiful face indeed, framed by golden hair thicker than her sister's. Nevertheless, when I held out my hand to shake hers, her pallor, despite the sweet smile that was almost a part of her features, took me aback. Perhaps it was owing to the fatigue of the journey.

The three of us sat down in the main room and I told Catherine that the new officer might come and have lunch with us today. Fiona asked, 'Captain Niyazi?'

'Right. Wasfi.'

Catherine told her sister, 'You'll have to get used to that. Here they address people by their first name. I was surprised at first when they'd say "Miss Catherine" or "Mister Mahmoud" but you have to know that from now on you're "Miss Fiona".'

Smiling, she replied, 'It's much nicer that way. Not so formal.'

This chatter made me lose focus on the conversation and I started observing Fiona. She had a calm yet strong presence, exerting no effort to impose herself. I asked myself idly whether the chief of police and his respected deputy had gone to see her off in obedience to a recommendation from some important person in the embassy or elsewhere, or to take another look at this beautiful woman. What surprised me too was that there was something else there, despite her beauty, that made her in no way arousing, as though she were a picture or statue of a perfect woman and not one of flesh and blood. I asked myself, 'Could that be why she's never married?'

I realized, however, that Catherine was asking me excitedly, 'Did you know that?'

I hadn't been following their conversation and she noticed that, so she repeated her question, 'Did you know that Captain Wasfi is interested in antiquities?'

'There hasn't been time to ask or find out.'

Fiona nodded her head in confirmation and said, 'He is extremely cultured and speaks English exactly like the English.'

She fell silent for a moment before continuing, 'He behaves exactly like an English gentleman.'

She spoke in a neutral tone and I couldn't understand whether she was praising or criticizing him.

As I rose preparatory to leaving, I said to Catherine, 'Now you'll have someone to talk to about your antiquities.'

Catherine walked with me to the door and whispered in my ear in Arabic before I left that it would be better to bring Wasfi to dinner so that Fiona could rest. She also said that her sister had been advised by the doctors in Ireland to live in a warm dry climate for a while as she was suffering from a bad chest.

As I left, I mumbled, 'Then perhaps Upper Egypt would be best for her. You know our situation here now.'

Fiona wasn't wrong. Wasfi conducted himself at dinner like a true gentleman. He knows the etiquette of the dinner table much better than I. He praised Catherine's taste in preparing the food and addressed her and her sister with extreme politeness, delivering witticisms that made them smile or laugh.

After dinner, he became engrossed in a conversation about antiquities with Catherine. They talked about books and mentioned names I don't know. He said he'd read everything about the antiquities of Siwa and intended to visit them all.

At this, Catherine shook her head and said bitterly that he might find great difficulty in doing that as the most important antiquities were situated in the midst of the houses and they didn't allow outsiders to walk around in them. She had tried and failed. Wasfi said confidently, 'We'll find a solution to that, I'm sure.'

I thought in astonishment, 'Have you still not learnt your lesson, Catherine? After all the disasters your visits to the temples have brought about? I had thought that, after the terrible sorrow that overcame you when you heard of Maleeka's death, when you stayed for days locked up in your room, you'd never go back to this perilous hobby. But no.

205

You never change. I really must get you and your sister out of here quickly. You are a danger to yourself and to others.'

I came back to their conversation to find her asking Wasfi with great interest, choosing her words, for some reason of which I was ignorant, with care, 'Since you've read so much, I'm going to ask you whether there were Greek temples in Siwa, and where you imagine they might be found?'

Wasfi replied, choosing his words with equal care, 'The matter calls for research on the ground. The Bilad el Roum temple – the temple of the Land of the Greeks – might be one of them, though. The name leads one to think that it was a Greek or Roman temple. Certainly it didn't resemble the Ancient Egyptian temples.'

Catherine said, 'I read that the first traveller to see it said of it that it was the most beautiful of the temples of the oasis. However, the temple was destroyed completely after that. There isn't a single column remaining, just some stones scattered in the midst of swamps close to Lake Khameesa. It's been almost completely obliterated.'

In spite of myself, I cried out, 'How fortunate!'

They turned towards me in astonishment so I said, 'It's spared people the trouble of studying it!'

There was a moment of silence that Fiona broke by asking with her by now familiar smile, 'Did I hear you say that this temple was near a lake?'

Catherine said, 'Indeed. Lake Khameesa, to the west of here.'

Fiona said, 'Why should it have been obliterated? It may still be beneath the waters, and they may still say prayers in it!'

Wasfi and I looked at her wonderingly while Catherine smiled and said, 'It's possible. Go on, Fiona!'

Fiona continued, looking at us, 'Don't you know the story of the people who live in a palace under the water? Why shouldn't what happened in the story of King Corc and his daughter in Ireland have happened to your temple? Let me tell you, and then perhaps you'll believe me!' Catherine said enthusiastically, 'Yes, Fiona! Do tell!'

So her sister began:

'Once there was a rich king who lived in a beautiful palace in the middle of a broad green valley, but for all his riches his real treasure and the one that he took most pride in was a gushing spring of water in the courtyard of the palace. Ireland knew no waters sweeter or purer than these and people used to come from far and wide to drink of it for its magical properties. As the throngs rushing to the palace increased, though, King Corc grew worried that the water would stop flowing and his peerless source of water run dry, so he considered the matter and surrounded the spring with a high wall and stopped the people from approaching it. And whenever he wanted to drink he would send his beautiful daughter Fior with the key to the door of the spring to fetch some water in a golden bucket that he had made for this purpose alone. He did not like to give the key to any of his servants because he was afraid that they might steal some of the water. Yes indeed, so fearful was he of his wealth deep in the ground. One day he held a great party to which he invited the princes and nobility. The palace glittered with lights, musical airs flowed mellifluously through its quarters, and tables groaning with every sort of food and drink ran its length.'

I followed Fiona's story and watched her, and Ni'ma came immediately to my mind, so I started comparing them. Fiona spoke calmly and simply, as though this palace in Ireland was a well-known place that we would see, albeit at a distance, in the midst of the green meadows of the Irish countryside, should we but open the door. Ni'ma, on the other hand, lived her stories. She fell under their spell and would herself become, amidst her tears, the imprisoned princess, the enchanted king or the abandoned lover, and her face would shine with joy

207

when victory was achieved. Thus she and I would become two inside the story – kings or poor men, lovers or ascetics. Which of the two ways was better?

Here suddenly was Ni'ma's beautiful prince, in the middle of Fiona's story! He enters the king's party and it's love at first sight. He cannot take his eyes off Fior's bewitching face and neither can she drag hers from him and his face afire with love. He invites her to dance, she melts in his arms, and they circle the hall with the grace of two butterflies flapping their wings to the music, while the musicians play their finest and without stopping, as they have never played in their lives before, as though they don't want this ethereal dance to come to an end – though finally the dancers have to sit down to dinner.

I was following Catherine's happy glances and Wasfi's eyes, which hardly stopped darting from side to side in childish eagerness to hear Fiona's story. 'At dinner, the king sent his daughter to fill the bucket from the precious spring and her beautiful prince accompanied her across the courtyard of the palace, but when she bent over to fill the golden bucket she found that it was very heavy and her feet slipped and she fell into the water. The prince tried to save her but to no avail. The waters of the spring started to rise and pour forth, running through the open door and covering the whole courtyard. The prince hurried to seek help from the palace but the waters that remained imprisoned behind the wall burst out in joy at their freedom and kept flooding the courtyard and rising faster and faster until, when the prince reached the hall, the water was up to his neck. In the end, the waters spread till they covered the whole of the green valley in the middle of which stood the king's palace, and that is how the Lough of Cork was formed.'

Fiona fell silent for a moment, looking from one of us to the next. Then she said, 'But the strange thing is that the king and his guests did not drown, as might have happened in such a flood, and nor did the beautiful princess Fior drown, but she returned the following night to resume her dance with her handsome prince under the water. And every night from that time on, the banquet and the dance have been renewed on the floor of the lake, and so it will continue until someone has the luck to snag the sunken golden bucket that was the cause of all that happened.

'So are you certain that no one can see this temple of yours below the water?'

She received no reply, so she went on in the same confident tone, 'I say that because, until today, if you pass by the Lough of Cork and your sight is strong, you can see through its pure water the towers and walls of the palace, and in the evenings you can hear the music and song of the outspread banquet, though only in the summer because the lake freezes over in winter!'

The magic of the tale held us all, and we continued to look expectantly at Fiona, hoping that there would be a continuation to the story, but Catherine suddenly laughed and clapped, saying, 'I was sure, Fiona. I was certain you'd do it.'

Then she turned to us and said, 'I think Fiona is the last of the line of the Irish storytellers. We had hundreds, maybe thousands, around whom the people would gather, but now they are becoming extinct. Fiona, though, still knows by heart all the stories, isn't that so?'

Fiona made a gesture with her hand and said, 'Never mind that. Fortunately there are still many others, but now, tell me, what did you understand from the story?'

We looked at one another for a while, but Catherine said, 'Don't ask me. I've known the story since I was small and I know its meaning. The king was punished because he kept the poor people from the water.'

Fiona said, 'That was when we were small. But how do you understand it now?'

Catherine shrugged her shoulders, smiling.

Fiona said, 'That too is an answer.'

Then she turned to me and said, 'And you?'

I hesitated a little and then said, 'I think it's a beautiful story.'

A serious expression passed over Fiona's face and she said, 'You're right, but you have to say what you understood from it. The story doesn't end with its telling. Its listeners have to finish it.'

I thought hard for a while. Then I said, 'Maybe the story means that what we see may not be the truth, and the clear surface of the water may hide a life we do not know, and the truth may escape us under any surface. Is that the meaning?'

Fiona smiled and said, 'Maybe. Didn't I tell you that the story is fashioned anew by everyone that listens to it? And what about you, Mr Niyazi?'

A frown appeared on Wasfi's boyish face and for the first time he lowered his eyes, making himself look like a schoolchild being examined, but he said, 'I'm not good at solving puzzles, but I don't understand how what happened could be a punishment for the king, as Mrs Catherine says. On the contrary, the story says that the king, the princess, the prince and the guests are living an eternal life under the water in an unending party.'

Catherine interrupted him to say, 'But don't forget that all of that is in a prison under the water.'

I said, 'Perhaps the palace, before it was drowned, was a prison above water. Perhaps the whole world is a prison!'

Addressing her sister in a joking tone, Catherine said, 'Observe, Fiona! Now my husband's dark side is at work. But don't worry, another story may well put him back in a good mood!'

At that moment, however, Fiona seemed distracted. Her lips were pursed, she was supporting herself with her hands on the table, and her face had suddenly turned red.

She put her hand over her mouth and her body began to shake as she exerted an effort to stifle short staccato coughs. Then she tried to rise, putting the table napkin over her mouth, but she sat down again, the coughing racking her body, her breathing now a painful rattle in her throat, as she tried to catch her breath. Wasfi and I stood up in fright. Catherine was also standing next to her gasping sister, her arms around her shoulders, and she addressed me, trying to master her fear, and pointed to a bottle at the end of the table, saying, 'Quickly, Mahmoud. Pour a spoonful of the medicine.' Fiona, however, gently pushed her sister's hand from her shoulder and made a gesture of refusal, which she repeated several times, still coughing, and when the crisis was past she gripped Catherine's hand hard and raised her tear-filled eyes to her standing sister. Then she looked at us and said vehemently, as though angry at herself, and still panting, 'I'm sorry. I've spoiled the ... meal, and the first ... the first time ...'

We muttered meaningless expressions of protest, but Fiona, trying to catch her breath, was addressing her sister and pointing dismissively at the bottle of medicine, saying, 'It doesn't do to take too much of it. It doesn't help at all. I took a dose before dinner in fact.'

Then she pulled herself together and went on, 'The doctors in Ireland told me that my illness isn't at all infectious. Otherwise I wouldn't have permitted myself ... you two ... and Catherine.'

I protested, 'Why talk of such things now? What matters is for you to recover your health.'

In firm tones she repeated, 'All the same, I would never have allowed myself.'

Catherine bent over her sister and kissed her on the cheek, saying in tones she tried to make cheerful, 'You only infect people with good things, Fiona. I wish I could be infected by you.'

The evening came to a rapid end. I went with Wasfi as far as the station and we were silent and oppressed. Halfway there, however, I stopped suddenly and asked him, 'Why do you think Fiona told us the story of that sunken palace? And why did she ask for our opinions?'

Wasfi stopped too, looked, somewhat surprised, into my face, and said, 'I think, Your Excellency, that she told us the story to entertain us. I forgot all about it in the crisis that overcame her.'

Resuming my progress, I said, 'You're right.'

Something inside me, however, told me that she didn't tell her story frivolously. At the very least, she had wanted to get to know us. And then what? At that moment, Wasfi was saying, in a tone of pity, 'These bouts used to come to her sometimes while we were in the caravan and everybody would feel sorry for her. On those occasions, she'd usually go away from us or avoid us. We discovered that she hated anyone to show concern for her at such moments. She wouldn't reappear until the crisis had passed, and then with a smile on her lips, as though nothing had happened.'

The following morning I was on the verge of sending Sergeant Ibraheem to summon Sheikh Sabir so that I could introduce Wasfi to him, when the sheikh himself surprised me by appearing in my office. Rarely had he done so since the incident with Maleeka and the firing of the cannon. He said he'd heard of the arrival of the new officer and had come to welcome him in the name of the *agwad*. I received him with lukewarm expressions of politeness, then introduced him to Captain Wasfi and explained that from now on the latter would be responsible for liaising with him with regard to everything that concerned the collection of the taxes. Wasfi, however, surprised me when he started talking about how happy he was to meet 'His Reverence' Sheikh Sabir, of whose learning he had heard so much before coming to Siwa.

I couldn't prevent myself from asking him, in front of the sheikh, 'Where did you hear about him?'

He answered with a certain excitement, 'Corporal Wahba el Salmawi, who came with me. He's from Marsa Matrouh and lived here for a while and he knows all the *agwad* of Siwa.'

'I know him,' said Sheikh Sabir.

Then the captain asked permission to leave 'for one minute' and returned with a small oval box of red velvet in his hand and addressed Sheikh Sabir, saying that his father had gone on pilgrimage to Mecca this year and brought back with him things from the Hejaz, for the blessing they contained, and that he wanted Sheikh Sabir to accept this modest gift. Astonishment appeared on Sheikh Sabir's face too when he opened the box and took out a string of yellow prayer beads, which he turned in his hand, saying, 'Pure amber!' Then he repeated his thanks to Wasfi, saying that it brought great blessing from the Sacred House, and that he would say many prayers for him and for his father, the pilgrim.

When Sheikh Sabir had left, I said to Wasfi, overcome by anger, 'What do you think you're doing, Captain?'

He didn't understand why I was angry and said, bewilderment on his face, 'His Excellency Saeed Bey advised me to pay compliments to the *agwad*, so I took the opportunity to do so.'

'Nevertheless, you should have asked my permission first! You don't know that sheikh. He's a man who . . .'

Then I fell silent because I didn't know what to say. If I started I'd have to explain everything, which I didn't want to do, not now at least.

Looking disappointed, Wasfi said, 'I'm very sorry, Your Excellency. I shall not repeat the mistake.'

Then he continued somewhat hesitantly, 'I brought with me prayer beads for the rest of the *agwad*, and for Your Excellency, of course, so if you'll give me permission . . .'

I waved my hand to dismiss him, saying, 'Do as you wish, Captain. Follow Saeed Bey's advice.'

No sooner had he left than I heard an urgent knocking on the door.

Sergeant Ibraheem entered, sketching a salute, and said, 'Excuse me, Excellency. Permit me to ask, why did Sheikh Sabir come to Your Excellency's office today? Since the incident, he's always stood at the door of the station and sent someone in with his requests.'

'He wanted to be introduced to the new officer. Why do you ask?'

Ibraheem was silent for a moment. Then he said, 'Forgive me, Excellency, once more, but I fear that man. He hasn't spoken to me once since my leg was cured. When he meets me in the road, he looks at me as though he doesn't know me. Not a word.'

I waved my hand dismissively. 'Don't concern yourself, Ibraheem.'

'I am not concerned. I just wanted to tell Your Excellency that I don't trust him in my heart. And I have heard things in the oasis. I have heard that he was the one who incited the *zaggala* to attack the station that day.'

'And I'm aware of that, without having to ask anyone from the oasis. He was presiding over a meeting of the *agwad* that morning and saw the *zaggala* marching on the station, yet neither he nor any of his *agwad* tried to stop them. He had known very well since the night before that they were going to attack and he made no attempt to inform me or warn me. I know all that, so what's new? What matters now is that he collect the taxes and hand them over without problems.'

'But for how long, Excellency? This calm itself scares me. I'm afraid for you and for the madame and even for her sister.'

'What's her sister got to do with this?'

'May God protect us all, but a man with revenge to take will not forget it, Excellency, and such men are insane. I had a colleague in the army, a very decent man, from a good family, who could read and write. He was promoted till he was on the verge of being made sergeant-major. He devoted himself entirely to his work and we never saw him go home to his village as all the rest of us did. All the same, one day someone came and killed him. There was an ancient feud with another family going back to the days of their forefathers. The other family wanted to hurt his, so they didn't kill just any peasant in the village and have done with it; they wanted to chop the head off the family, so the poor man lost his life through no fault of his own.'

'You worry too much, Sergeant!' I said.

'I'm sorry, Excellency. You and I are going to stay here because that's our job and how we earn our living, and whatever God has in store for us will be. But why don't you send the madame and her sister away from here as quickly as possible?'

'I'll think about it, Sergeant. You're dismissed.'

After he went out, I got up and started pacing the office, avoiding the window, for I didn't want to see anyone. Ibraheem had put into words what I'd been thinking about ever since Fiona came. I was no longer comfortable with Catherine's surprises. She might leave the house tomorrow and cause a new disaster. After her mourning for Maleeka, or her apparent mourning for her, she returned to being exactly the way she was. It was as though nothing whatsoever had happened, just as in the oasis, from which, the moment Maleeka was dead, all talk of fires, scorpions and other calamities disappeared, as though all the oasis had been waiting for to return to its former ways was her blood. Poor girl!

Last night, during the conversation between Catherine and that 'gentleman' Wasfi, I sensed new disasters on the way. I shall try to delay the departure for Marsa Matrouh of the caravan that the captain came with for a few days so I can make arrangements for her and her sister to travel.

Him, a captain! Of course!

A Military College graduate. From a rich Circassian family, certainly! I didn't envy him, but why had this fortunate young man come to this wretched oasis? He must certainly have the contacts to get himself out of such a dangerous assignment. So why had he come? And why was he buttering up Sheikh Sabir? Like you, Ibraheem, I don't trust him in my heart. So now new worries pile themselves on top of the old. Even Tal'at is making an appearance now to remind me of himself. His Excellency the deputy chief of police! Good for him! I never wanted to be like him or in his place, but what did I want? Once more, what is my problem?

The problem is precisely you, my dear major! It's no good in this world being half good and half bad, half a patriot and half a traitor, half brave and half a coward, half a believer and half a womanizer. Always in the middle. I didn't kill Maleeka but I let her be killed. I wanted to save young Mahmoud but in the midst of the attempt I let Ibraheem break his leg. I was a supporter for a time of the nation and the revolutionaries, and when it came to the test I denied them. And then I did nothing. Never was I one person, complete on the inside. Tal'at was more honest with himself. Since he'd been a traitor once, let him follow the road to its end. He sold himself and pocketed the price he'd asked for. I, I sold myself for no price at all, content to be bitter at myself, the British and the whole world without knowing what I'm asking for. Even in love I was always happy to settle for pleasure, then stop and not go to the end of the road. I let myself lose Ni'ma, whom I loved. I didn't get involved in a proper relationship before Catherine, but that's another story. I think that, inside, I've finished with her, after what happened to Maleeka, who lies every night between me and her, keeping me from her and her from me, and bursting in on my dreams.

Last night was an unending nightmare. She came to me with a scarf over her face and nothing of her showing except her huge eyes. She was running along the shore of a lake that was edged with greenery and I ran after her till I could almost take hold of her hand, but I couldn't catch up with her, no matter how hard I tried. The lake shore was transformed into a vast desert and I fell to the ground, impotent and exhausted, so she turned towards me and I screamed in terror when I saw the face of a hideous ghoul-woman with eyes like glowing coals, holding in her hand a rib of palm as large as a palm tree, which she thrust into my chest, burying me in the ground, which swallowed me up. Before she could bury me completely, however, I looked at her again and saw that beautiful face of hers that I had only ever seen once, the smooth chestnut hair fluttering around it and tears pouring from her eyes. Then I woke, panting and unable to draw breath, as though I really had been buried under the ground.

I remained standing in my room at the station catching my breath with difficulty, as though I had entered the dream anew.

I went back and sat at my desk, saying to myself for the thousandth time that there was nothing to be gained by thinking about things that couldn't be changed. I would never escape from the eyes of Maleeka. I would never escape from Catherine or Sabir or Ibraheem, or from the face of Tal'at, which had been peering at me since Wasfi had brought him back. I would never escape.

Let me then think about something else. Something beautiful; and what was there in my life more beautiful than Ni'ma? I would try to recall her whenever escape routes were blocked, but she too was punishing me. She was refusing to let her face visit me again. I couldn't blame her at all.

I turned my face to the window. Nothing but blue sky and small, light, scattered clouds. From the forecourt of the station came the voice of Wasfi, high pitched but implacable, giving orders to the troops.

*　　*　　*

I shall gradually come to understand him. There's no call for haste. It isn't even that important if I don't understand him.

On the first Friday after his arrival, I accompanied him, along with some of the soldiers as usual, to perform the prayer in the Great Mosque at Shali. Lately, they've made a space for us that is almost separate from the rest of the worshippers, and some of the sheikhs shake hands with us without saying anything, after which they leave the mosque in a hurry. This time, after Sheikh Sabir had shaken my hand, staring at me with his glassy eyes, he took the hand of Captain Wasfi and presented him proudly to the *agwad* of the Easterners and the Westerners one by one. Then he turned to me and said to me in an aside, 'The *agwad* would like to welcome the new officer, with Your Excellency's permission, naturally.' I nodded my consent and left the mosque with the rest of the soldiers. Later I found out that they'd invited him to lunch in Sheikh Sabir's garden and that they'd exchanged gifts.

I understood of course that the *agwad* were making a fuss over Wasfi as a way of stressing my isolation and of slighting me by displaying far more respect and good feeling towards the underling than they did to his superior. I supposed too that Wasfi wanted to prove how successful he was in his new job. So far I have no objection to what he's doing.

His relations with the *agwad* may have contributed to calming the people of the oasis after all that has happened, even though Ibraheem hasn't stopped warning me against imagining that the problem is over. In any case, Ibraheem was relieved that his duties as my orderly excuse him from having much to do with Wasfi, who treats all the soldiers strictly and severely. He's always organizing exercises – marching, running and sometimes even firing – from first thing in the morning.

The soldiers fear and obey him. He asked my permission as soon as he arrived to conduct these daily training exercises for the troops, and I agreed, saying to myself, what's the harm in maintaining the troops' fitness and constant readiness when we are indeed living in the midst of danger?

I didn't, however, take Wasfi with me on my nightly patrols to the edges of the oasis, which have become rare. There hasn't been much call for them now that the Bedouin raids have almost come to a stop.

I was very concerned at that time with Fiona's condition. I hadn't succeeded in delaying the caravan, which, on the ministry's instructions, had had to return quickly to transport those shares of the tax that had been collected, and Fiona's state didn't permit her to undertake another long and arduous journey. Her and Catherine's expectations that the warmth and the dry atmosphere would help to improve her general health and her cough proved ill founded, especially as they couldn't leave the house. In fact, they moved from one room to another following the sun's rays, and spent most of their time in the back courtyard, which resembled a terrace, open to the air and with high walls, which was flooded by the sun all day long and where Fiona would sit, a heavy woollen abaya covering her chest and shoulders.

Captain Wasfi kept asking after the health of 'Miss Fiona' and I'd answer him tersely. One morning, however, after she had spent the whole night in ceaseless coughing, Catherine at her side, I told Wasfi that it wasn't improving. Disquiet and sorrow appeared in his face and he said he wanted to suggest something that he didn't know whether I or Miss Fiona would accept. I wondered whether he wanted to ask for her hand in marriage! I looked at him so that he would continue his speech and he said that Corporal Wahba, who had come with him, had told him that they had herbs and plants in this oasis that were to be found nowhere else in Egypt, and that many people came from Marsa Matrouh, and even from Alexandria, to be treated with these herbs, which had magical effects.

I said I could well believe that because it was treatment with such herbs that had saved Sergeant Ibraheem's life and I was astounded that that hadn't occurred to me till now.

Then I thought, how can I ask for the help of Sheikh Sabir, or anyone else in this oasis, now that I've become the enemy whom no one even speaks to? I told Wasfi that I'd present the idea to Miss Fiona and leave it to her to decide.

The same day I told Fiona of our conversation and talked to her about my experience with Ibraheem. She looked interested and said, 'Let's try, Mahmoud. What can we lose? This bitter medicine that the doctors in Ireland prescribed for me no longer helps at all.' I looked at Catherine and, unconvinced, she knitted her brow, but Fiona insisted.

I went back to the station and summoned Wasfi, and with him Corporal Wahba el Salmawi.

I'd seen him before but hadn't charged him with any task. The corporal had a huge body, Bedouin features and a Bedouin accent that I found repulsive. I asked him what he knew and he repeated in front of me what he'd said to Wasfi.

'Do you know who it is that treats people with these herbs?'

An expression of regret on his face, he said, 'I'm sorry, Your Excellency. The last person the people of Matrouh recommended and to whom they'd go in Siwa for treatment has renounced the world and shut himself up in his garden.'

Wasfi said, enthusiastically, 'Let's try with him.'

Wahba repeated warningly, 'He meets no one, Captain.' Then he looked at me and said slowly in his deep voice, 'Even if we told him we were coming from His Excellency the district commissioner, he would refuse to see us. I know him.'

I realized that Wahba knew about what had taken place in the oasis, so I made no comment, but Wasfi said with the same enthusiasm, 'Will you allow us to try, Your Excellency?'

I was silent for a moment, during which Wasfi watched me eagerly. Then I repeated what Fiona had said: 'What do we have to lose?'

Wasfi gave the salute that he never tires of delivering, then said in commanding tones, 'Follow me, Corporal.'

After a little, I heard horses leaving the forecourt of the police station.

15

Catherine

Did you say his name is Sheikh Yahya? I know him.

I told Mahmoud and Fiona about my meeting with the sheikh and said it was the day of that other visit to our house, knowing Mahmoud would understand. Fiona said, 'If you know him, Catherine, let us try him. I don't mind going with you to meet him.' Mahmoud objected. 'It's not possible,' he said. 'If he refused to meet an officer and a soldier he's known for a long time, what would make him . . .'

I, however, could see Fiona's eagerness, so I interrupted him by saying, 'If I'd been in his place, I would have refused too. It was like a military order to a man who, as you say, has forsworn the world, to break his seclusion. But perhaps, if we went to him, just us, on our own, just two women seeking help, things might be different.'

In Arabic Mahmoud said to me, 'For you, especially, to go out in these circumstances is dangerous, and you know it. Dangerous for you and dangerous for Fiona too.'

When Fiona heard her name on his lips, she said in a tone of entreaty, 'Please agree, Mahmoud. I beg you. I don't expect miracles, naturally, but if there were something that would relieve this cough, even just a little . . .' Then she fell silent.

Mahmoud took his eyes off Fiona and appeared to be sunk in thought. Then he said, 'I don't feel at ease about the two of you going out unaccompanied. I shall send some soldiers with you.'

In almost one voice, we exclaimed, 'No!' and then laughed.

He stood there hesitating for a moment, then left. All the same, I'm sure he'll send some soldiers to follow us.

I put on my riding dress and Fiona wore a grey dress and put a woollen shawl round her shoulders. Then we waited for a long time for Mahmoud to send us the two donkeys. I supposed he must have had difficulties in finding someone willing to hire anything to us at a time when the whole oasis was against us.

I recounted to Fiona, in summary, the story of Maleeka. I told her only about her visit when she was a ghoul-woman and about her death. She didn't show great surprise when she heard the legend of the ghoul-woman, but an expression of sadness passed over her face when she heard of her death, which still remained a mystery – murder or suicide?

Fiona said, 'Don't be angry with me, Catherine. Whether she killed herself or not, either way she was murdered. Whatever their customs here may be, whether we like them or not, they are their customs and they are happy with them. What business is it of ours whether they see ill-omen in widows or not? It's their way of life, which has lasted on the basis of their traditions for hundreds of years. I imagine that no death or murder occurred as a result of this custom until outsiders came.'

I defended myself. 'I didn't do anything. She's the one who came from her house when it was forbidden for her to leave.'

Fiona said nothing.

I felt I was having to justify myself before my sister. How would it have been if I'd told her the whole story?

It was only with the greatest difficulty that I had got myself out of the crisis. I kept to my room for a number of days after hearing of her death, days during which her image never left me, and nor did my sorrow. I would think through every second of our encounter and what it had led to. I would try to understand what had happened and to judge myself. Was it she who had seduced me? I who had seduced her? And was there in fact any seduction, or only fear? She was extremely sweet when she entered. She had grasped the impossibility of our understanding one another through language, so she'd devised the business of the two statues. But then she'd become angry with me and with herself because she'd been unable to make me understand what she wanted, either with words or with the statues. What had she wanted, in fact? When she put her arms around me, her embrace was as delicate as that of a child. It was I who allowed the idea of Sappho and her passionate words of love to women to drive everything else out of my mind. Was I really in thrall to the influence of the poetess of Lesbos, or afraid of it? Desirous of it or rejecting of it? I pushed her away and she tore my dress. She was afraid. Perhaps she'd knelt on the ground in front of me and embraced my legs to show that she didn't want to harm me. As for what happened next, there's nothing but fog in my mind. Why did she kiss my breast? What precisely happened at that instant? Did my naked breast take her by surprise and did that make her kiss it, or was it I who took her in my arms? Then it was my turn to be afraid, so I snatched up the palm rib and started beating her, pursued by those accursed verses.

I don't know exactly what was going through Maleeka's mind. It may be that she was entirely innocent. My concern was to judge my own behaviour, and I reached the conclusion that that truly was not I. At the worst, it was a moment of weakness, a moment of confusion brought about by the killing loneliness of this oasis. That was it indeed – nothing but a moment of delusion. Thus, thanks to my own strength of will and nothing else, I pulled myself back from the brink of fear and weakness. I am not responsible for what happened. What happened was not important, and I am not guilty of Maleeka's death. Given this, would Fiona too possibly understand and confirm my innocence, if I told her the whole story with all its complications? As far as I'm concerned, I've decided to turn this page once and for all.

We sat in silence in the sun waiting for a messenger from Mahmoud, who, fortunately, has not been assailed by the slightest doubt about what took place between Maleeka and me, beyond her having attacked me and torn my dress.

Finally we heard the braying of the donkeys and someone calling Mahmoud's name. I opened the door and found a tall, well-built policeman at the bottom of the stairs mounted on a donkey, and with him a glowering boy pulling two others. Fiona also came to the door and waved with her hand, her smile widening as she said, in extremely broken Arabic, 'Good morning, Mr Salmawi!'

The policeman returned her greeting and she told me in an aside, 'He was with me in the caravan. He knows a little English and he's very good hearted.'

The sun flooded the open area that stretched before us and the fortified town to her left. Nevertheless, Fiona felt a cool breeze and went back into the house, returning after a short while wearing the striped blue mantle in which the women of the oasis envelop themselves. As she pulled it tightly around her, she said, 'Isn't it pretty?' I looked at her in astonishment and said, 'Well, at least it keeps you warm.'

With a certain pride, she said, 'They call it *tarfottet*. A woman on the caravan gave it to me.'

The children stood watching us from a distance, calling out in their high-pitched voices what I took to be insults. Salmawi scolded them, waving his rifle jokingly at them, and the children ran away.

I asked him in Arabic, 'Is it far?' He answered, 'About a quarter of an hour.' Fiona hadn't ridden a donkey before and laughed with pleasure like a child as she tried to get on, but I warned her that the donkeys sometimes suddenly bucked and went off course, throwing their riders, and advised her to hold on tightly to the halter.

Salmawi went ahead of us on the road, the frowning boy, as usual, running behind. We left Shali behind us and turned east towards Aghurmi on the dirt track that leads to the temple. This is the path Maleeka travelled as she returned, bleeding, from our house, and was the last thing she saw in this world. Enough! Didn't I give myself an undertaking I'd never think about her again?

From behind the walls, I could hear the familiar songs of the *zaggala*, but the smell of figs and other summer and autumn fruits disappeared and that of manure spread on the ground took their place. I told myself bitterly that it was the first time I'd noticed the changing of the seasons. I hadn't been out of the house since Mahmoud had made me a prisoner there and Fiona arrived. It was as though my relations with the world had been cut off years before and I'd never been along this track in my life!

The columns of the temple appeared in the distance, but before we got there, Salmawi turned off to the left, so we followed.

Finally we arrived at a garden from behind whose walls all that appeared were the banners of the palm fronds as they clacked monotonously in the breeze, which also brought us the smell of mint, jasmine, lemon and many other fragrant perfumes.

We stopped in front of the open door and Salmawi sent the boy who had accompanied the two donkeys to inform the sheikh. The boy was gone for a long while and I saw Fiona, full of hope, looking around her with her ever-present smile. She said, 'This is a strange place, Catherine. When you see all this greenery and all this water you forget you're actually in the middle of a sea of sand.'

'But the sand isn't far way, all the same. If you look beyond the greenery, you'll see it everywhere.'

At that moment, the boy returned with another boy of similar age and they informed Salmawi that the sheikh was in retreat and couldn't see anyone.

I told Salmawi angrily, 'Impossible! I shall go in myself and speak to him.'

I moved towards the door and Salmawi stood in front of me, spreading his arms to block the way, and said politely, in his deep voice, 'Madame. That's impossible. Even under ordinary circumstances, women here don't go in to see a man on their own and without permission. Now, though, Our Master the Sheikh would get very angry.' Then he was silent for a moment before going on, 'And it will make His Excellency's position in the whole oasis more difficult.'

So this Salmawi knows everything.

I stopped in my tracks in impotence and frustration. Fiona asked me to tell him that we wanted to ask the sheikh's advice, and even if he refused to meet us, perhaps he could explain a treatment to us, or inform us as to the name of someone else he trusted.

Salmawi talked to the two boys again, and then we stood and waited some more. I looked at Fiona. She hadn't lost her calm but disappointment showed itself clearly on her face as she said in a tone of resignation, 'If this doesn't work either, we can only go back.'

At that moment, however, I saw the two boys returning at a run. They said something to Salmawi, whose face brightened and who gestured to me and Fiona to stand back a little from the door. After a short time, I saw approaching that same Sheikh Yahya who wore his glasses tied to his ears with string, leaning on his stick.

He seemed to me to have aged greatly since I had first seen him. He stood inside the door, his face flushed with anger.

He didn't look at me or at Fiona but addressed thunderous phrases to Salmawi in the language we don't understand, while Salmawi tried to placate him, waving his hands in supplication. The sheikh, however, was about to turn his back on us and retreat when Fiona asked me quickly to tell him that she had heard that he was in retreat, worshipping God, and that the best way to worship God, as far as she was aware, was to help those in need.

In a loud voice I translated for the sheikh what Fiona had said, starting with the words, 'My sister says to you . . .'

Without looking at me, he answered in a voice that shook but was completely clear, 'Tell your sister that no one speaks in God's name. He alone assesses and judges.' To which Fiona replied, 'Despite which, it is a sin in all religions for someone to turn away any needy person that knocks at their door.'

'Unless the one who knocks be a murderer or have hate in their heart,' he said.

Fiona responded, 'My heart holds no hatred for anyone. I came seeking your help and you have refused to help me. God knows, though, that I do not hate you.'

He came towards us a little without passing through the garden door and stared from behind his glasses into Fiona's face, saying, 'And your sister? And the district commissioner?'

I was translating for them mechanically, and Fiona said, 'I can't answer for my sister or for the district commissioner but I know that hatred is a sickness in any heart. God has afflicted me with the disease that I came to you to seek help with, but he has spared me the other.'

I then said, 'And for myself, Sheikh Yahya, I too hate no one.'

Staring with his dim eyes into Fiona's face, he said, in an aside, 'But do you love us? Do you and your husband love our land and our people?'

He didn't wait for a response, but turned his back and returned the way he had come, resting his weight on his stick and on the boy's shoulders.

Fiona stood, following him with her eyes until he disappeared, and I too remained where I stood, as though paralysed, observing him vainly. She moved towards the donkeys, coughing hard and putting a hand over her mouth while gesturing with the other that we should go back.

Salmawi said in his tremulous voice, 'She had some medicine with her in the caravan that helped when the bouts of coughing came.'

I said roughly, 'She doesn't have that medicine with her, and it doesn't work any more.'

Urging us to hurry, Fiona said, 'Let's go. I don't need any medicine now. But I really did hope the sheikh would help me.'

'God damn him!' I exclaimed.

Fiona frowned in my face, saying, 'Don't you see, Catherine? You're just proving that he's right!'

Even more angrily I said, 'I'm not a saint like you!'

She replied, 'And I'm not a saint, and I don't like anyone to address me by that term. I used to be too shy to say so to my father, who coined the expression, but I implore you not to use it. I am not a saint. It's enough for us just to be humans. It's more than enough.'

On the way back, Fiona was completely silent. She bent over her donkey, and it seemed to me that her whole body was on the point of collapse, and I started saying to myself, 'Don't you dare die, Fiona! If you're not a saint, then become one, and make a miracle to cure yourself of this illness! What anyway is this disease that isn't infectious but is on the verge of killing you? Make a miracle, since the medicine of Ireland doesn't work and this accursed sheikh refuses to try. I do not believe at all in the business of their magical herbs, or that the sheikh could have an effective medicine, I just did what you wanted.

'He spoke of my hatred, and my animosity! My animosity and Mahmoud's? He's the one who bears animosity. Whom do we bear animosity towards? I don't even think about them, since they keep themselves away from us. I do not hate the sheikhs despite their ignorance and narrow-mindedness. In fact, I loved this sheikh until I saw what he did today. No. "Love" is too strong. I mean that I liked him on that day. I found something in him different from the rest of the sheikhs.

'But I know the truth now. He's the worst of them. God damn him a thousand times over, however much that angers you, Fiona. I don't forgive easily, like you.'

229

When we arrived home, Fiona was so exhausted that she put her arm round my shoulder as we climbed the worn stairway. I put my own arm round her waist and we rested at each step, as she was breathing with difficulty. When I opened the door, she collapsed on to the first chair in the room, saying between breaths, 'I haven't left . . . the house . . . since I came here, which is why . . . I'm not used to moving. Don't worry, Catherine. I'll sleep a little and then I'll be better.'

I looked at her face as I forced myself to smile and said, 'I'm not worried, Fiona. I know it's just a passing crisis, like the others.'

In truth, I wasn't worried. I was terrified.

In the morning, I woke up in a bad mood.

Fiona stayed in bed and I didn't have much conversation with Mahmoud during breakfast, though I did ask him to invite Captain Wasfi for a cup of tea in the evening.

He said, wonderingly, 'Didn't you tell me Fiona is tired?'

'That's why I want him to come. The change and the company may be good for her. This isolation that we live in is killing.'

He said doubtfully, 'I don't think that Wasfi's company . . .'

I interrupted by saying, 'Are you jealous?'

He looked at me in astonishment. 'Of that child?'

I went on, irritably, in spite of myself, 'So invite him today, then. And tell him too that I'd like to take a look at whatever books he has on Siwa.'

I spent the day with Fiona in her room on the second floor. I took her her breakfast in bed and she didn't object, as she has done before. She always insists on coming down to take breakfast with me in the main room, no matter how bad her condition, having first washed and got fully dressed, as though we were about to go out to an important meeting. This morning, though, she stayed in bed, and her smile did not succeed in hiding her extreme exhaustion. I stayed with her and proposed to her that she move into a room on the ground floor with us, so that going up and down the stairs didn't wear her out, but she preferred to stay where she was.

In the evening, we were sitting in the main room waiting for Mahmoud and Wasfi, Sergeant Ibraheem having come earlier to inform us that they would arrive at sunset.

The rest had done Fiona good and she was a little better. She had arranged her toilet with care and tried, as usual, to appear normal.

Mahmoud entered like a whirlwind after two knocks on the door, trying to hide the great excitement that shone from his eyes. Wasfi was behind him, smiling with a certain bemusement and carrying a heavy bag.

Mahmoud waved in our faces a parcel he was holding, saying, 'Imagine what happened!'

'And how are we supposed to know?' I asked.

But without even waiting for a reply from us, he began talking rapidly and enthusiastically. 'Corporal Salmawi came to see me,' he said. 'I mean I was in my office getting ready to leave when the corporal came in carrying this parcel. A boy had brought it to him. Can you guess from whom? Can you guess what's in it?'

Fiona said, 'The curiosity is killing us, Mahmoud! You say what's in the magic parcel!'

Mahmoud took hold of the parcel again and raised it in front of his face, looking at it as he said, 'In it are medicine and a bottle of oil. Who sent them? None other than Sheikh Yahya! He advises Fiona to rub her chest with the oil and cover it with wool all night long. The drink you take first thing in the morning.'

'The sheikh?' I said. 'Just imagine!'

Then I went on doubtfully, 'But he refused to see her yesterday or to listen to anything about her condition, so how can he have chosen this treatment?'

Wasfi intervened. 'I asked that too, Mrs Catherine,' he said. 'Salmawi answered that he noticed the sheikh taking long looks at Miss Fiona's face and listening to her cough.'

'Is that enough for a diagnosis?' I asked.

Fiona interrupted me. 'It's enough that he thought of helping us, Catherine. I was certain that, despite his anger, he was a good person.'

I laughed. 'Of course! Everyone's good as far as you're concerned, Fiona!' I said.

In a sharp tone she said, 'No. Only the good ones. His treatment may help. He seems to be an experienced sheikh.'

'Of course it'll help,' said Mahmoud enthusiastically. 'Their medicines work miracles.'

We all sat down around the table and Wasfi put his bag next to him as he said, 'We shan't be staying long anyway. His Excellency has to rest a little because he will be going out tonight on patrol in the desert.'

'And you too?' I asked.

He replied, a note of regret in his voice, 'No. His Excellency wants to go out on his own.'

'One of us has to stay behind at the station,' mumbled Mahmoud.

I started pouring the tea and Wasfi asked, somewhat diffidently, whether his tea could be very weak, and Mahmoud said that Wasfi was very careful of his health and drank tea and coffee only to be polite.

'Maybe he has other ways of passing the time,' I said, and he raised the heavy bag that he'd put down next to him and said, smiling, 'Just reading. I've brought all the books you asked for.'

After I'd handed round the tea, I took the books from him and started reviewing the titles. I found they were the very same I'd brought with me from Cairo – Von Minutoli's celebrated *Atlas* and the pictures he drew for the temples on his visit to the oasis in 1820, a translation of the book by the

German writer Rohlfs on the oases, and other books I knew. I did, though, find a new article in the British *Geographical Journal* by Jennings-Bramley on the Western Desert and its tribes. I asked his permission to read it and return the journal after a few days. He said I could take all the time I needed because he had in fact read the article, and had known even before he read it that all Siwa's Egyptian temples, including that of the oracle, go back to the last period of Egyptian cultural revival, just before the Persian invasion, and that the latter had been built by King—

Mahmoud, who was following the conversation with annoyance and boredom on his face, interrupted Wasfi by saying, 'So, according to what you say, Wasfi, while the Persians were getting ready to invade Egypt, we were preparing for them by building temples? Marvellous! The king thought that building the temple was of greater benefit to the country than building an army, even when he knew the Persians were coming. Why not?'

Wasfi looked a little disconcerted at Mahmoud's provocative tone and extricated himself from the situation with the cliché 'Times change!'

I intervened to rescue him and said, 'Mahmoud, to the Egyptians the temple wasn't just a building but a means of protection. It was a symbol of the whole country, its roof decorated with stars like the sky and its floor the Egyptian earth, from which sprouted the plants drawn on the columns, which were themselves towering shoots of papyrus. And the god who protected this land from ruin and enemies manifested himself in the Holy of Holies.'

Making a show of great earnestness, Mahmoud repeated, 'Marvellous! Marvellous!'

He managed to disconcert me too, and I mumbled, 'That's what they believed, Mahmoud.'

There was a moment of silence and then Wasfi asked me, 'I've read that in the later periods they used to worship Amun in Siwa as the god of the setting sun. I know they saw him as being one with the god Ra, god of the sun, but why did they worship him here as the setting sun?'

I said, 'You're right. I read that too and I've thought about it. You know, Captain Wasfi, that the sun, or the western horizon, was the kingdom of Osiris to the Egyptians, the kingdom of the dead and the land of judgement, which the Egyptians thought was located somewhere in the Western Desert. Maybe they considered Siwa, being the westernmost place in Egypt, to be also the last stopping place of the sun before it left this world.'

Mahmoud let out a sudden laugh and said, 'So here Amun became a god of death too!'

'And of eternity as well!' said Wasfi in a voice loud with excitement.

Then he added, in his usual refined tone, 'Eternity, Your Excellency! The western horizon is the world of eternity.'

Mahmoud continued to stare at him, trying to hide his irritation. Then he asked him why he was so interested in these historical excavations when he was a police officer of recognized competence. Couldn't he have found a better hobby or pastime?

Wasfi replied, 'This is no mere pastime, Your Excellency. I am trying to get to know the history of my country and my forefathers. I study their remains and their greatness, which dazzles the world, so that we may learn from them. If I could have my way, I would make teaching the history of Ancient Egypt and its antiquities compulsory in the schools from an early age. They would learn how strong the state was and how well organized the government and that we must become strong like them in order to regain the same glory—'

Mahmoud interrupted him to say, 'But you know that since the occupation the history studied in our schools is that of England only. Egyptian history is banned in our schools now, though of course we could always teach our children the

234

importance of order and strength from the history of England too.'

Wasfi puckered his brow, having decided that Mahmoud was mocking him. He said, 'I think, Your Excellency, that they have banned the teaching of Egyptian history so as to spare the students study of the period of civil conflict and treachery, and thus the pollution of their minds.'

'What treachery are you referring to, Captain?'

'That of Urabi and his fellow mutineers, of course.'

Fiona said, 'Do you mean Urabi Basha, Captain Niyazi?'

'You know of him?' asked Wasfi in astonishment.

'I was young at the time of the revolution,' she replied, 'but my father, like many Irish of his time, considered Urabi Basha a hero for resisting the British occupation of his country. His picture hung in his study and it remained there for a long time.'

Wasfi said, 'Then he didn't know, and you of course didn't either, that Urabi betrayed his sovereign the Khedive and spread anarchy through the country. Fortunately, however, his rebellion ended in crushing defeat.'

Trying to hide her anger, Fiona frowned and said, 'The uprisings of many of our leaders in Ireland against the British ended in defeat but we still consider them heroes. At least they tried.'

'But Urabi . . .'

Exasperated, and her pale face flushed with anger, Fiona said, 'Why don't we change the subject?'

Then she immediately apologized with an artificial smile by saying, 'Politics always causes rifts. Maybe it's better to talk about antiquities.'

Thank you, Fiona, I said to myself. I had no idea myself how to put an end to this difficult conversation.

And I'd invited Wasfi precisely to talk about antiquities. I didn't join you in the attack on him, even though he deserved more than just reproach. He was virtually defending Britain's occupation of his country! What a disgrace!

It made more sense now, though, to keep my mouth shut, because I needed him. Not to mention that I was watching Mahmoud and expecting him to get angry and lash out at Wasfi – but he didn't open his mouth! Though what's surprising about that? When have I ever succeeded in understanding Mahmoud's conduct? He remained silent and stared at Fiona during her brief flare-up as though seeing her for the first time. However that may be, I must improvise something now to banish this heavy silence. And I have to make everyone happy.

I gave a broad smile and spoke with a show of enthusiasm. 'Really, Fiona's suggestion is much better. Let's leave politics and go back to antiquities. I want to ask Captain Wasfi if he's interested in the Greek antiquities in Egypt too. Does he consider them Egyptian antiquities, and does he also consider Alexander and the Ptolemies Egyptians?'

Unexpectedly Mahmoud finally now spoke. 'And do you consider the British who are occupying your country Irish because successive generations of them have lived there?'

I raised my forefinger in Mahmoud's face and said, jokingly, 'Don't drag us back to politics. We've agreed that we've finished with that subject, and the comparison isn't very exact.'

Then I addressed myself to Wasfi. 'But last time you were trying to say something about the temple of Bilad al-Roum. What exactly have you read about it? I'd be most interested to know.'

Wasfi made an attempt to master his chagrin and speak normally. 'You must have read about it as I have. It was probably a Greek or Roman temple, because they called it the "Doric Temple". It's clear that its columns were of the Greek Doric order and not of the Egyptian.'

'Unfortunately we can't be sure,' I said, 'because it's been completely destroyed.'

'You're right,' said Wasfi, 'but I read too that there are caves carved out of the rock in the neighbouring area. All of them have been robbed and there are no carvings to be seen, but they were probably Greek or Roman tombs.'

I thought for a moment, then asked him, 'Do you intend to visit the temple, Captain Wasfi? Khameesa isn't far away and it's rich in antiquities not to be found elsewhere. If you're thinking of visiting it, I could go with you.'

With a certain hesitancy, he replied, 'If His Excellency permits.'

Mahmoud, who had bowed his head and was paying no attention to our conversation, said, 'On your leave day you are free, Captain, to go where you wish. But you, Catherine ... Would you take Fiona with you on such a trip?'

I responded, quickly, 'I mean after things have improved. Soon, of course, when the weather is better.'

Fiona paid attention when he mentioned her name and said, addressing me, 'Of course, Catherine. I have to go with you on a visit to the lake. Perhaps we'll discover something under the water there!'

We laughed out of mere politeness. The party had come to an end and the evening died the moment talk of politics had begun and I hadn't succeeded in reviving it. On the contrary, Mahmoud had succeeded in embarrassing me, so I kept quiet. Wasfi seized on the moment of silence that followed to gather his books and put them in his bag, after leaving the journal on the table and thanking me for the tea, of which he hadn't drunk two sips.

He got ready to depart, so Fiona, seated, extended her hand to shake his and said, 'Try to visit us from time to time, Captain Wasfi.'

That would give him great pleasure and he hoped that the new medicines would help her to get better quickly. I walked a few steps with him, thanking him for the visit, and Mahmoud accompanied him to the door. I heard Wasfi say, 'I'll give orders for them to have the white stallion ready for Your Excellency. I know you like him.'

At the door, however, Mahmoud said suddenly, 'I'll go back to the station with you.'

He waved goodbye as he left without looking in our direction and the moment they'd gone out Fiona stood up and said, picking up the parcel, 'I'm going upstairs to rest a little. Perhaps we can begin trying the sheikh's medicines tonight.'

I followed her with my eyes as she walked slowly towards the small staircase and painstakingly mounted its steps.

If only you knew how much I hope this treatment helps, even if I'm not convinced by it. I too, though, like you, dream of a miracle of any kind. You performed a real miracle yourself when you wrested the chagrin and anger from the sheikh's heart and made him send you these things, so complete the miracle and let yourself live . . . and let Mahmoud live too!

Yes, Mahmoud loves you, there can be no doubt. How long have I known that? Perhaps from the first instant, when he stood at the door, taken aback and disconcerted at the sight of you. And I feel it now, when he tries to keep his eyes off you. Sane or insane, he's not a good actor. They're the same gestures and facial expressions that I saw at the beginning of our relationship, when he was trying to escape from love by retreating into himself and by silence, by avoiding confrontation and by depression. This time, though, I think his confusion is greater and his sorrow deeper. He knows, of course, that winning you is less likely, and I know his love for you and I'm not angry. I don't feel even the natural jealousy of an abandoned spouse. I tell myself, it's fair! It's the necessary retribution. I stole Michael from you, so if you now perform the miracle of getting better, I shall give him to you, or give you to him. But will you accept? Do you love him in return? I haven't seen any love for him in your eyes. I mean, that kind of love. Or perhaps the saint would consider such a belated exchange of men a sin? If that's the case, then it doesn't matter, Fiona. Perform the miracle of getting better, and then leave him to me, by which I mean leave him to himself, for we haven't been lovers since we came to this oasis, and we haven't been spouses since Maleeka's blood came between us. He no longer touches me and I too no longer want him to touch me.

How did it all happen? If I could talk to an innocent young lady like yourself about things of that sort, I'd ask you. In fact, though, I have no one but myself to depend on. I have to look more deeply inside myself to find out what happened. Or rather, I have to forget it all and leave it behind me. I have to resume my work and my search. That alone is the way out that will bring back the true Catherine.

I was leafing through the journal that Wasfi left without concentrating when I was surprised by Mahmoud's familiar knocks, followed by his opening the door and rushing in.

He took in the room with a quick look and then came and sat down next to me.

I asked him, 'Are you going to rest a little before going out on patrol?'

He laid his arms on the table and put his head between his hands, saying, 'No. I'm not going out tonight. I postponed the patrol until tomorrow. I felt tired.'

I smiled to myself. I know that tiredness, Mahmoud! I know it very well!

16

Mahmoud

Light white clouds that herald no rain but veil the sun and the heat.

From the window of my office I watched them gathering and then moving apart in widening circles. It would be a hard day for Fiona and Catherine. She's unlucky, Fiona. Our main problem here is the killing heat, but she has come at a time when at night we search for the slightest warmth. I hope Sheikh Yahya's medicines do her some good. Yesterday I saw the worry in Catherine's eyes as she looked covertly at her sister. Fiona was indeed as pale as death. No, don't think of death! Didn't she get excited and redden as she answered Wasfi when he described the revolutionaries as traitors? No, her health will surely return with these medicines, and the sparkle will return to her eyes as she tells her Irish tales in the evenings, and that pure gaze of hers that pierces the soul will remain.

Enough!

I rose and went to the window and looked out over the forecourt of the station. Haven't you had enough yet, my dear captain, of the marching, running and jumping exercises that you've been at with the soldiers since sunrise? The poor wretches are perfectly ready now to do battle with any army, but to what purpose? At the moment of danger, nothing can save you from the shell of a cannon (so long as it fires!). Maybe I'll test your courage by sending you on patrol with them into the desert to look for the Bedouin. Flattery won't help you then the way it does with the *agwad*. Either you chase them away or they make you their prey!

You didn't bat an eyelid when Fiona said that defeat didn't strip revolutionaries of their heroism. You fell silent out of good manners because you were my guest, but I saw the chagrin in your eyes. And who precisely are those Egyptian 'forefathers' of yours whose antiquities you're studying, my dear blond Circassian captain?

During the revolution I met a few good Circassians who loved Egypt as their homeland. Most, though, considered themselves the masters, and they conspired more than once to kill Urabi, the 'peasant', and were happy to see him defeated, just as you were. How then do the antiquities of the ancestors of these peasants, whose glory you want to restore, concern you?

Perhaps you're thinking specifically of the pharaohs! Perhaps you see them as your forebears for being masters who ruled over Egyptian slaves. You too were masters clinging to the skirts of the Turkish masters, and when the slaves rose up against you, you went for help against them to other, British, masters, and you beat them and then became masters too. And me? What did I consider the revolutionaries to be? At the investigation I said they were 'miscreants', so what difference is there between you and me?

How I hate myself!

I was still sitting at my desk when I heard a sudden row in the courtyard, and the strident voice of Wasfi as he issued his training orders ceased. I got up again and looked through the window and saw the soldiers standing at ease while Corporal Salmawi spoke to Wasfi, who was absorbed in reading something. Then he turned and gave an order to two of the soldiers, who set off at a run in the direction of the station while he hurried towards the stairway.

He burst into my office, Sergeant Ibraheem behind him, but Wasfi turned to the latter and said in commanding tones, 'Go out and lock the door behind you. I wish to be alone with His Excellency, so let no one in.'

Ibraheem executed the order, his face filled with astonishment and displeasure, while I tried to look calm as I asked him, 'What's happened, Captain?'

Not forgetting to deliver a salute, he handed me a folded piece of paper, saying, 'Thank God Your Excellency didn't go out on patrol yesterday. A boy threw this piece of paper tied to a stone into the courtyard of the station, then ran off. Corporal Wahba el Salmawi saw him and tried to run after him but the boy was too fast. I have sent two soldiers to try to catch and arrest him.'

I opened the paper, which contained two lines of writing in large sloping letters: 'The district commissioner should not go out alone on night patrol these days. People are waiting to kill him.'

I looked at the piece of paper. How easy it would be to find out who wrote it. The number of those who know how to write here can be counted on the fingers of one hand. But why send this warning? Who in this oasis would not be happy to get rid of me, and fast?

I refolded the paper, placed it on the desk and looked at Wasfi in silence. Rigidly at attention as usual, he asked me, 'What is the meaning of this threat, Your Excellency? I hope that the soldiers will come across the boy who threw the stone and we can interrogate him. Does Your Excellency suspect anyone, so that we can arrest him right away?'

I answered with a smile, 'Can we arrest everyone in the oasis?'

Confused, he responded, 'Of course not. But maybe we could ask Sheikh Sabir to ...'

I interrupted him to ask, 'Wasfi, do you really not know the meaning of this threat? Have you not heard till now from Sheikh Sabir or any other of the *agwad* what happened here before your arrival?'

The confusion was written clearly on his face when he said, 'Your Excellency, I want ...'

'You want to help. Thank you, but there's no need to send soldiers either. They'll never find the boy and they won't be able to identify him because they didn't see him. You may leave now, Captain, and resume your training of the troops. The training will be of use if the local people think of making another attack on the station.'

Wasfi went out and I heard Sergeant Ibraheem's familiar knock at the door.

As he entered, extreme agitation on his face, he said, 'Forgive me, Your Excellency, but what's happened?'

I looked at his face for a moment, his anxiety increasing by the minute until his body started shaking. Since he had been saved from death the lines on his faces had increased and his true age become clear, but he interrupted my silence by saying, at the end of his tether, 'Tell me, God reward Your Excellency, what has happened. I think of you – no disrespect intended – like a son, as God is my witness.'

'I know that, Sergeant Ibraheem, without your having to tell me. You too have a special place in my heart. The whole business is . . .'

Then I decided I couldn't care a damn so I told him everything that had happened, and his face creased and he said in sorrowful tones, 'Do you remember what I told Your Excellency the other day? They never forget. Be on the lookout . . .'

He paused suddenly, then continued in a rush, 'And be on the lookout too for that captain!'

'Why do you say that? What do you know about him?'

'I don't know anything but all the soldiers complain about him. He isn't a decent man like Your Excellency. And I'm frightened by his eyes, which are like a cat's.'

To reassure him I said calmly, 'Fear nothing, Sergeant Ibraheem. You may go now.' He gave the military salute that he so often forgot but paused again before going out and said, wagging his finger, 'But you should have no doubts about Corporal Wahba Salmawi. He's a good man and I've known him for a long time.'

'Thank you. You're dismissed now, Ibraheem.'

After he had left, I tried to distract myself by writing replies to the latest correspondence from the ministry so that I could send them with the next caravan, but it didn't work. I couldn't concentrate on anything.

The letter doesn't bother me and the threat has been there since I came. I almost see it as overdue! Better the event than the wait, as we say. If they'd ever wanted to carry it out, nothing could have stopped them. So they too are settling their scores, after the two periods of calm that we've experienced – the first after my supposed heroism in saving their son, and this, which we're still living through, after the firing of the cannon. The disasters that they attributed to Maleeka have stopped happening, though the threat of disasters from Catherine has not. Now she wants to go out again, to Khameesa, and to drag Fiona with her into yet another adventure! I will never permit it. Her nasty surprises never cease; why did I involve myself with her in the first place? And did I get involved with her or did she get involved with me? It doesn't matter. During our first nights together, she reminded me of Ni'ma so I was satisfied with what I had before me. I shall never find Ni'ma again, so I ought to take care to keep Catherine, but since we got to this oasis something has been broken, I don't know what. The daytime of our relationship has reached a sunset at this last stopping place on the western horizon, as Catherine described the place. Our marriage crumbled into sand and then Maleeka's storm wiped it out completely.

Why did Fiona come here at this time?

No. Let me think of something else. To work! But my mind isn't in a mood to calculate the figures and write the reports to the ministry. Why not write a letter to Brigadier General Saeed? From time to time he too writes me letters full of brotherly greetings. I cudgel my brain to read between the lines in them news of the Protected City or even of the ministry but find nothing. It is this caution that he has used to keep himself safe through the vagaries of the times without losing his integrity. Why wasn't I like him? I took out his last letter and read it again:

Your Excellency my dear brother Mahmoud Effendi Abd el Zahir. The expressions of brotherly love now in full measure attached, and the yearnings of which the Creator, glory be to Him and exaltation, alone is aware dispatched, should I attempt an exposition of all that the heart contains, such an exposition for ever would extend, and never reach its end. God willing, you are all, with His help and favour, in the best of health and on the topmost rungs of enjoyment . . .

'The topmost rungs of enjoyment!' How can I reply to this good-hearted man without lying?

It was no use. I got up and started as usual moving about the spacious office. That too was no use.

Whatever I think about, she comes back to me. What am I to do? Catherine says that her father always used to call her the Saint. Why did this sick saint come here to add more agony to my soul's agony? It's not her saintliness or her goodness of heart which have captured me. My interest in such things is feeble; the period when I used to attend the meetings of the Masons spoiled me. I didn't lose my faith entirely, but I became used thereafter to not giving much thought to what was 'forbidden' and 'permitted'. I abandoned Masonry after reading Afghani's attack on it and his renunciation of it. I hated it too when I saw the European Masons supporting the British in Egypt. Despite this, I retained faith in the mind and in logic above all, and a little of the old faith too has survived. I experience true repentance every year in the month of Ramadan. I don't go near alcohol or women, I perform both the obligatory and the supererogatory prayers, and I read the Koran. At the end of the fasting month, though, I go back to being exactly the way I was. And from time to time, when my spirit is disturbed, I find comfort in prayer, so I pray a lot. Catherine knows nothing of all that. She takes me as she finds me, or perhaps more accurately, she doesn't care. But what about her? It seems to me all she knows about her religion is the silver cross that she sometimes hangs on her chest, saying, 'I inherited it from my grandmother.' And Fiona? In her evening tales there are no lessons or morals and I haven't heard her saying prayers under her breath. She just tells beautiful stories. In fact, she . . .

Enough!

A knock on the door. I gave thanks for it, whatever it might bring! As though calling for help, I shouted at the top of my voice, 'Come in!'

Sergeant Ibraheem opened the door and said that Corporal el Salmawi was asking to see me. I gave him permission to enter, and the sergeant opened the door and called to him. When the corporal entered, his huge body filled the doorway, so he moved to the side a little to let Ibraheem out. I didn't know why he had come. I myself wanted to hear from him in detail what had happened when he went with Catherine and Fiona to meet Sheikh Yahya, but I thought of what Ibraheem had said and asked him whether he had known the sergeant in the oasis when he came with the army. He replied that he had known Ibraheem but only a long while after that, when they had fought together in Urabi's army at Kafr el Dawwar.

I thought of the Bedouin of Alexandria and asked him with some astonishment, 'You fought with him in Urabi's army?'

'Indeed, Your Excellency. We fought together, and he's a courageous soldier. He risked his life once to save me from death in battle. I was coming out of the trench when firing started, and he jumped out and pulled me back with him.'

He fell silent for a moment. I said, 'It seems saving people's lives is a hobby with Sergeant Ibraheem.'

He understood nothing and remained silent, so I went on, 'But they dismissed you from the army after the war, as they did Ibraheem and the rest of the troops, isn't that so?'

'They did. But then later they needed me in the police in Marsa Matrouh. They don't have many trained troops there.'

'And why have you come now, Corporal?'

He said he'd been going to ask to see me before but the business with the boy who'd thrown the stone had delayed him. They'd searched for him and found no trace. Now, though, he wanted to inform me that Sheikh Yahya had sent him a letter with one of his grandsons asking to see me as soon as possible.

After a moment's silence, I said, 'That's strange, but he can come and see me here whenever he wants.'

'How can that be, Your Excellency? He has vowed not to leave his garden until he dies.'

'So I'm being asked to go to him?'

'It's up to Your Excellency, but if you wish to go, allow me to go with you.'

'You'll have to, because I don't know the way.'

On our way to Sheikh Yahya's garden, I wanted to pass by the house to let Catherine know, and to find out whether Fiona had started to try the treatment. When I got down from my horse, however, one of the soldiers of the guard that I'd put in front of the house stopped me, saying, 'There's a woman from the oasis inside.'

I exclaimed, 'Another woman from the oasis in my house? What disasters will this one cause?' I sprang towards the steps, but Salmawi stopped me with a gesture from the first step, saying imploringly, 'Wait a moment, Your Excellency, till we find out from the guard what happened. As Your Excellency put it, there's no call for more disasters.'

The guard was eager to tell what he knew. He'd seen a woman going up to the house walking very slowly and supporting herself on the shoulder of a boy. From the way she walked it looked as though she was a very old woman, and he'd become sure of that when she came close and he saw a part of her face that was uncovered. She wanted to climb the stairs but he prevented her, at which she addressed him in speech that contained words of Arabic and words in the language of the place, which he had difficulty in understanding. She knew the madame and wanted to see her.

Salmawi asked him, 'Did she say her name was Zubeida?'

'Yes, Corporal,' answered the soldier. I looked at Salmawi enquiringly and he said, 'I know her, Your Excellency, that old woman who speaks a bit of Arabic. She was with us in the caravan and Miss Fiona took a liking to her. She wanted to buy her *tarfottet* mantle, but she gave it to her as a present.'

The soldier continued, 'All the same, I didn't let her go up, Excellency, but sent the boy, and he knocked on the door and gave them the message. The younger lady came to the door and waved to Zubeida to go up and she hugged her at the door. Then they went inside together.'

The guard finished his story in the same state of excitement with which he'd begun and pointed to the boy, who was sitting on the sand and watching us from a distance. As though to defend himself, he said, 'That's the boy who came with her. He'll tell Your Excellency how I tried to stop her.'

I wanted to go on up the steps, but Salmawi approached me and whispered in my ear, 'Even if she is an old woman, Excellency, a woman a hundred years old, no man can enter the house so long as she's inside.'

Pointing to the cloak thrown down on the stairs, he went on, 'So long as she's left her cloak in front of the door, men aren't allowed in. It's their custom, and the boy sitting there will tell if you go in. Now we can rest assured that the old woman won't harm anyone, so let's continue our errand, Excellency.'

I hesitated for a moment, then remounted, as did Salmawi. He was the one who was giving the orders now, and I was following them. No matter. I would heed Ibraheem's advice and trust him until I had put him to the test. We set off in the direction of Aghurmi. After crossing the patch of open desert in front of the town, we proceeded along the road that goes through the walled gardens. At the sound of the horses' hoofs, the singing inside would stop, and a few *zaggala* would appear at the entrances to the gardens. I made up my mind not to pay them any attention after the looks of hate and murmurs whose meaning was not hard to grasp from the first garden we passed. Some of them greeted Salmawi warmly, repeating his name so I would understand that their greetings did not include me.

I had been riding ahead of Salmawi on the road but he drew alongside me as we were crossing a small water channel, and I asked him, 'Salmawi, do you know why the sheikh wants to see me?'

'All I know is what I told Your Excellency. Maybe he wants to talk to you about the condition of Miss . . .'

His deep voice trembled suddenly, making me think that he was on the verge of tears.

Pulling up my horse, I asked him, in amazement, 'What's going on, Corporal?'

He bowed his head and said, controlling himself, 'Forgive me, Excellency. I was just thinking. Sheikh Yahya only saw the young lady once, and when he was angry then at . . . And all the same, he loved her and thought to send her the medicines. If Your Excellency had seen how she was in the caravan! She would talk with the troops and the Siwan women and the Bedouin women and their children, God knows in what language. She didn't speak their language and they didn't understand hers but all the same they talked to one another in words, signs and laughter throughout the trip. When she got one of her coughing fits, some of the women would weep to see her going off far away on her own.'

249

I spurred my horse and shot forwards, Salmawi following me. Enough! Enough! Enough! The horse was galloping and I was looking straight ahead, paying no attention to the insults of the *zaggala* or to the fact that we were passing Gouba Spring, and I realized that we had passed it only when I saw the columns of the temple of Umm Ebeida. All the disasters had started here!

I was making straight for the temple at a fast pace but my guide called out to me from behind as he tried to catch up, 'Wait, Excellency! Where are you going? It's this way.'

He pointed to a narrow path that turned off to the left, so I returned and followed him.

Eventually we found ourselves at the door to the sheikh's garden. A small garden compared to those we had passed; from the surrounding wall I calculated that it couldn't be more than half a feddan. Salmawi clapped his hands and called out a few phrases and a boy appeared, who kept his gaze fixed on me while Salmawi spoke to him. The boy said nothing but disappeared and after a little returned and gestured to us to follow him.

At the entrance to the garden were many palms, as usual, and some fruit trees, which had not yet borne fruit. Behind these was a jungle of olives. Scents, most of which I could not distinguish, reached my nose. A few moments after passing through the door, the boy pointed out to us reed mats on the ground on which cushions had been arranged in the shade of jostling palms. I sat and Salmawi remained standing, and when I gestured to him to sit, he continued to remain at a distance, squatting on the ground as though he might get up at any moment. And indeed, he did leap up to receive the sheikh, and I stood too.

Sheikh Yahya walked towards us slowly, leaning on his stick, and Salmawi went up to him, shaking his hand and saying, 'Peace be upon you, Master,' and tried to kiss his hand, but the sheikh pulled it quickly away.

I too went forwards and shook his hand, and he kept mine in his for a moment while observing me from behind his glasses with a searching look. Then he said, 'Sit down.'

I had seen him before, with a delegation of *agwad* on my arrival, then many times at Friday prayer, where his glasses had caught my attention, though I couldn't recall that I'd spoken with him. It seemed to me that he'd aged since the last time I saw him at the mosque. In any case, he was certainly over eighty.

Salmawi took his arm and helped him to sit on one of the cushions, and the sheikh leant his back against a palm tree and said with a smile, 'Thank you, Salmawi. You could see that I need help.'

The corporal replied, 'On the contrary, it is we who need your help, Master.'

Addressing him with some acerbity, the sheikh asked, 'What's all this "Master" nonsense, Salmawi? I'm not one of God's Chosen Friends. Enough of such talk.'

The sheikh turned his gaze to me where I sat opposite him and directed his words to me. 'The message was delayed in getting to you, Mr Commissioner. Thank God you didn't go out on patrol yesterday.'

Salmawi, who had once more squatted down between me and the sheikh, said, 'I swear I knew in my heart it was you who sent the message, Master. But how did you learn of the plot they'd hatched?'

The sheikh muttered, 'Master! Master!' and I looked at Salmawi and gestured a warning at him, so he got up of his own accord and sat down far enough away for him not to be able to hear our conversation.

Once Salmawi had moved away, the sheikh turned to me and said, 'Nothing's a secret in this town. Have you seen the boys who go around everywhere, moving among the houses and the gardens? No one pays any attention to them but they know everything, great and small, and they pass on the most important news.'

Then, after a moment's silence, he addressed me with a line of verse:

> He who does good, ne'er are his rewards expunged.
> God's pact with Man is never broken.

'You saved a boy called, like you, Mahmoud, so he in turn wanted to save you. It was he who brought me yesterday the information that you were intending to go out on patrol, and it was from him too that I learnt they were lying in wait for you.'

'Who are they?'

The sheikh shook his head, saying, 'That is something I will not tell, Mr Commissioner. I do not betray my people or inform on them. It is enough that you should take your precautions.'

He seemed distracted for a moment. Then he said, 'And you must give me an undertaking too that you will not look for the boy Mahmoud or try to interrogate him.'

'Rest assured, Sheikh Yahya,' I said. 'I promise you I will neither look for him nor interrogate him. I thank you both for thinking of saving me.'

'Don't thank me but be on your guard,' he replied. 'That will save you and us more blood.'

Without meaning to I blurted out, 'I'm not afraid of death!'

He responded quietly, 'Indeed, you long for it.'

'Do you know men's thoughts too?' I asked.

'Only the devils eavesdrop on those, Mr Commissioner, and I am not, thank God, one of them. But why did you announce in the courtyard of the police station for all to hear that you were going out on patrol at night? It had been your habit earlier to ride out into the desert, sometimes alone, sometimes with your troops, and your patrols have kept thieves from the oasis. But you used not to tell anyone. So why did you do so yesterday when you knew your life was in danger? I cannot read what is in men's minds, for only God, most glorious, knows that, Mr Commissioner, but I can read what you do and what you say.'

Having said this, he occupied himself with fixing firmly in place the string that tied his glasses to his ear. Then he fell silent.

After a while, I said, 'So be it. But you too, two days ago, refused to meet my wife and her sister and said of me things that were repeated to me. I know too that, like all the people of the oasis, you do not love me. So what made you suddenly concerned for my life, after the firing of the cannon and after what happened to Maleeka?'

His face flushed with sudden anger as he said, 'Why do you not stay silent? Why open that subject? Maleeka wasn't just my niece; she was dearer to me than the most precious of my daughters!'

Like one stung, I shouted, 'Your niece? I didn't even know she was your relative. No one told me.'

'Now you know, and what difference does it make?' said Sheikh Yahya. 'What did you expect me to do when I saw your wife and she reminded me of everything that happened to Maleeka because of her and you? You killed her.'

To defend myself, I said, 'It was she who went out as a ghoul-woman and stirred up terror in the oasis.'

'It wasn't the first time she'd been out. Ever since she was small, she'd been used to disguising herself in boys' clothing and going out and no one would recognize her, but you tore off her the robe with which she'd disguised herself and threw it into the public highway, causing a scandal. Then what happened in the oasis happened. And that wasn't enough for you, Mr Commissioner. You went and asked that revenge be taken on her. Revenge for what? Did she kill your wife?'

With real sorrow, I said, 'When I went into the house I saw my wife defending herself and I saw that her dress was torn. I truly believed that she wanted to kill her.'

'Stupidity! Why should she want to kill her? The last thing she said, as I heard, was that she was looking for friendship with someone who wasn't one of the people of the oasis, who hated her and whom she hated. She went to your house looking for affection and you met her with hatred and then killed her.'

'Did she not kill herself, Sheikh Yahya?'

He straightened his back a little and said in a voice that trembled with anger, 'Maleeka did not kill herself! Why should she kill herself when she loved the world so much? She ... she found beauty in everything, in plants and in the mounds of the temples, and thanks to her I came to love those antiquities that people fear. Maleeka ...'

I asked him insistently, to bring him back to the subject, 'So they killed her?'

'Who will say? Who will confess that he buried the knife in her heart? All of them, all of you, took part. Even the ancestors who invented the story of the ghoul-woman ...'

The sheikh fell silent suddenly, relaxing his posture once more and looking as though he was making an effort to control his anger. He bowed his head and a cloud of sorrow seemed to pass over his face. Then he said, after a long time, in a low voice, 'Sometimes, in the middle of the garden, I find a beautiful flower or plant whose seed I haven't sown and the like of which I've never seen before. I tend it and keep away the harmful weeds and other plants. I water it more carefully than the other plants but after a while it shrivels up. I fail to either keep it alive or nurture new shoots from it. I wanted Maleeka to live but she was lost.'

I put into words something that had been going through my mind all this while: 'But Sheikh Yahya, that would be an even stronger reason for you to have let them kill me yesterday!'

He raised his head and said in an exhausted voice, 'Had I not learnt long ago to hate blood and killing. But I am a human being, Mr Commissioner. Never, from my earliest years, have I learnt to master my temper, though I do try to keep it in check. I have learnt, if I become angry, to regret and repent. I now ask you and your wife to forgive me. Maleeka loved you and for her sake . . .'

He fell silent, a catch in his voice. Then I said, 'Should it be we who forgive or you, Sheikh Yahya? If you knew how much regret I too feel at what happened to your niece!'

'But regret on its own is not enough. What matters is repentance.'

'How can there be repentance now, when what has happened has happened? She's dead, and that's the end of it.'

He looked into my face for a while and said, 'If a person doesn't forgive himself, how can he ask others to forgive him?'

Then he gestured with his hand and said, 'But that's not what I invited you for, Mr Commissioner; rather I wanted to talk to you about your wife's sister.'

My heart leapt and I hoped that nothing would appear in my face to expose me before this sheikh whose dim eyes could read what was in my soul.

'She is a good and courageous woman,' he said. 'But I saw her face at close hand two days ago and I heard her cough.'

Then he became distracted again, as though he were thinking of something else, and he said with some astonishment, 'I've known during my life the like of her in every religion, sect and race. Few are born with the God-given gift of tolerance and purity of soul. It is a gift from the Giver for which they can take no credit. They are few because He, glory be to Him, has not wished that we be angels. He has known that we are mutinous and sinful and must repent and struggle every day so as to reach purity of soul through our own actions and efforts.'

He fell silent once more, so I said, to encourage him, 'You were speaking, Sheikh Yahya, of her cough. What did you want to say?'

Without looking at my face, he said, 'I would wish to say nothing, but I am afraid, my son – and I pray God that I am mistaken – that hers is that sickness for which no one knows a cure.'

In panic, I exclaimed, 'No! The doctors in her country didn't tell her that! They said she needed a dry climate.'

'I hope that may be so. I said, I hope I am mistaken, but I wanted to alert you so that you and her sister may consider well what has to be done. It may be that her condition is indeed due to a build-up of extreme humidity in the chest, and a delay in treatment.'

I muttered in confusion, 'And those medicines that you sent her yesterday. Won't they dry out the water in her chest and cure this humidity?'

'God alone heals, Mr Commissioner.'

'Of course, but . . . will these medicines cure her?'

He gave a weak smile that multiplied the wrinkles on his face as he addressed me, saying, 'Did you listen well to what I told you, Mr Commissioner?'

I didn't grasp what he meant immediately, and he continued, looking into my face, 'Anyway, what I sent you is what I had ready. God may guide me to other things. If her condition is humidity in the chest, though, the best thing would be for her to bury herself in hot sand. But it's winter now.'

He paused for a moment, then continued, 'I used to know how to administer that treatment but I don't leave this place, and no man can treat a woman by this method. Today I sent her a woman who knows the treatment.'

'Zubeida?'

He nodded and said with some sadness, 'However, as I said, it only works when the sand is as hot as fire and we're now in the cold of winter . . .'

I clutched at this hope. 'Warm days come – in fact, sometimes there are even hot days – in winter.'

'True, but the heat has to remain for days and weeks on end, so that the warmth can penetrate deep into the sand.'

'Let us pray that the hot weather comes.'

Smiling again, he said, 'Would that our prayers to the Omnipotent were a little more ambitious.'

I bowed my head in thought. So, in the space of a day and a night, this sheikh had sent medicines for Fiona, sent a message warning me about the killers, sent this woman Zubeida, forgiven me and Catherine, and asked us to forgive him! What is this? Is he too a saint . . . I mean, is he a 'Friend of God', even though he denied that? If that were true, then the friend of God is bound to succeed in curing the saint. But he spoke of 'that sickness for which no one knows a cure'. At one sitting, he gives me life through hope and then kills me with despair!

I became aware that the sheikh was addressing me and saying, 'I pray that God may decree a cure for her, and I shall pray often for you, that you make peace with yourself.'

'What do you mean, make peace with myself?'

As though he hadn't heard me, he went on, 'And that you make peace with the people, Mr Commissioner. I know that won't happen from one day to the next. I know that it may take a whole lifetime.'

Then, as though remembering something, he said, 'It would be better if you don't tell what you have just heard to your wife and her sister, unless you've decided to send her away from here to look for a cure elsewhere.'

'Where? She tried the doctors in her own country and they sent her here.'

'Then say nothing. Don't make her lose hope.'

As he said this he was pressing down with his hands on the ground in preparation for rising, so I stood up quickly and took hold of his hand to help him. Salmawi saw us, hurried over, grasped the sheikh by his forearms as though embracing him and held him thus until he had stood him on his feet.

257

'Thank you, Salmawi,' said Sheikh Yahya. 'Try to pass by tomorrow and I may be able to give you new medicines for the commissioner's house.'

He held out his hand and shook mine with a firm grip, despite his age, and then shook hands with Salmawi. Then he turned around, leaning on his stick, and disappeared among the trees of his garden.

On our way out, I asked Salmawi, 'Why did you address the sheikh as "Master", and why did that anger him?'

Salmawi answered excitedly, 'He's the best person I've met in this oasis, Excellency. Did Your Excellency note that he only saw the young lady for a few moments, yet he took an interest in her treatment and sent her the new medicines even though he was angry with . . .'

He fell silent, but I understood what he wanted to say.

On the way back, Salmawi said in his tremulous, rough voice that always made me think that he was on the verge of tears, 'The young lady too, Your Excellency. You didn't see how she was in the caravan. Everyone . . .'

I said sharply, 'You told me that before, Corporal. Don't talk about her as though she's going to die!'

Enough lamentation!

And I said to myself, 'Alas for me were she indeed to die!'

17

Catherine

Another cloudy morning.

There will be a little warmth for Fiona and much dejection in my heart, which I will have to subdue, though I can't read now in this weak light. If I want to help Fiona, I have to help myself. I have said before, I will not allow this oasis to defeat me. A time will come when I shall go out on my own, even if it costs me my life, just as Maleeka went out knowing she would pay the price. Whenever I try to put her out of my mind, something occurs to bring her back to me. If she doesn't pursue me in my dreams, something else happens. Everything that happens in the oasis reminds me of her, and Mahmoud won't let me forget. He took me by surprise when he told me she was a relative of Sheikh Yahya's and of the sheikh's love for her. He spoke as though he were attacking me as he passed on to me what the sheikh had said about Maleeka's coming to our house to seek our friendship, or perhaps just mine.

He wants me to feel ashamed of myself because I struck her and drove her away. I reminded him once more that it was he who made a spectacle of her and threw her out on to the public highway, so what fault was it of mine? He wasn't convinced. Even more, he wants me to recognize this sheikh as a saint and proclaim his virtue day and night because, despite what we did to his niece, he sends medicines and herbs to Fiona to help her.

What can I tell him? It's true that every now and then he sends herbs for Fiona to take, steeped in water or boiled in the morning or evening, and he sends oils of various colours for her to rub on her neck or chest, along with precise instructions. But what's the result of all that? Each time Fiona says that her health has improved thanks to the latest treatment she's tried, and that it needs time, that's all.

I, though, see no improvement from these primitive medicines. Her pallor and thinness increase day by day. The only thing that's changed is that the bouts of coughing come at less frequent intervals, though they are much more intense than before, as though all that these medicines do is to suppress the cough in the chest until the scattered crises are gathered into one violent crisis that makes her face turn blue and her eyes bulge, filling me with terror. She doesn't complain but I can see for myself. So what has this sheikh done that we have to thank him for?

At least he's trying, Catherine, as is this woman Zubeida. Their generosity does not, however, extend to me. The woman brought a present of dates and almonds for Fiona and I could, with difficulty, understand the few words of Arabic interspersed in her speech, but she had no difficulty communicating with my sister, who doesn't know Arabic, through signs and sounds. I was astonished to hear Fiona using, in her conversation with Zubeida, Siwan words and expressions that she'd learnt from her. I try to do as she does, for language is my field. I get close to them and listen to their conversation, but the crafty old woman rarely says anything to me directly. What hurts me more is that she avoids looking at me. Nevertheless, I have written down some of the words that I've been able to extract from their talk. I smiled when I thought of her first visit to us, when we looked at her in bewilderment as we tried to understand. She would cup her hands and move them as though using them to remove something while pointing to the ground and saying in Arabic, 'Go down! Go down!' It was only later, from Mahmoud, that we heard about the treatment by burial in hot sand. But still, the heat that killed us in the past few months now refuses to return.

Fiona greatly loves this brown old woman with her wrinkled face, who puts copious amounts of kohl around her narrow eyes. She seems happy to have her there whenever she talks to her. She astonished me when Zubeida first started coming to our house by taking hold of her hand and looking in wonder at the henna with which she stains her palms. Then she asked her in Siwan, *neesh*? ('and me?'). I was amazed that Fiona would be interested in such a thing in her deteriorating condition, but Zubeida understood and agreed immediately. The following day, it wasn't just Fiona's palms which were stained, she also tattooed with henna the back of her hands with spiral lines that looked like little branches with leaves and a small bird in the middle. Fiona was very proud as she spread out her hands with her broad smile to show the design to me and Mahmoud.

So long as it makes her happy!

So long as it makes them both happy for Zubeida to visit our house day after day! If one of her grandsons doesn't accompany her, she comes on her own, riding her donkey and always bringing gifts for Fiona. At the end of each visit, though, she points to the sky and the pallid sun and slaps palm against palm in a gesture of resignation. So we must wait for the heat, then.

Is Mahmoud up to the wait?

He too grows thinner by the day. He always used to have an appetite, he was virtually a glutton, but since Fiona's arrival he hasn't been able to finish his meals. I see him at table with his head bent so that he doesn't have to look at her face, but he swallows his food with difficulty, as though he has something in his throat. He has completely stopped drinking too – not even one glass in the evening as was his habit when things were going well for him. Is he seeking sainthood too? He has become calm and meek, which has relieved me of the madness of his changing moods. And in the last two days, I've noticed that his hand shakes. I understand and I wish I could tell him that you cannot escape loving her by running away from her face.

I cannot forget the night he entered the house more miserable and downcast than I had ever seen him, and looking as though he were about to cry. He took me aside and asked me, swallowing, if it wouldn't be preferable for us to send Fiona back to Alexandria or Cairo to seek better treatment. I understood immediately that it was another attempt to flee, by sending her far from his gaze. I said quietly that I agreed totally, but did he think that Fiona's condition permitted travel in a caravan and having to withstand the cold nights of the desert? It would be a death sentence. The question 'For whom?' escaped from him in a tremulous voice. I ignored the slip of the tongue and said, 'Let's wait till the weather improves.' I watched joy struggling with despair in his face as he said, with resignation, 'Let's wait.' At that moment I almost felt pity for him, as I do when he tosses and turns in bed, sleepless for most of the night and then pursued by nightmares from which he wakes in terror. Despite this, he's a complete stranger to me now, as though we had never been man and wife.

Fortunately, Fiona is not aware of any of this. In her innocence, she cannot imagine that her sister's husband could fall in love with her. Her imagination would be incapable of grasping the idea even if I were to tell her that what had been between Mahmoud and me was over. I'm just waiting for her to be cured, or for her condition to improve, and hoping that during this period I can get somewhere in my search. In any case, I shall leave with her. That is a final decision. I shall have done with everything concerning Mahmoud, Maleeka, this oasis, Egypt and its people. All that will be behind me soon.

I took advantage of a ray of sun that entered the main room and started reading what the historian Arrian wrote about the last days of Alexander; he, like me, was enthralled by Alexander. He isn't one of those who criticize him harshly for what he did during his wars. Rather, he sees the greatness in the Macedonian king's character. I changed my place every few minutes to catch the daylight that filtered in through the window. Then I heard Fiona's footsteps.

She stood at the entrance to the main room, wearing her winter clothes and with a woollen mantle over her shoulders. She looked a little rested this morning compared to yesterday. I think I did the right thing when I insisted on her moving to a room on the ground floor, with us. This had spared her the effort of climbing the stairs to the upper floor. She sat down next to me and pointed at the book, saying, 'Am I interrupting your work?'

I smiled and held it out to her, saying, 'It's a book I've read many times before. I almost know it by heart.' She took it and looked at the cover. 'Another book about Alexander? I read it too, in my father's library. I know you're interested in Alexander because of what happened to him in this oasis, but why all these books? What do you find so fascinating about him?'

'His tomb!'

Fiona laughed out loud. 'His tomb? I thought what interested you was his life, not his corpse! Besides, I've read a lot about him and I don't like what he did at all. He spilt a great deal of blood and destroyed many cities. What he did at Tyre on Mount Lebanon is a sufficient example. It made His High and Mightiness very annoyed that its people should resist his attack on the city and that he should be obliged to lay siege to it for a long time before he broke through its defences. So he killed thousands of its people, by slaughter and crucifixion.'

'I know that and all the rest, Fiona. But I was thinking before you came that he did great things as well as committing those massacres. He built new cities everywhere and tried after invading Asia to unite East and West.'

'Naturally! To unite them as slaves in his empire! Have you ever heard of an empire that didn't proclaim noble goals? Don't the British today say that the mission of their empire is to spread civilization and its benefits to the world? Just take a look at this civilization, steeped in blood from Egypt to India to I don't know where!'

I didn't want to get into an argument with her. Her mood always worsens when the conversation turns to something that reminds her of the British and their massacres in Ireland, and especially Connaught, our province, on which the British declared open war time and again.

'Anyway,' I said, 'I'm not interested in his empire or his wars, with which many historians have already busied themselves. I'm preoccupied with his tomb, as I told you. He asked to be buried here in Siwa but they buried him in Alexandria, so where is his tomb there?'

She replied with astonishment, 'Millions of tombs of the mighty and the poor alike have been destroyed and disappeared with the passing of the years, so what's strange about Alexander's grave being one of them?'

'The strange thing about it is that we've found many tombs and relics of ordinary Greeks in Alexandria but we haven't found a stone or any other trace giving the slightest indication of the whereabouts of the sepulchre of their king, the man who built the city, and whose sepulchre, or temple, the historians say was the heart of Alexandria, and which emperors, poets and many famous people visited when they went there out of simple curiosity, or to come into contact with his divine grace.'

Fiona knitted her brows and thought for a while. Then she said, 'You're right. I remember now that I once heard you discussing the matter with my father, and I think he supposed that the tomb must have sunk into the sea after the earthquake that struck the coast, isn't that so? But he didn't deny that Alexander was buried in Alexandria.'

'And nor do I, but I ask myself why every trace of him has disappeared there.'

I explained to Fiona my idea about the possibility of Alexander's body having been removed secretly from the city that he built to the oasis that he had wanted to be his last resting place.

Fiona recovered her smile and said, 'If you think they hid his grave here, then let him rest in peace, Catherine. There's no need for us to go digging him or his memory up. We have plenty of his like and inheritors of his mantle!'

I smiled too as I told her, 'You needn't worry at all. I'll never disturb his rest wherever he may be. I'm not mad and I'm not searching for his sepulchre or grave. That is a search that needs many men and a lot of money, which I don't have. All I'm looking for is evidence – no, even just a pointer. I'm thinking of a paper I might publish with some convincing evidence, so that others can go on with the work.'

'Maybe I didn't understand properly, Catherine. Did you say you're looking for evidence that would support your theory?'

'Yes.'

'How, then, did you reach your conclusion?'

'By intuition.'

'But they taught us at school not to reach a conclusion until we had evidence, and you're starting the other way round. You've imagined the conclusion and now you're looking for the evidence for it. Don't you find that strange?'

'No. Many discoveries have come about thanks to such craziness.'

'And much craziness has led to nothing but more craziness!'

She was laughing but stopped suddenly and said in a serious tone, 'Forgive me, Catherine. I was joking, of course. Pay no attention to what I say and go on with your work.'

'Of course I understand that you're joking and I'll never give up my work. I'll never ever give it up.'

Then, on a whim, I asked her suddenly, 'Tell me, though, why did you give up Michael?'

I regretted the words as soon as I'd said them but it was too late.

She was taken aback and looked at me for a while before saying, 'Why don't you let Michael lie in peace too? He's in a world where he's not bothered by the things that bother us.'

'Sorry. I didn't mean it.'

She was silent again, thinking. 'That business causes you a lot of disquiet, Catherine. You raised it with me before you got married and I answered you, so will it help you with anything now if I tell you, yes, I loved Michael? And of what use is this conversation now? Weren't we both there for him to choose from and didn't he choose you, and didn't I agree of my own free will? Why aren't you satisfied with that?'

I didn't answer, so she went on, 'But I will tell you that I was astonished when you agreed to marry Michael. Why did you agree when you didn't love him?'

'I don't know, but I paid the price.'

'And so did he.'

'He made my life hell. He never stopped quarrelling.'

'I witnessed one of those quarrels. He was criticizing your translation of the Greek in an article, I believe. He said there were mistakes in your translation, and you replied that he was jealous of you.'

'Indeed. He *was* jealous of me.'

'So let's forget all of that past, then. The important thing now is that you love Mahmoud, isn't it? Your long letters before and after you were married made me very happy. I gathered from them that you'd at last found a man you truly loved, as he did you. Was I wrong?'

'No.'

She looked me straight in the eye and asked calmly, 'Why aren't you happy, then, he and you?'

Her question took me by surprise and I mumbled, 'We aren't the way we used to be. Things happened in this oasis.'

'I hope you will be able to overcome them. I won't pry into your secrets but you both deserve to be happy.'

Overcome with emotion, I said, 'Teach me, Fiona, how I can find that happiness! All my life long I put my trust in work. I inherited that from my father, I suppose, just as you inherited from my mother that ... calm and tranquillity. My father used to encourage me always to persist. He taught me that my goal should always be work – to learn a new language or write an article or perhaps one day write a book. I did as he told me, but where's the happiness and peace of mind?'

'You're much cleverer than I am, Catherine, so how can you ask me for advice? When I was young I always used to feel jealous of you every time you learnt a new language or read me a translation or a study you'd made. Then later on I became proud of you. I would feel as though I too had achieved something, and I believe now that you will indeed find happiness through work. So don't pay any attention to what I tell you, or anyone else. You know your road better than we do, so don't give up.'

So Fiona has sensed the collapse of my relationship with Mahmoud. Of course, she's too intelligent to be fooled by the show we put on, pretending that all is as it should be. But even if I were to find the courage to tell her everything, how could I explain when I myself don't understand? If I told her, for example, that our marriage had died with Maleeka, how could I explain the real story of that to her? Our one and only real encounter remains alive. No matter how often I tell myself that nothing happened and that I have turned that page, I still live the shudder that swept over me when she kissed me and I pressed her head to my breast. The dampness of her tears and saliva is still there; they never disappear, no matter how I deny them. I try to reassure myself that I have lived my entire life as a normal woman and that I used to take great pleasure in making love to Mahmoud, and then a thought insinuates itself into my mind that mocks me – that Sappho herself enjoyed making love with men. She was more normal than I am. She, at least, was a mother who loved her daughter, while I'm sterile. No, I'm not yet absolved.

Would Fiona still be proud of me, as she said she was, if she heard all this? She says she used to be jealous of me, then became proud of me! Why? She isn't aware, then, that it was I who was usually jealous of her. All my life I've seen her as the ideal of beauty and the goodness that wins people's hearts. She is the closest person to my heart but still I always envied her all that, and maybe I'm still jealous of her even now. She didn't want to tell me whether she had loved Michael or not. She left my question hanging. Maybe she's right – let's leave him to rest in peace! And let's leave her own question about why I married him hanging too. I don't know the answer, so let's leave all the ghosts of the past alone. The ghosts of the present are more than enough. The ghost of Maleeka alone is enough.

Let me then indeed get back to work. Work will at least make me forget the search for that peace of mind that never comes. Fiona counsels me to keep going – is there any alternative? It seems that something pursues me to make sure I keep going.

I devoted myself for several days to reading whatever writings by the historians I had available about Alexander's end, going over again what I knew, questioning it in the light of whatever new information I could find. Maybe that way I would find the evidence Fiona wanted before talking about the conclusion. My intuition and obsession were not enough. She was right. Always, as usual, right!

I set out the facts, in the hope that they might reveal something. What happened after he died? They wanted to carry out his wishes and have him buried in the Oasis of Amun next to his father, and they bestowed great honours upon him, building him a wagon of vast size as a mobile sepulchre that would transport his corpse from Babel to Egypt, and they decorated the sides of the wagon with pictures and gilded statues that told the story of the king-hero-god. It was pulled by dozens of mules, the jingling of whose hundreds of bells could be heard from miles away as it proceeded along the highway on its funereal passage to Egypt, across the deserts, valleys and forests and through cities he had built and others he had destroyed.

The wagon took two years to cover the distance from Babel to the Nile valley, but it never completed the journey to its goal in the Oasis of Amun as he had requested. Ptolemy, the king's deputy, received it and diverted it to his capital of Memphis in Upper Egypt, and he erected the king's sepulchre there, so that Alexander might be a witness and guarantor of the glory of his ambitious follower, who lost no time in announcing himself king. When the capital was transferred from the south to Alexandria, he took the corpse there and built a sepulchre between the miraculous lighthouse and the splendidly endowed library that he had built. It was no longer simply a sepulchre then. It had become a temple to the god Alexander, son of Zeus-Amun, with columns of the Grecian Doric order, the objective of crowded processions of pilgrims on his annual festival, while others came at any moment to seek his blessing and worship the embalmed god in his marble sarcophagus, which, after a time, they exchanged for another of glass, whose transparency made his form appear more brilliantly. The centuries passed and the temple remained a place to be visited by all the great who passed through Alexandria, among them Julius Caesar and Mark Antony – both accompanied, no doubt, by Cleopatra – and then in later years by many of the Roman emperors. All of them abased themselves before the conquering, never defeated hero, and they may have envied him, as no one after him ever achieved the same glory.

Suddenly, however, after six long centuries, mentions of the sepulchre and the corpse disappear altogether. Following the adoption of Christianity as the Roman Empire's only religion, a zealous emperor issued an order for the closing of all the temples to the heathen gods, including that of Alexander.

But where did the embalmed god in his glass sarcophagus go, and where his temple? Why was no trace of him left behind? The historians have no answer to these questions. Did he drown in the sea, as my father used to say, or was he obliterated by the action of time, as Fiona said?

Why does my mind refuse to accept this truncated end to the long and majestic legend?

Is it my mind which refuses, or is it that I'm clinging on to the hope of myself having some great achievement in life? Why not? Life is very short, as Alexander understood, and those who have the capacity to leave some trace behind them shouldn't hesitate or prevaricate. He conquered the world and I dream only of seeing him in the arms of his father Amun, his last testament thus realized, so that I too, through this, may realize some modest glory! Something to compensate for my failure with Mahmoud and with Michael and to make me forget for ever the ghost of Maleeka. Even should I not succeed, it is still an attempt worthy of my time. Whatever happens, peace of mind will remain beyond reach.

Despite this, my intuition provides the story with a logical and believable ending. Christianity did not put a swift end to paganism in Alexandria or in Egypt. There were Christian martyrs who accepted torture and death in defence of their divine beliefs, but there were also martyrs to the pagan gods who were content to be tortured by the Christians and to sacrifice their lives for the sake of Amun, Isis, Horus and others. Why should there not have been among these loyal followers of the gods adherents of the cult of Alexander, son of Amun-Ra? There were many of them in those days, so what if, after the closure of the temple, they transported the body of their god secretly to his father's oasis? It would be the ideal place. It was far from Roman rule, Christianity had not yet entered it, and the worship of the Egyptian gods continued to flourish there for centuries, far from the eyes of any power that might govern Egypt. It would have been logical then for his loyal worshippers to think of moving him here and carrying out his last wishes after centuries of exile. My mind says why not, and my sixth sense says he is close, but where is the evidence?

I also reread everything the travellers who had visited the oasis had written about the temples of Siwa and its antiquities. I paused as I always do at the description of the obliterated Doric temple near Lake Khameesa. The area and dimensions of the temple as described by the French traveller Cailliaud are those of a typical Greek temple. More important still is his reference to the style of the columns as Doric, and his statement that it was the only one of its kind in the oasis. Where, though, is that temple now, for me to deduce from it any evidence for anything?

Captain Wasfi could have helped me and we could have gone together to look around there, in places I could not have gone on my own. But Mahmoud continues to impose imprisonment. I'm not allowed even to invite Wasfi for a discussion. Fiona will have nothing to do with him after he described the revolutionaries as traitors, and she doesn't welcome the sight of him. Why such a puritan, Fiona? He's talking about the revolutionaries of his own country, so he can say what he likes, and Alexander the Great wasn't the English Cromwell, who declared open war on Connaught and slaughtered its people, so why take your anger out on the Macedonian king? Also I need Wasfi now to help me. I have to think of a way.

Before that, however, there's something I have to make sure of myself. What am I to do?

'Why not, Catherine?' said Fiona heatedly. 'Go out!'

I looked at Zubeida, on whose wrinkled face were written refusal and doubt. I had tried, with Fiona, to explain to her in Arabic, Siwan and sign language that I wanted to borrow her donkey for a short while and return it safely to her. She, however, kept repeating stubbornly, 'The *izit* is sick.' The donkey was sick! I tried to convince her with gestures that I wouldn't tire it and wouldn't be late; in fact, I'd be close to the house. Fiona tried to reassure her and pointed downwards with her forefinger, saying, 'Soldiers downstairs,' meaning they would protect me, and the donkey, if anything happened. Then she put her hand on Zubeida's shoulder and said with her bewitching smile, 'I'll buy you another *izit*!' At this, Zubeida agreed to lend me the donkey, but grudgingly.

I hadn't told Fiona the whole truth. I had seized the opportunity of Zubeida's unaccompanied visit and said that I was thinking of making a short outing in the vicinity of the house if the old lady would agree to lend me her donkey. Fiona agreed at once, saying, 'You really need to go out and take the air a little instead of staying a prisoner with me in the house.' Her words intimated that she blamed herself, and I didn't object that she had nothing to do with my being a prisoner. I needed her help to persuade the stubborn old woman.

The moment Zubeida agreed, I put on the clothes I'd prepared so that I'd look like a Siwan woman. I donned a flowing dark-coloured dress with long trousers underneath, then wrapped tightly around me Fiona's *tarfottet* mantle, which hung from the top of my head, and draped it over my face, completely covering it but for a space for the eyes.

As I was slowly descending the steps, my heart beating, I noticed that the soldiers of the guard were looking at me in astonishment. Too bad! I'd be back before they could think or do anything.

I mounted the donkey the way Zubeida did, dangling my legs on either side, and urged it quickly down the road to Aghurmi, the road of Maleeka, Sheikh Yahya, Gouba Spring and many other things. I felt certain I'd disguised myself well. Some *zaggala* were coming out of their gardens when they heard the bray of the donkey and gave me a passing glance, then returned to their work. All the same, my heart started beating faster. What did it mean, then, when I said I was afraid of nothing? Here I was, afraid! Was that another delusion with which I lied to myself?

I didn't have much time to think about that or anything else. I urged on the slow donkey, which was indeed weak, as its mistress had claimed. Often it stopped on the road and started braying, as though it were moaning, but we got there in the end.

I looked around me. No one.

I tied the donkey to the palm tree beneath which young Mahmoud had stretched out. Then I entered the temple. I had hidden my sketchbook and pen beneath the cloak, so I took them out and made my way quickly towards the wall from which I'd copied the text. I looked it over and traced the letters with my fingers. I hadn't been mistaken. It was indeed a prayer to Amun-Ra and none other. I wanted to be sure of the reference to water. I would not fool myself. I had to try to decode the symbols forming the columns of partially erased demotic writing. As I reread them, I discovered that I had made mistakes in copying some of the lines when I had written them down the first time. I rested the sketchbook against the wall and tried to be very precise in copying what I saw in front of me, but I still made mistakes because of the speed with which I was working, so I would rub out what I had written and do it over, reproaching myself for the error. I had no time to lose!

I had barely written out one page before I heard a murmur that changed into a clamour, which changed into yelling voices, just as my heartbeats changed into a drumming in my ears. My hand shook and the sketchbook fell from it, and I had bent down to pick it up when I saw the angry faces of the *zaggala* surrounding the entrance to the temple.

I was bent over, so the first stone didn't hit me, but the stones followed one another, raining down on me. I put my hands and arms over my head and face and screamed just as they were screaming. Then there was the sound of a horse and a shot and the stoning stopped as the *zaggala* turned and looked in the direction from which it had come.

After the silence that fell, I heard the deep voice of Salmawi and that of Sergeant Ibraheem calling out, then saw them together. Salmawi stood in the midst of the *zaggala*, his rifle slung over his shoulder, and started talking to them, smiling and patting their backs, while Ibraheem charged towards me and asked me anxiously, 'Are you all right, madame? Did anything hit you?'

He looked at the stones scattered about me on the ground and said, his apprehension increasing, 'Did those rogues hit you, madame?'

'No, Sergeant . . . Ibraheem.'

I wouldn't scream. I wouldn't moan. Many parts of my body hurt but I'd been able to protect my head and face. I wanted to be sure, so I felt them with my hand. There wasn't any blood.

Salmawi succeeded in dispersing the *zaggala*, talking to them in a loud voice and joking with them, while Ibraheem asked me in a sorrowful voice, 'Why, madame?'

Trying to keep my voice normal, I answered him with the question, 'How did you know I was here?'

The guards had informed the corporal. Zubeida's cloak was still on the threshold of the door, so they knew that it wasn't she who'd left, but . . .

Corporal Salmawi came up and said, 'Excuse me, madame, but we must return as quickly as we can before those men change their minds and before His Excellency hears what happened. We came without telling him anything.'

I picked up the sketchbook and walked with firm steps towards the palm tree. At least Zubeida's donkey hadn't come to any harm.

Salmawi mounted his horse and almost had to pick the sergeant up and put him on, the latter riding pillion behind him. Then he preceded me, his rifle in his hand, and I mounted the donkey and followed. There was no longer any point in my disguising myself, so I let the cloak fall open and left my face uncovered, feeling my wounds and suppressing my moans.

Mahmoud charged into the house like a madman.

On his reddened face there was anger such as I had never seen.

Zubeida also left in a temper as soon as I arrived, shouting words of blame and reproach that I didn't bother to try to understand, and for the first time she didn't hug and kiss Fiona as she went out.

Fiona sat at the table opposite me, her head bowed, sorrow and defeat on her face.

Before Mahmoud could get a word out, I said, 'I'm sorry. I was wrong and I'm sorry.'

He opened his mouth to speak but the words choked in his throat, his face turned an even brighter shade of red, and in the end he exploded with, 'Madame is sorry?'

Then he resumed, his tongue tripping over the words, 'I . . . I . . . I'm the last one to know?'

He came towards me, extending his arms and spreading his hands out as though he intended to hit me with both of them, or strangle me, but he suddenly raised a hand and struck himself on the forehead, stammering out again, 'I'll . . . I'll . . .

I'll throttle Salmawi, and Ibraheem with him. Me, the last to know? I swear I'll . . .'

'Wait a moment, Mahmoud!'

When Fiona stood up and addressed him, he fell suddenly silent. Her face was the colour of ashes but she spoke in a clear voice, suppressing her violent emotion. 'You should direct all your blame at me, Mahmoud. Catherine is not at fault. I'm the one who asked her to go out and get some air.'

He stood looking at her uncomprehendingly. Then he said, 'You too? But why?'

He turned and rushed out as he had entered. Fiona put her hand on my shoulder and repeated the question in a faltering voice.

'But why, Catherine?'

18

Mahmoud

I woke earlier than usual, in the midst of deep darkness.

Another night of little sleep.

And that name. Deird? Deirdre? Deiradra?

It's been going around in my mind from the moment I opened my eyes but I can't manage to remember it. A difficult name, and a more difficult story, Fiona.

The name won't come back to me and the details are slipping away. In the story there's an evil king, who wants this innocent girl Deirdre, who is in love with a beautiful cavalier. I don't remember whether the king kills her beloved and his two knightly brothers or someone else does. And does the beautiful girl kill herself out of grief over her beloved or does she die of sorrow? The details evaporate but I remember the ending perfectly. The king is determined to part her from her beloved even in death. He buries her far away from his grave and there's a river, or a canal, between them. A plant grows up from her grave, though – ivy, perhaps. It grows longer and longer and it spreads over the ground and across the water and, on the other bank, intertwines with a shoot that has grown up from her beloved's grave, and from their embrace grows a bush. The king orders that the bush be cut down and the two shoots cut back, but they spring up again and embrace again and again and again, until the king despairs and stops having them cut back. In death their love frustrates the will of evil.

It wasn't our smiling Fiona who told that story last night, but another Fiona, one whose face had emptied of blood and delivered her words sadly, one by one. When she'd finished,

Catherine asked her eagerly, 'Why did you cut the story short and leave out the beautiful poetry?' and Fiona replied, as she got up, 'That's enough for now. I'm tired this evening.'

Indeed, her painful coughing went on all night. It's getting worse day by day and with it my feelings of impotence. Sheikh Yahya's herbs haven't worked the same miracle as with Ibraheem, so what's to be done? Catherine refused to agree to the two of them travelling to Cairo in the hope of finding better treatment and asked me the question I already knew the answer to: how? The journey would kill her. But her staying here will kill her too and kill me along with her. If Sheikh Yahya's intuition about her condition is correct, there's no hope, and there's still a long time to go before the hot weather when we can try the last possibility. Will she hang on till the summer comes and the sands get hot? Will she live? She has to live. If anyone deserves life in this house, it's her alone. Not me and not Catherine.

The sound of coughing became a little quieter, then stopped. I've grown able to distinguish the different types of cough quite clearly since Fiona moved to the ground floor. My hearing has become sensitive even to the sound of her breathing. What do I want from her? Nothing except that she live, just as Sheikh Yahya said that he wanted Maleeka to live so that the world could have some meaning. Why, then, can I not rid myself of her face, which pursues me at home, in the office and on the road, when I'm alone in bed and when Catherine is lying next to me? To what end will it lead us, that thing which comes unsought and cannot be escaped?

The cough started again, harder this time, and my heart began pounding. I had to go out, to get away. I jumped out of bed and Catherine didn't wake. Neither my movements nor her sister's coughing wake her. She has returned to her heavy sleep after the nights of moaning and groaning caused by the bruises made by the stones. The only worries that keep her awake are the temples of the ancestors! I wish that that day instead of throwing stones at her they'd . . .

No. Forgive me, Fiona. I don't wish any harm to your sister!

I washed quickly, dressed, and left the house.

The dark was still intense and there was a long time to go before the first streaks of dawn. I found no one awake at the station except for the soldiers of the night guard, whom my arrival at that hour greatly surprised. But as I crossed the courtyard I saw a phantom, whose identity I could not distinguish in the dark, moving as though to leave the place.

It was taken aback by me too, and came forwards, greeting me in embarrassment, then stood silent.

'Welcome, Sheikh Sabir,' I said.

I had seen him once following the assault on Catherine at the temple. He came to make a show of apologizing for what the *zaggala* had done, his words, as usual, hinting at other things. They carried a reproach to Catherine, 'because the lady went to the temple where these "ignorant" people suspect that she is practising magic', and a reproach to me because, since I'd permitted the lady to go to the temple, it would have been better to send a sufficient number of guards with her. Privately, I conceded that he was right, but I contented myself with thanking him and said I would take care it didn't occur again. Wasfi insisted that Sheikh Sabir should direct us to the *zaggala* who had carried out the assault so that we could flog them in front of everybody and make an example of them to others, but I said, decisively, that I accepted the apology of Sheikh Sabir and considered the matter closed.

In the dark courtyard, we stood facing one another without speaking. Finally, I said, 'Has anything happened, Sheikh Sabir, that requires the intervention of the police?'

He replied, with growing embarrassment, 'Not at all, not at all, Mr Commissioner. I was with the captain and . . . we were going over the accounts for the taxes.'

I laughed in spite of myself. 'You were going over them at this hour, Sheikh Sabir?'

'Yes. He told me before the dawn prayer. He likes to work early.'

'It's the early bird, indeed, that gets the worm. Goodbye, Sheikh Sabir.'

I left him and climbed the stairs to my office. One of the guards wanted to wake up Sergeant Ibraheem but I forbade him. I told him, 'We'll start work at the proper time, as we do every day.'

As soon as I went in, I felt cold, so I closed the open window and sat alone in the dark room. I need to be on my own and have this peace in order to think.

Think about what exactly? I'd become an addict of thinking about myself and every page I turned I found to be worse than the one before. Would that I weren't I! Would that I were my brother Suleiman, for example, that I were a merchant in Damascus and he an officer in the police. Why not?

The same father, the same mother – it's just a matter of luck. It would have been perfectly possible for luck to have taken my side, and then I would have been him. I haven't seen him for years and I've never seen his wife and children. His features have faded in my memory. He cut all his ties to the past and built a new life far from us, and I don't blame him for it. He never failed to fulfil his obligations, and during his mother's life he used to send her money, even though he was just starting his business and needed every piastre. Still, it hurt me deeply that he didn't come when I sent him the telegram announcing her death. He responded with a message of condolence in which he said there was no point in his turning up after the funeral and burial were over and it made better sense for him to distribute what he would have spent on the journey in charity, for the rest of the departed's soul. I had hoped at the time that he'd come and we could weep for her together. I was the one that needed him, though perhaps what he did was the more correct. If I had been

Suleiman, I wouldn't have lived this life of uncertainty. If I'd been Suleiman . . . If I'd been . . .

The marquee is large and I'm standing receiving condolences for Mahmoud Abd el Zahir, but all the chairs are empty and no one comes. A sheikh is sitting reciting the Koran on a high wooden bench but he opens his mouth and closes it without making a sound and no one comes. Then the marquee is a large garden crowded with people where lots of children are playing and I walk on my own, bearing on my outstretched hands the folded white cloth. I have stopped an old man and I ask him where the burial area is and he gestures without stopping and says, 'Straight on,' so I follow his directions and I find myself on the shore of a river that is edged with willow trees, whose branches dangle in the water, and I take hold of the hands of a beautiful young girl and we laugh together and I say to her, 'Can you imagine? I was dead but I came alive again!' and she says proudly, 'That's because of me.' We get into a boat on the river and I discover that she's Ni'ma and I laugh and ask her, 'When did you change the colour of your hair?' and she answers, 'When you left me.' Suddenly, though, she screams and points behind me and lots of people appear on the riverbank pointing where she did and I turn and find a huge crocodile, its mouth wide open, descending on the boat.

I take hold of Ni'ma's hand and we jump out of the boat together. We run quickly over the water and once again we're in the middle of the marquee amid the empty chairs and the voice of the reciter, which doesn't come out even though his mouth is opening and closing.

Ni'ma says in annoyance, 'Why doesn't that sheikh at least recite?' I go up to him angrily and find that he's not reciting but laughing. I know who he is from his eyes so I take hold of the front of his robe and say furiously, 'You, Sheikh . . .'

Then I shouted, 'Come in!'

Ibraheem's knocks on the door woke me with a start from my doze.

His words mixed with the remnants of the dream so I couldn't concentrate on what he was saying. I understood from his sorrowful tone that he was reproaching me because I hadn't allowed them to wake him. Was he no longer of any use in the station? I mollified him and asked him to bring me a large mug of tea. Then I fell fast asleep and didn't even notice the bustle of the start of work at the station or the morning light that entered the room though the shutters were closed. Eventually I got up and opened the shutters and started walking rapidly about the room to restore some warmth and energy.

When Ibraheem returned he remained standing in front of me as I sipped my tea from the mug, my hand trembling and causing a few drops to fall on the desk in spite of myself. I put the mug on the desk and asked him, 'Do you want something, Sergeant Ibraheem?'

He looked hesitant for a few instants, then told me that Sheikh Sabir had come that day before dawn and met the captain.

'I know,' I said. 'I met Sabir and he said he was checking the tax accounts with the captain.'

'Accounts? And why would they check them in secret, Excellency? It's not the first time. The sheikh often comes in the middle of the night and they go into the office on their own where no one can hear them, and he leaves before anybody in the station is awake. Is that "checking accounts"?'

'You're dismissed now, Sergeant, and stop spying on the captain or anyone else. If there's something going on, we'll find out about it in due course.'

'How can that be, sir?' he protested. 'When will the due course be? We have to take steps before it's too late.'

'We shall, God willing, take steps. Dismiss now, Ibraheem.'

He left, grumbling. How can I tell him, 'These things are of no importance to me. Anything that might befall me has already happened'?

*   *   *

282

I spent the day working at the station, inventing things to do. I inspected the storerooms and started writing letters to the ministry about the supplies and the ammunition they needed to send with the next caravan to make up for what had been used. Captain Wasfi came to review the accounts concerning the amount of taxes collected. He said that he'd gone over them with Sheikh Sabir that morning and that they were in conformity with the ministry's requests. I deduced that he'd heard about my encounter with Sabir and come to review the accounts, which he should have done long before. He sat in front of me following me with his eyes, which never stop moving and get on my nerves, so I cast a glance at the lists and thanked him, setting them aside. He also had other papers in his hand, however, which he presented to me, saying, 'These came to me with the last caravan. Your Excellency might care to take a look at them.' They were old issues of the newspaper *el Muqattam*, which I hate. I read a few headlines quickly and then handed them back to him, saying, 'It seems the young Khedive is not like his father. It seems he doesn't like the British a great deal.'

'He will!' said Wasfi.

He spoke with great confidence, so I asked him, 'How so?'

'Our government cannot do without the British. We need them.'

I said, smiling, 'But the other night you were extolling the greatness of our ancestors the Ancient Egyptians and praising their remains. Cannot the descendants be as worthy of ruling the country as their grandsires?'

'Not at present. First we have to learn many things from the British. See, Your Excellency, how it is the British who reveal to us the Ancient Egyptian antiquities and their greatness, while we know nothing about them. Mrs Catherine almost sacrificed her life in pursuit of knowledge, and what did the ignoramuses whom she was trying to serve do to her?'

I said nothing, so he continued heatedly, his eyes jumping around even faster than usual, 'I wasn't able to explain my point of view to Your Excellency the other night because Miss Fiona interrupted me. I wanted to say that the strife caused by the mutineers prevented us from progressing. Your Excellency must have seen with your own eyes the chaos that the country lived through during those days and which my father told me about.'

'What exactly did your father see and tell you about? What was his position at the time?'

'He was a brigadier general in the army.'

'And did he preside over a commission of inquiry with the Urabists?'

He said in surprise, 'No. No, I don't think so. Anyway, he's now on reserve, but he remembers every detail of the riots and the strife. He told me that one of those traitors, I think his name was Mohamed Ebeid, went so far as to contemplate murdering Our Master the Khedive! Imagine, Your Excellency, the ruination that could have overtaken the country!'

With a quiet laugh, I said, 'I do, Captain!'

Then I went on in the tones of one who wants to bring the conversation to an end, 'So, to be brief, you can see that the Urabists committed crimes against Egypt because they wanted the people of the country to rule it.'

He pursed his lips in distaste and said, 'That, sir, is the sickness that brings ruin in its wake! When the common people interfere in government, chaos follows, and weakness. Just look, Your Excellency, at France! Since the day the revolutionary upheaval began there and the common people participated in government, the country has gone to the dogs. Even when God gave them unequalled military geniuses like Napoleon, the British were able to defeat him and crush him because the government of France was at the mercy of the mob. England, on the other hand, was administered by strong politicians.'

'Masters.'

'Politicians, sir.'

'Exactly, masters who are politicians.'

I stood up saying, 'We must discuss these matters some other day, Captain.'

He too stood and said, 'That would give me great pleasure. I shall learn much from Your Excellency.'

He saluted with his usual correctness and when he opened the door to go out, I said to him quietly, 'Listen, Wasfi.'

'Sir?'

'Urabi Basha had more honour than ten khedives put together. And Lieutenant Colonel Mohamed Ebeid had more honour than all the traitor khedives and bashas who sold us to the British.'

He stood at the open door looking at me as though stunned. Then I said quietly, 'Dismiss!'

I sat back down at my desk, a voice inside me mocking me and saying, 'But it's twenty years too late to say that, my dear major! And you should have said it to someone other than Wasfi!'

Why, though, had his words revived that memory? What takes me back, at this moment of hopelessness, to the days of glory? The fact that I was there!

I was there, in the house of Sultan Basha, Speaker of the House of Representatives, along with Captain Saeed and Lieutenant Tal'at, providing security for the meeting. The whole of Egypt was there – the members of parliament, the high officials, the sheikhs of el Azhar, the priests of the Church, the notables from the countryside, even the princes of the khedivial house. I was close and saw the tall handsome peasant officer standing, his face red, its muscles working as he brandished his sword.

The Khedive was far away in Alexandria and had accepted the notice the British had given him to exile Urabi from Egypt and dismiss the revolutionary government. Urabi spoke and said that there was no solution but to remove the Khedive, and those present applauded him. Tal'at took out his revolver, intending to fire it in the air as a salute to Urabi, but Saeed told him off and pulled the hand holding the gun down. When Urabi said, 'Anyone who's with us, rise!' most of the people there stood up, though Sultan Basha and the rural notables remained in their seats. At that moment I caught a whiff of the betrayal that was coming, and Mohamed Ebeid felt it too, and waved his sword and said, in the heat of his fury, 'I will kill him myself, Urabi Basha, and then you can execute me afterwards!' Urabi, also furious, said, 'Make that madman shut up!'

'That madman', my dear Basha, was, however, the only one who died fighting the British, out of all those who were present at the meeting, while Sultan Basha held the invading army's stirrup, and your father was probably there helping him, Wasfi!

And it was the same Mohamed Ebeid, and those who were with him, that I described as 'miscreants'!

So there's no call to pat yourself on the back in front of Wasfi or anyone else. No call for belated bravado.

I sent Sergeant Ibraheem to the house to inform Catherine that I wouldn't be coming home for lunch and until evening fell I stayed at the station for no reason at all, not work or anything else.

When I returned I didn't find Fiona but saw Catherine with her papers and books spread out on the table, reading and writing by the light of two large incandescent lamps. She has done this often recently, protesting that she doesn't have a study. I didn't say anything but felt sure that a new disaster was in the making. After the stoning incident, we'd reached the point of ignoring one another completely – in an almost friendly way. How was it that we'd failed to discover this comfortable arrangement before?

She was wholly engrossed, and responded to my perfunctory greeting with one equally so. I asked her about her sister and she said she was tired tonight and had gone to sleep without having dinner. Then she went back to her papers, closely examining some large pages full of drawings and reliefs and moving from these to write notes on other pages. I watched what she was doing for a moment, then said I was going to go and sleep.

'Without dinner too?'

'I'm not hungry.'

'I'll be there in a little while.'

'Take all the time you need.'

I climbed quickly into bed but once again sleep refused to come. I wasn't thinking about anything but lay with my eyes open, feeling that again sleep would not visit me tonight. Then a soft cough would come from a distance, a sudden flash of lightning would fill the room, and my tense body would relax and a strange peace fill me – an easeful despair and final surrender: there is no escape, so do not even try; accept what happens; accept the blessing of experiencing something you never experienced before. Now you love without desiring even to touch. It's not important that you understand. It's not necessary that you be happy. She has come. You fell in love with her and all you want from her is that she live. That's the beginning and end of it all, so don't try!

After a long while during which I didn't close my eyes and I strained my ears, Catherine came quietly into the room. She changed her clothes without making any noise, then slipped into the bed. I turned over and she said in a whisper, 'Did I wake you?'

'No. I wasn't asleep.'

In a low voice that betrayed an excitement she couldn't suppress, she said, 'Mahmoud, I've found a sign!' and she went on mumbling, as though to herself, 'I've found a sign. I've found a sign.'

I said, 'Marvellous,' then turned over and closed my eyes.

*   *   *

287

Another dark dawn and two nights without sleep.

I saw the guards outside the door. They'd wrapped their heads in woollen scarves, lit a fire and were gathered in a circle around it, warming their hands. I stopped for a moment, so they moved away from the fire and stood to attention. I told them they could go now and sleep.

'But the relief watch hasn't come yet . . .'

'It doesn't matter.'

They saluted and hurried off.

I didn't find Wasfi in the station courtyard, where he usually was. Corporal Salmawi had taken over the morning roll-call for him and he caught up with me as I was preparing to mount the stairs. I asked after the captain and he said that he'd gone out early, before dawn, with some of the soldiers, to meet the caravan coming from Kerdasa, promising to be back quickly, before the start of work, but it seemed that they must have taken the wrong road because soldiers from the caravan had already arrived and handed over to the corporal boxes of ammunition and some letters, which he'd left on my desk.

So there were no new officers, nor any reinforcement troops for Wasfi to train!

Too bad!

Ibraheem met me at the top of the stairs and went ahead of me as fast as his gammy leg permitted. Then he opened the door, entered after me and closed it.

Before I'd seated myself at my desk he was saying, in great agitation, 'What did I tell Your Excellency?'

'What did you tell me, Sergeant Ibraheem? Keep it short because I'm tired this morning.'

'What did I tell you about Sheikh Sabir and Captain Wasfi?'

Without waiting for me to reply, he went on, 'He came to him in the middle of the night, as usual, before the captain went out, and I was able to hear some of what they said.'

He was silent for a moment and then he continued in agonized tones, 'He's got his eyes on your position, my son,

288

and that accursed sheikh is encouraging him! I warned you they were plotting something.'

I laughed as I said, 'District commissioner? At his age? Why not? The sooner the better, Ibraheem. If it were in my hands, I'd make him commissioner today and go back to . . .'

He interrupted me angrily. 'A pox on anyone who wants Your Excellency's position!'

To calm him down, I said, 'So there's nothing to worry about. And it's not Sheikh Sabir who appoints the district commissioners. Dismiss now.'

He left muttering, and I looked at the envelopes from the ministry placed on my desk. I knew well what was inside each – receipts for the ammunition, which I would have to sign, pay lists, new instructions from the ministry, promotions and transfers, etc.

Most of them were papers that I'd glance at and then file away for ever.

I opened the large yellow envelope and found in it only what I expected, though something in the middle of the list of incoming ammunition did catch my eye. Next to so many new rifles, so many boxes of cartridges, etc., there was '1 (one) box, dynamite'. Dynamite?

What use could that be in the middle of the sands? Perhaps the ministry stores had wanted to get rid of it so they'd sent it to the desert, probably so they could buy more!

There was a final letter that was not in the large envelope. I opened it and found lines uninterrupted by any figures. I went back to the top and saw that it was addressed to Captain Wasfi, and that it was his name on the envelope too. I almost resealed it to give to him when he returned, but I saw my name repeated often among the lines. So, it concerned me too.

I read the letter twice, and laughed.

What call was there for surprise? Even Ibraheem had been able to predict it!

Despite all the facts and figures that reached me from the ministry, I was unfamiliar with this department called the Directorate of the Special Order, and neither could I guess who might be its head, who signed himself only 'S.H.' He thanked Captain Wasfi for his well-documented report and said that His Excellency the advisor to the ministry was very pleased with his accuracy and congratulated him on his success in gaining the affection and trust of the *agwad*. His Excellency had been particularly interested in what the report had to say about the deterioration in the relations of the district commissioner with the inhabitants of the oasis and their attempt to attack the police station with rifles and the recklessness shown by the district commissioner in firing a cannon shell in the direction of the town without first consulting the ministry and without informing it of what had happened. His Excellency the advisor believed that, to quote him word for word, 'these are very serious developments in the wrong direction' and he was following the results with the greatest concern, asking, at the same time, that the captain continue to be entirely correct in his dealings with His Excellency the district commissioner as his superior officer. He should obey his commands according to standing instructions and rules until such time as the ministry was able to take the appropriate steps. His Excellency also confirmed his confidence in Wasfi Effendi and requested that he continue his contacts with the sheikh of the Easterners who sought to be appointed to the position of mayor. The man was to have hope without the captain's giving him any specific promise and without this harming his relations with the sheikhs of the Westerners. In closing, S.H. congratulated Captain Wasfi on Mr Harvey's confidence and instructed him to continue to send similar reports on all matters that might reach his ears concerning the *agwad*, the local inhabitants and His Excellency the district commissioner, and to take care to keep the correspondence secret. After this there was a postscript to the effect that His Excellency the Basha, Wasfi's respected father, had contacted him and that he could reassure the captain as to his health and that he was in the best of states, praise God.

I put the letter back in its envelope and placed it in front of me on the desk, laughing again.

What had happened to me? Why didn't I feel the slightest anger? Why didn't I feel anything at all? Did I deserve this punishment? Perhaps!

I heard horses approaching at a gallop and entering the courtyard of the station, followed, faster than I expected, by a knocking on the door. Wasfi came in.

He waved Ibraheem away as he entered, and closed the door. He hadn't changed his uniform and for the first time I saw him in front of me in a tarboosh topped with dust and clothes smudged with sand. He saluted, his face pale, and accompanied the salute with an anxious question: 'Was there anything, Your Excellency . . .'

Before he could continue, I held out my hand to him with the opened envelope, saying, 'This letter is for you, Captain. I opened it because it was with the official correspondence from the ministry, but you can regard it as unread. Dismiss.'

He stood there hesitating, turning the envelope over in his hands, but I repeated, in a tone that brooked no refusal, 'Dismiss!'

Only a few minutes had passed after he had left when there was an urgent knocking on the door. I gave permission to enter and Corporal Salmawi rushed in, his face like thunder.

'I wish to make a complaint, Your Excellency!' he said in that same tremulous voice that seemed always to be on the verge of tears.

'Calm down, Corporal. Who do you want to make a complaint against?'

'Captain Wasfi. He ran into me at the bottom of the stairs as he was coming down from Your Excellency and he slapped me in the face for no reason.'

'On the contrary,' I said to myself, 'there was a reason, Salmawi. He had to slap someone!'

I answered him, however, by asking, 'Had you committed any offence, Corporal? Had you done anything to make the captain angry?'

Trying to control his anger, he said, 'Not at all. He saw me at the foot of the stairs and he slapped me in front of the troops. Then he left without a word. He slapped me in front of the troops, Your Excellency.' Then Salmawi raised his bowed head and said, 'I want my rights, Your Excellency. We are Bedouin and do not accept humiliation. He would pay dearly if I sought satisfaction with my own hand.'

'Don't say that again, Corporal. Don't say it in my presence or behind my back. You have made your complaint and I will investigate it. If you are in the right, you will be given satisfaction.'

I didn't, however, see Captain Wasfi during the day. He sent a soldier to inform me that he felt tired and to ask permission to stay in his room, a request to which I immediately agreed. At least, he will relieve me on this one day, when I'm destroyed with fatigue, of having to listen to the racket of the training, his shouted commands, the yells of the soldiers as they run and jump.

I left the office and took Sergeant Ibraheem with me. His eyes were full of curiosity about what had gone on in the closed office with Wasfi and Salmawi, but I didn't give him an opportunity to ask. I said, 'We have work before us, Sergeant Ibraheem.'

I called the sergeant in charge of the stores and the three of us went to the stores and together checked the arms and ammunition that the ministry had sent us. Then the storekeeper signed the receipts and I took them and returned to my office, where I finished replying to the letters from the ministry. I could have put that job off until later but I needed to keep myself busy with something. I needed not to think.

As I left the office in the afternoon, Sergeant Ibraheem told me he felt tired and asked permission to take the rest of the day off. I examined his face and he did indeed look exhausted, but I asked him jokingly whether he was jealous of Captain Wasfi.

Disgustedly, he said, 'God forbid!'

'Naturally you can take as much time off as you like. Anyway, I'm not coming back later.'

He came closer and told me in a low voice that he had a request.

I looked at him enquiringly and he bowed his head and said in his whispering voice, 'I want you to swear to me, Your Excellency, that, if my time comes while I'm here, you'll have me buried in my village. Don't leave me among strangers in the sand.'

My heart shrank as I contemplated the wrinkled face but I tried to go on in the same tone as though he had said nothing. 'Life is in God's hands, my dear chap. You asked me the same thing after you broke your leg and look at you, strong as a horse. You, more than anyone else, are likely to bury us all and walk in our funeral processions.'

'God forbid, Excellency!' he said, interrupting me with a wan smile.

I followed him with my eyes as he limped slowly away, muttering, 'I would never forgive myself!'

I left the office and downstairs was surprised to find that Captain Wasfi had changed his uniform and tarboosh and was standing, elegant and erect, yelling to the soldiers in his commanding voice to dress their line and salute. I returned the salute from a distance and left without a word. I decided to postpone my investigation of him until the following day.

On the way home, I found the weather warm, in contrast to the morning.

There were just light transparent clouds, and the late afternoon sun was warm and calm and tempted one to relax under its rays. When I opened the door, though, I found the two of them sitting at the table. Catherine had spread out on it her many papers, which look like charts.

'Are we having pharaohs for lunch today?' I said in surprise.

Excitedly Catherine exclaimed, 'We'll delay lunch a little, with your permission. You're early, but I'm glad you're here. I want your opinion. I was just about to read what I've found to Fiona.'

Fiona turned to me and said, with her smile that spreads a little light over her wan face, 'Isn't it wonderful? At last Catherine has found what she's been looking for.'

She gave her staccato cough, her hand over her mouth. Then she continued, 'I think . . . I think that the historians . . . the . . . the . . . the historians will be interested in this.'

I transferred my gaze to Catherine and asked her in bewilderment, 'What historians? What will they be interested in?'

'The sign, the evidence. I told you last night but you weren't paying attention.'

I remained silent, looking at her enquiringly. She continued, 'You remember the day we went together to the temple of Umm Ebeida?'

'How could I ever forget it?'

With the same excitement she went on, 'The evidence was there, Mahmoud, but I didn't give it any thought. I copied it down myself but I didn't pay attention. I thought it must be just a supplication to the god Amun. Stupidly, I was concentrating on writings in Greek script, but he wasn't a god to the Greeks alone. He was the son of Amun-Ra, the god of the universe and the god of the sun, and the Egyptians worshipped him as such. Some of the columns were illegible, so I went back to the temple again to look at them carefully, and—'

Almost shouting, I interrupted her. 'Please, Catherine. What are you talking about? I don't understand a thing.'

Now it was her turn to shout. 'How can you not understand? Haven't I told you before that I'm looking for evidence of Alexander's tomb in Siwa?'

'Never! You're looking for evidence of Alexander's tomb here? In the desert, and at the wretched temple of Umm Ebeida? If I'd heard that from you before I would have said you were mad.'

With a triumphant smile she said, 'Naturally! And not just you! Many others too would have said I was mad. But listen, if you please ... Listen before you pronounce.' She started reading, stressing particular phrases, and looking from me to Fiona, as though to say, 'Do you see?' I focused my gaze on Fiona, whose face has become almost yellow of late, but I forced myself to listen to Catherine, who read as though reciting scripture and looked at us between every sentence and the next to make sure that we were following and understanding.

O Divine One of the Hidden Names, O Thou who Openest Thine Eyes and the Light Leaps into Life and Closes Them and the Darkness Falls, Justly Dost Thou Rule Thy Servants. Thou Shinest by Day over Their Land and by Night Thou Travellest to Oversee the Immortal Inhabitants of Thy Kingdom in the West. Grant Me Thy Blessing, O God. Increase Me with Thy Strength. Thou Art He Who Hath Thwarted All the Enemies in the Land and on the Horizons of the West. Accept This Prayer from Thy Servant Sanharib, Who Rules Thy Sacred Desert in Thy Name. Far from Here They plunged Thy Feet Far into the Water but Thou Returnest to Bless Thy Land and the Land of Thy Father. I, Thy Servant, Raise My Prayer to You in This Temple Erected to Thy Glory, the Temple of Thy Brother Pharaoh, Son of Amun.

Catherine stopped reading and looked at us proudly, though saying, in a tone of resignation, 'The name of the pharaoh is unclear, and in many places I've had to use my imagination where writing in the columns is illegible. For example, the sign for "water" is clear and I confirmed it when I returned to visit the temple, but the context – meaning the return to the land of thy father and so on – there I had to use my imagination because the writing is completely erased. But then, who is it who "thwarted all the enemies in the land"? To whom other than Alexander could this prayer be made?'

No one said anything for a moment. Then Fiona asked, 'Is that everything?'

'Yes,' replied Catherine.

Then she continued, turning her gaze to me, 'Until circumstances allow a visit to the remains of the temple at Bilad el Roum. I believe that is the place meant in this prayer. I believe that it is the sepulchre, or that the sepulchre is in a hidden tomb next to it. The Egyptians are experts at hiding the tombs of their kings to keep them out of the way of thieves, as you know.'

With surprising vehemence, Fiona said, 'But . . . but what you read isn't evidence of anything, Catherine!'

Catherine protested. 'How can that be? I went to great efforts to explain . . .'

Fiona interrupted her, and now it was she who was making the effort, to wrest the words from the midst of her disjointed breathing, despite which she persisted with what she had to say.

'This prayer . . . or encomium . . . could have been made to any god . . . or any ancient king . . . and in the most important part, you say you resorted to imagination. Isn't that exactly the criticism that Mi . . .'

She didn't complete the name but I understood she meant Catherine's first husband. Catherine responded obstinately,

'That's because he was without imagination. Time will show that my theory is correct and the tomb of Alexander is here.'

In an extremely quiet voice, Fiona said, 'Perhaps. I'm sorry, Catherine.' She fell silent, but I noticed that the blood had gone from her face and that she was breathing hard as she leant with both her hands on the table and, with difficulty, stood upright. Then she staggered and I ran to support her with my hand before she could fall.

Catherine screamed too and ran to support her sister with me. Together we moved her to the bed and Catherine started moistening her face with water and holding scent under her nose. Her breathing was weak but she opened her eyes once and tried to smile at her sister. Then she closed them again.

I contemplated the body lying stretched out on the bed and the face, which was turning blue, and I asked Catherine quietly, 'Is she dying now?'

She screamed in my face, striking my chest with her two fists, 'No! No! Don't say that! She's fainted lots of times before and revived. She'll revive now! Right now! Yes, she must.'

I didn't remove my eyes from the sleeping face. The eyes were closed but they remain graven on my memory.

I said, 'The sun really has got warm again . . . and Zubeida will be able to . . . I mean Sheikh Yahya's medicines will work . . . but I'm not going to wait.'

'What do you mean? And where are you going? Are you going to leave me on my own now when you can see how she is? Have you gone mad?'

She was screaming and I screamed too as I went out, saying, 'I'm not going to wait!'

She followed me with her cries.

At the station I saw Captain Wasfi again.

He came towards me as I was adjusting the horse's saddle and hanging the satchels on either side. He didn't ask me where I was going but stood in front of me and said, his face ashen and a look of determination in his eyes, 'Your Excellency, I wanted to explain to Your Excellency . . .'

'Explain nothing,' I said. 'I don't want to hear any explanations. It's life itself that's at fault.'

'Pardon. I didn't understand Your Excellency's meaning. What is life at fault about?'

'You'll work everything out on your own. Or rather, you worked it out long ago.'

And as I mounted, I said, as an aside, 'But I advise you all the same to set things straight with Salmawi.'

Contemptuously he said, 'Salmawi? And who might he be?'

'He is who he is. Forget what I told you and do as you wish, but don't send him or anyone else after me. Or, better still, send him and Sergeant Ibraheem to the house immediately. The madame may need something from them. Understand?'

'Yes, sir!'

I spurred the horse on and exited the station. I didn't stop at the house but took the road to Aghurmi, galloping through the gardens in the late afternoon light. As usual I saw a few *zaggala* and boys standing in front of the gardens but I paid them no attention. I drew close to the place where one turns off to the left to go to Sheikh Yahya's garden. Your advice was of no use to me, you goodly sheikh, and your medicines were of no use to Fiona. Maybe the medicines will work for Fiona, and it was just your advice to me that didn't. What's to be done, Sheikh Yahya, when all the wisdom in the world cannot bring rest to the heart? The fault indeed lies with life itself. I didn't choose my life. I didn't choose to come to this oasis or that Maleeka should enter my house or that Fiona should come to the heart of the desert.

All I asked was that she live, nothing more. I came to you so you could help me, but you didn't see me.

298

I suddenly became aware of the noise of donkeys and an army of *zaggala* riding them appeared in front of me, deliberately taking up position so as to block the road. The horse suddenly reared, then stopped and started impatiently pawing the ground. They were looking at me challengingly, in silence, shaking their legs where they dangled in their long white trousers with a monotonous motion. I patted the horse's neck as I shouted in fury, 'No!'

I have waited for you to do something for an age and you did nothing, so don't delay me now! Then I spurred my horse on, saying, 'Don't let me down now, my friend!' I charged towards them at full gallop and the *zaggala* were seized by sudden terror and jumped to the ground, while their donkeys collided and brayed and cleared the road for the horse, which dashed through the middle of them, knocking into them on either side, and they started running off in all directions, their owners shouting and uttering curses.

Do what you like. Nothing will do in this faulty world but what is itself faulty.

I galloped till I reached the temple.

Its columns stood out very clearly in the ruddy rays of the sun, which was preparing to set.

The entrance columns, from which the stone flew to smash Ibraheem's leg, seemed tall to me, but I couldn't see the carvings engraved on them, the carvings that had so preoccupied Catherine that it hadn't bothered her, as she deciphered their spells, to see her sister dying before her eyes. No, don't talk of death! But anyway, could these carvings really deserve such concern? All that foolishness, and around her sister she could see the shadow of death?

On! No time to lose. The sun's disc had started to drop below the horizon of immortality that Wasfi extols. We won't let it go alone!

I leapt from the horse. There were many ghosts here, around this temple. I could feel them without seeing them. Ghosts of the pharaohs? Ghosts of the palm trees? Ghosts of the murderers? Who had sent them after me? Sabir and Wasfi? Tal'at? Harvey? Catherine?

A murmuring and a muttering filled my ears. Braying of donkeys, horses' hoofs, singing and the beating of drums. All the sounds of this small, closed world. No! I must finish the job before I lose my mind. I must settle accounts swiftly.

I grasped the horse's neck and turned its head towards me, and it stared at me with its bloodshot black eyes. What are you trying to tell me? That there's no time left? That maybe you can take me to some other place where we can make a new start? But it's not in my fate to be saved. If pain, toil and the thrusts of betrayal and injustice were a price that could purchase salvation, I would have been saved, and everybody else would have been saved with me. So off with you! I took the saddlebags, smacked his rump and shooed him away, but he dawdled, unwilling to move. I chased him to the edge of the palm trees and left him on the road, where he remained standing, snorting and pawing the ground with his hoofs. Let him. The important thing was for him to be far enough away.

I returned to the temple and stood for a moment contemplating it, the bags over my shoulder. So this was the glory the British were revealing to us so that we could know we had once been giants and were now dwarves!

The ancestors, jolly good! The grandchildren, though – fit for nothing but occupation.

Wasfi was very proud of this discovery, which kept the masters masters! This nightmare had to end. I didn't believe what Sheikh Yahya had said of Maleeka, that she had loved these accursed ruins and seen beauty in them, and that he had loved them for her sake.

I didn't believe it! Maleeka and Wasfi could have nothing in common!

The sheikh, as his mind wandered, imagined things, and all these phantoms of the past had to disappear.

I took the sticks of dynamite out of the saddlebags and entered the temple. A lot of sticks here, beneath the entranceway that supports the whole structure. Then to the inside. Here remains of columns formed entrances and chambers full of carvings, carvings of the dead.

All was well. What I had was enough. More sticks beneath the walls themselves. Not a trace must remain of the temple. We had to be done with all the stories of the ancestors if the descendants were to wake from their delusions of greatness and their false complacency. One day they'd thank me! They'd have to thank me!

I extended a fuse from beneath the columns and the edifice to the outside.

The horse was still where I'd left it, snorting angrily. All was well. Was that the sound of his hoofs pawing the ground, or of other hoofs, or more of those tricks that my hearing played on me?

It didn't matter. I had to make haste. I lit the end of the fuse that extended from the bottom of the structure and stood and waited. Why did the spark move so slowly? On, holy fire! Devour the holy temple so that we can be done with all these fables!

Then something happened. Much hubbub and many approaching voices. On!

Explosions and a shower of stones flying through space. I would have preferred the whole temple to catch fire. What do you say, Catherine? Will these stones do to build a new, solid flight of steps? Will they do for a house?

Or perhaps another tomb? Do what you like with them but you won't find any carvings on them from now on. I swear I'll not leave you a single carving!

Forgive me, Maleeka, you were braver than I. And forgive me, Fiona, because I couldn't wait, and forgive me, Ibraheem, for I've gone on ahead of you as I promised you I would, though the stones fall around me and not on top of me. Why, then, am I waiting outside? Is cowardice going to take me again at the last moment? No! I'm coming! On! Into the temple!

I run but fall to the ground before I get there. Before I fall, I see it bounding towards me. The stone smacks against my head, I fall, and sleep overcomes me, but I wake again and put my hand to my head and neck and feel the stickiness and warmth of blood and touch the large splinter that has fastened itself in my neck. I try to pull it out with my listless hand but fail. There is no pain. And suddenly a light blazes up inside me. Yes, now I see everything, understand everything in life that I failed to grasp. I try to raise my head but can't. The light dies down to be replaced by the onslaught of heavy slumber and I hear a deep, tremulous voice crying my name as though weeping, and I say, as I close my eyes, 'Thank you. Thank you for coming too late.'

Postscript

In writing this novel, whose events take place at different historical epochs, I have drawn on a number of books and studies, and the reader interested in comparing reality with imagination has the right to consult these and participate with me in certain speculations around them.

1. *Siwa Oasis*, by the late archaeologist Ahmed Fakhry, was my point of entry to this work, having caught my attention with its indication of the connection between District Commissioner Azmi and what happened to the temple of Umm Ebeida in 1897. I have tried in this novel to understand the character and the event. Fakhry's book, which combines the accuracy of a vastly erudite scholar with the style of a talented writer, was of the greatest use to me in evoking the atmosphere of Siwa in the nineteenth century, especially in terms of two customs – the internecine wars and the treatment of widows.

2. The customs of the nineteenth century have now disappeared and Siwa has become an authentically Egyptian region whose inhabitants speak Arabic, which is the language of instruction at all the various levels of education in the oasis, albeit they preserve their original language for communication among themselves. Siwa continues to be distinguished by its rare beauty, which in ancient days enchanted Herodotus (on the basis of hearsay) and Greek, Arab and foreign travellers with its forest of palms and olives, its gardens, its sweet and salt lakes, and the springs that well up in the midst of this green land encompassed on all sides by yellow sands. The pyramid-like remains of Shali still stand in the middle of the

town, after having been 'melted' by heavy rains in 1926. I add my voice to those of the other lovers of this beautiful oasis who point out the need to ensure that efforts at modernization and development respect its unique character.

3. Siwa remains the land of Alexander the Great, who consulted the oracle in its celebrated temple, which towers there to this day. For the picture that the novel draws of the most famous of famous Macedonian kings I sought the help of a number of works of history, of which the most prominent is the *Life of Alexander* by the Roman historian Curtius, who shows a greater interest therein in Alexander's human side than in the conquests and military feats on which other books concentrate.

I also read with great pleasure *The Memoirs of Alexander the Great*, a fictitious autobiography by the living Greek writer Nestor Matsas, translated into Arabic by the Tunisian man of letters el Tahar Guiga, who has added to the work numerous footnotes that greatly enhance the text.

4. Alexander's tomb: people of my generation will remember the sensational headlines that proclaimed the discoveries of the Alexandrine Greek waiter Stylios and how close he believed he had come to stumbling across the tomb of Alexander under the Mosque of the Prophet Daniel, the sole result of these efforts, however, being to threaten the mosque's foundations, thus causing the authorities to curtail his activities. To this day, a Polish archaeological mission continues the search for the tomb in Alexandria. Others, however, search for it in other likely places and probable sites across three continents. The instigator of the theory that his tomb is in Siwa is the Greek scholar Liana Souvaltzi, who commenced digging in the oasis in 1989, her work leading to the discovery of several new archaeological sites there. While she claims that she was on the point of discovering the tomb itself, her researches were stopped in early 1996 following a disagreement with the Department of Egyptian Antiquities.

Souvaltzi then wrote a lengthy book entitled *The Tomb of Alexander the Great at the Siwa Oasis* in which she seeks to refute the accusations directed against her by the Department of Egyptian Antiquities and asserts that she was on the track of the most important archaeological discovery of modern times. Who knows?

5. For the events of the Urabi Revolution I had two main sources, Abd el Rahman el Rafi'i's *al-Thawra al-'urabiya wal-ihtilal al-ingilizi* (The Urabi Revolution and the British Occupation), and Wilfred Blunt's *The Secret History of the English Occupation of Egypt*.

6. Last but not least, I offer my special thanks to my friend, the great poet and writer Dr Nassar Abdallah, from whose valuable counsel I benefited on more than one occasion during the writing of the novel. Thanks must also be extended to the two most demanding readers and critics of my work, my two dear daughters, Dina and Yusr. They did their duty and I can only hope that I have benefited from their perceptive comments.

7. One word remains to be said. In the Author's Note before the novel begins, I mention that I have found no information on the life of the real-life district commissioner Mahmoud Azmi or on what happened to him after the incident at the temple. It is worth noting, however, that it is said that the stones from the temple were used to build a new flight of steps for the police station and to repair the district commissioner's dwelling.

Bahaa Taher
Cairo

October 2006

Translator's Note

In the seventh and eighth decades of the nineteenth century, Egypt witnessed major upheavals. Khedive Ismail, ruler from 1863 to 1879, bankrupted the country through his major infrastructural projects (which included the completion of the Suez Canal, in 1869), his foreign conquests, and his lavish lifestyle. By 1875, one third of Egypt's revenue was going to service debts on foreign loans at extortionate rates, and in 1876 the country stopped making payments. A European commission to manage the debt imposed on Ismail the same year had evolved by 1878 into the Dual Control, which gave France and Britain supervision not only of revenues but also of government. In acting so implacably, the Western powers may have been motivated by their desire to control the Suez Canal, which was vital to their colonial interests further east. Deposed by his nominal suzerain, the Ottoman Sultan, in 1879, Ismail went into exile and the 'experiment in autonomy that Muhammad Ali (Ismail's grandfather) had begun'[1] came to an end.

The new khedive, Tawfiq (1879–1892), acquiesced in the stringent austerity measures imposed by the Dual Control. These caused hardship to many sectors of society, including the army, which was greatly reduced in size, and gave rise to a nationalist movement with the slogan 'Egypt for the Egyptians'. In 1881, Colonel Ahmad Urabi, a member of this movement, presented Tawfiq with demands that challenged foreign control of the country. Popular support for Urabi ultimately forced the khedive to appoint him minister of war.

In May 1882, alarmed by these developments, Britain and France sent a naval force to the waters off Alexandria, Egypt's largest port. On 11 June, popular resentment fired by this move – or, according to some accounts, instigated by the then governor of Alexandria, Umar Basha Lutfi, in collusion with the khedive and intended to undermine Urabi's credibility by demonstrating his inability to maintain order – exploded into riots. A naval bombardment of the city by the British, aimed at toppling Urabi, took place on 11 July 1882, leading to large-scale loss of life among its defenders and citizens. These events were referred to subsequently either (sympathetically) as 'the Urabi revolution' (Arabic: *Thawret Urabi*) or (dismissively) as 'the Riots' (*el Hoga*). By September 1882, British land forces had defeated the Egyptian army under Urabi at Tell el-Kebir, the khedive had sought protection with the British, and the British domination of Egypt, which was to continue in various forms until 1956, had begun. By 1895, when the novel opens, Egypt was tranquil under Tawfiq's successor, Abbas Hilmi II (1892–1914). Real power, however, belonged not to the ruler but to the British consul general and the British 'advisors' appointed to steer the work of each ministry.

This bare-bones account is not intended to imply that *Sunset Oasis* should be read as an 'historical' novel but to clarify references to events with which the reader may not be familiar. The short glossary that follows includes further information on individuals and institutions as well as definitions of the few words that, to avoid awkward or lengthy equivalents, have been left untranslated in the text.

Humphrey Davies, 2009

1 Thompson, Jason. A History of Egypt from Earliest Times to the Present. Cairo American University in Cairo Press, 2008, p.249.

Glossary

Abdallah el Nadeem (1843–1896): pioneering journalist and political activist, whose magazine *el Lata'if* became the organ of the Urabists.

Basha: Arabised form of Pasha, a Turkish title awarded to high-ranking officers of the administration and army in the Ottoman Empire.

Circassian: member of an ethnic group originally from the Caucasus, many of whom were imported into Egypt as military slaves during the Mamluke and Ottoman eras and who came to form an elite whose dominance of the Egyptian military continued even after the country's emancipation from direct Ottoman rule.

dahabiya: a large boat with cabins used for travel on the Nile.

dhikr: literally 'remembrance', i.e., remembrance of God, and hence a ceremony in which Sufis, adherents of the mystical school of Islam, constantly repeat His name, or that of one of His attributes, often to the accompaniment of rhythmic movement, in order to produce an ecstatic sense of closeness to the Divine.

feddan: a measure of land equal to 1,038 square metres.

gallabiya: the common, floor-length, outer garment of Egyptian men and women, closed at the front but with an opening, sometimes with buttons, from the neck to the mid breast, and long sleeves.

Khedive: a title awarded by the Ottoman sultan from 1867 onwards to rulers of the Muhammad Ali dynasty. The 'young khedive' mentioned towards the end of the novel is Abbas Hilmi II (1874–1944), who succeeded his father, Tawfiq, in 1892, at the age of seventeen. Abbas Hilmi II was deposed by Britain in 1914 for refusing to accept Egypt's separation from the Ottoman Empire and thereafter the title was no longer used.

Rifa'i sheikh: a member of the Rifa'iya Sufi order. Rifa'is are reputed to possess the power to discover and expel snakes from houses.

Sheikh el Afghani: Jamal el Din el Afghani (1838–1897), a political agitator, philosopher and teacher, and a major inspiration of Ahmad Urabi. Born in Persia, Afghani was invited to Egypt by nationalist leaders in 1870 but expelled by Khedive Tawfiq in 1879.

Senoussis: members of a militant reformist Islamic order that exercised great influence over the peoples of the Sahara, and especially Cyreniaca and the western marches of Egypt, from its founding in the mid-nineteenth century. In the years leading to 1894, their leader, Muhammad al-Mahdi, ruled from Jaghboub, a town thirty miles to the west of Siwa in what is today Libya. 'Mahdi' is both a name and a title meaning 'Rightly Guided'.

Umar Basha Lutfi: governor of Alexandria at the time of the British bombardment. A Circassian and close to the royal court, Umar Basha Lutfi has been accused of instigating insecurity in the city at the urging of Khedive Tawfiq, in order to justify the intervention of the British.

Urabi: Ahmad Urabi (1841–1911): army officer and nationalist leader who led Egyptian opposition to foreign domination of the country. Defeated by the British army at Tell el Kebir in September 1882, he was initially exiled but eventually returned to the country, where he died in obscurity.

Zeitouna Mosque: one of the oldest mosques in North Africa, dating from the eighth century, and a major teaching institution.